WORD
AND
SPIRIT

a monastic review

1

In honor of Saint Basil the Great
†379

ST. BEDE'S PUBLICATIONS
Still River, Massachusetts

Published with ecclesiastical permission.

LIBRARY OF CONGRESS CATALOGING IN PUBLICATION DATA
Main entry under title:
In honor of St. Basil the Great.
   (Word and spirit; 1)
   Bibliography: p.
   CONTENTS: Danielou, J. The Fathers and Christian
unity.—De Vogue, A. The greater rules of St. Basil.—
Gribomont, J. Intransigence and irenicism in St. Basil's
"De Spiritu Sancto." [etc.]
   1.Basilius, Saint, the Great, Abp. of Caesarea,
330 (ca.)-379—Addresses, essays, lectures. I. Basilius,
Saint, the Great, Abp. of Caesarea, 330 (ca.)-379.
II. Series.
BR45.W67 vol. 1   [BR1720.B3]   282s   [281'.4'0924]
ISBN 0-932506-07-0 — [for vol. 1]   79-20045
ISSN 0193-9211 — [for series]

CONTENTS

To
Archbishop Joseph Tawil,
A zealous bishop in the
tradition of St. Basil the Great

PREFACE

WORD AND SPIRIT, a monastic review of which this issue is the first, will be published once a year, centering on a vital scriptural, theological, or spiritual theme; or commemorating the anniversary of a significant event in the history of the Catholic Church. Its main purpose is to promote a critical interest in the myriad aspects of our Christian heritage with its riches, difficulties, struggles, crises, and achievements. To be ignorant of an inheritance is always an impoverishment. Christopher Dawson expressed it admirably when he said, "A people unaware of its past is like a man who has lost his memory." *Word and Spirit* is an attempt to remind us of the rhythms of our past with its many protean elements—Hellenistic and Judaic, pagan and Christian, saintly and shocking— seemingly cyclic yet somehow linear.

$$* \qquad * \qquad * \qquad * \qquad * \qquad * \qquad *$$

It is fitting that our first issue should be dedicated to Saint Basil the Great who died in 379, exactly 1600 years ago. The dedication is appropriate not only because of the timing but because Basil himself is one of the great legacies from antiquity, a man imbued with all the riches of the Judeo-Christian, and of the Hellenistic cultures.

Born of a prominent family that had known saints and martyrs, he had been given the best education of his day, having for classmate the future Emperor Julian the Apostate. After his studies he turned to asceticism. He traveled a lot and grappled with the monasticism of different kinds and countries. Being not only a reformer (yet cast in a practical mold) but also a patriarch and an inevitable founder, he drew up from his experiences a code of life which spread on its own merits and is still observed by thousands of men and women to this day.

Whether considered as a bishop, theologian, thinker, writer, law-giver, or guardian of orthodoxy, Saint Basil is an epoch-making figure. Today, 1600 years after his death, his rule is followed, his letters are studied, his theology is discussed and there is no doubt that he will live as long as men can read and pray.

What Saint Benedict is to monks of the West, Saint Basil is to monks of the East—their patriarch. He has put his seal on eastern monasticism for the rest of time, not by mere mandate but because of the practical and spiritual depth of the rule he wrote. He has been ranked with Saint Ambrose and Saint Leo as one of the bishops whose influence helped to mold not only the immanent world order of his time but all subsequent Catholicism as well. He cannot be ignored.

S. M. Clare

THIS ISSUE:

A general survey of the life and times of St. Basil is provided in an essay by the late *Maisie Ward*, reprinted here with the kind permission of her husband, Frank Sheed. *William Meninger* then discusses the advantages and disadvantages of having a saint in the family—even when one is a saint oneself.

Two essays focus on Basil as a father of monasticism. *Adalbert de Vogüé* gives a critique of his Rules, contrasting them with the monastic legislations of Pachomius and Augustine, while *Basil Pennington* considers one aspect of these Rules—the instruction on manual labor.

The complex issue of the division among Christian churches in Basil's time, and his efforts to restore unity, is the subject of an article by the late, illustrious patristic scholar and theologian, *Jean Cardinal Daniélou*. Basil's "ecumenism," and particularly his decisive role in the Arian controversy, is likewise dealt with in a magisterial essay by the renowned Basilian authority, *Jean Gribomont*.

Working from the same text as Dom Gribomont, the Treatise on the Holy Spirit, *Cyril Karam* explores some of Basil's theological and spiritual themes and their implications. And, finally, *Brian Keleher* studies St. Basil's contributions to the liturgy.

The issue concludes with two pieces which, though not directly on St. Basil, deal with themes closely associated with him: *Abbot Keating's* exhortations to newly professed monks, and *Louis Dupré's* meditation on the Agony of Jesus.

ACKNOWLEDGMENTS

Grateful acknowledgment is made to the following for permission to use previously copyrighted material:

"Saint Basil and the Cappadocians" by Maisie Ward originally published in *Saints Who Made History*, copyright 1959 by Maisie Ward, published by Sheed and Ward, New York. Reprinted with permission of the publisher.

"The Fathers and Christian Unity" by Jean Danielou, SJ originally published in *The Eastern Churches Quarterly*, Vol. XVI, No. 1, 1964. Reprinted with the permission of the publisher.

Greek/English text of the Anaphora of Saint Basil reprinted from *The Divine Liturgies of our Fathers among the Saints, John Chrysostom and Basil the Great with that of the Presanctified*, edited by J.N.W.B. Robertson, London: David Nutt, 1894.

WORD AND SPIRIT

SAINT BASIL AND THE CAPPADOCIANS

Maisie Ward

*(Late wife of F.J. Sheed, author,
and co-publisher with him)*

Gregory the Great signifies for us the first Pope of that name, but to the Cappadocians of the fourth century the great Gregory was Thaumaturgus—the Wonder-worker. He was a century earlier than Basil (329-79), who often spoke and wrote of him; Basil's brother, Gregory of Nyssa, wrote his life. Their grandmother Macrina would often tell the two boys of this great bishop, repeating his very words.

When Gregory became Bishop of Neocaesarea there were only seventeen Christians there; when he died there were only seventeen pagans. So deep was the impression he had made that Basil tells us how—in an age when the liturgy was rapidly developing throughout the Christian world—men of Pontus and Cappadocia would not lay a finger on the heritage bequeathed by their evangelist. Their liturgy had, he acknowledged, an archaic, indeed an unfinished look, because of this profound reverence for the man who had first brought it into being.

In the countryside Gregory recognized the need to win people to Christianity through a certain gaiety, to transform not destroy their ancient joys. Saints' days were to be kept with high festival; a populace baptized and transformed through the Christian message would learn later to worship with greater awe and solemnity. He was concerned to preach divine truth accurately to these simple folk but not to curtail their pleasures.

How could he announce to worshippers of many gods the Trinity in Unity of the one God of Revelation? It was in answer to his really anguished prayers that Our Lady appeared to him. With Mary came John the Apostle especially loved by her Son, and Mary told John to teach Gregory how he should unfold this great mystery. This is the first apparition of Our Lady known to history; the Creed itself remarkably anticipates Nicaea. Devotion to the Holy Trinity is marked in the men of Cappadocia—Gregory Nazianzen, Gregory of Nyssa and Basil himself, all disciples of the Wonder-worker—and it is to Gregory of Nyssa that we owe his namesake's creed in its fullness, since the last clause is not found in all the codices:

> And there is one Holy Ghost, who hath His being of God, who hath appeared [to mankind] through the Son, Image of the Son, Perfect of the Perfect; Life, the Cause of all them that live; Holy Fountain, Holiness, the Bestower of Sanctification, in whom is manifested God the Father, who is over all and in all, and God the Son, who is through all. A perfect Trinity, not divided or alien in glory and eternity and dominion.[1]

Intellectual ardor seems to have been the chief mark of Basil as he grew into youth and manhood—pursuing his education first at Caesarea in Cappadocia, next at Constantinople, where he was taught by Libanius, and finally at Athens. Men of sense, says Gregory Nazianzen, his close friend and fellow-student, realize that among all good things education comes first—not only the noblest part of it, which concerns our salvation, but also that culture which so many Christians reject as useless and even dangerous. What gift of God is useless, and what is without danger? he asks, passionately defending in his famous funeral sermon the mental culture which he and Basil received together at Athens. "The ignorant and uncultured want everyone to be like themselves, that they may pass unnoticed in the crowd and escape the reproaches their illiteracy merits. This principle once laid down and accepted, let us consider our hero."

When acutely bored by Bossuet's *Oraisons funèbres*, it may amuse us to remember that this is no original Christian style but derives with a few turns and twists from the Sophists of Greece. So, long before, Gregory Nazianzen had studied the same form closely and applied his studies to the man who was his hero. Things must be said that belong to the form—Basil had (for instance) been a fine-looking man before he had begun the conquest of his body by asceticism. Classical allusions must be introduced, comparisons elevating his hero in relation both to the heroes of Greek antiquity and of Scripture. But anything perfunctory in this discourse is conquered by a vitality rising up from the deep affection, the shared life, of those days at Athens.

Gregory had got there first and welcomed Basil, as yet merely his acquaintance. And if Basil owed to his own personality his unique escape from initiation—via a highly undignified ceremonial bath—into university life, Gregory makes it clear that to himself was owing Basil's first triumph in debate. The close friendship they formed was based indeed on this, but far more on their common aim. Both took the road to church even more eagerly than the road to the lecture room, both avoided feasts and shows, both desired philosophy above all else; and for the young Christian, philosophy implied the ascetic life.

Basil gathered around him some sort of confraternity which made them, Gregory claims, "famous among our professors and our companions, famous throughout Greece and especially among the country's notabilities...both of us were known and praised together; a famous pair known and boasted of as such among our teachers." Of higher fame in fact than any of the noted couples in classical literature—the Orestes, the Pylades, the Molionides of Homer. "But here I am boasting of myself without realizing it—a thing I regard as ridiculous in others." He cannot help it. Those days are so much alive. Then he profited through Basil's virtue, today through his glory.

Every effort was made to persuade the two friends to remain in Athens, and Gregory did agree to stay on for a time after his friend left in 355. For a short while Basil taught rhetoric in Caesarea; then came a visit to his home where his sister Macrina and his widowed mother were already living a secluded and ascetic life. His brother Gregory says bluntly: "The great Basil returned after his long education a practiced rhetorician. He was puffed up beyond measure with the pride of oratory and looked down on the local dignitaries, excelling in his own estimation all men of learning and position."

Thus the sharp-eyed younger brother, taking note of what might become a critical situation. "Nevertheless," he continues, "Macrina took him in hand and with such speed did she draw him also towards the goal of philosophy that he forsook the glories of this world, and despised fame gained by speaking and deserted it for this busy life where one toils with one's hands."

Somewhere between these two accounts what happened to Basil emerges. He speaks himself of all he owed to Macrina, he speaks of a conversion when, after leaving Athens, it was as though he had awakened from sleep. This is not to deny the excellence of his university life, so much as to show us that something startlingly greater had shown itself suddenly before the eyes of his spirit.

Yet it is difficult to fix the chronology of his early life or to evaluate the various influences working upon him. From Gregory Nazianzen one would judge that they had long determined on leaving the world together and that Basil was only waiting for Gregory to join him. But Gregory would not come; he admits his promise, but to have kept it would have distressed his parents.

THE RULE OF ST. BASIL

Newman attributes to Basil's disappointment at the non-arrival of Gregory, his decision to spend a year studying the ascetic life as it was lived in the wide deserts. But we must not forget the influence of Eustathius, Bishop of Sebaste, who did in fact suggest this pilgrimage, nor yet that of Macrina. Anyhow it was common sense, having decided to follow the perfect life of renunciation, first to study it in its highest representatives. "And many did I find in Alexandria and many in the rest of Egypt and others in Palestine and in Coelo-Syria and in Mesopotamia." Basil was away for a little more than a year and returned full of admiration, but already he had ideals differing in some respects from what he had been witnessing. A study of his own ascetical writings, and a glance at the contemporary behavior of hermits and ascetics, show us the weaknesses which Basil became determined to correct in his design for monastic living.

Anthony wrote no rule, but Pachomius did—and for the East it was surprisingly moderate. (What appeared moderate in the East seemed to the Westerner appallingly severe.) But Pachomius looked on his rule as a minimum—his monks were encouraged to go beyond it, each according to his ability. They were often called athletes of Christ, and the competitions that resulted had a slightly comic resemblance to those of modern athleticism. While the young athlete tries to run faster or jump higher than his competitor, the young ascetic tried to fast longer, sleep less, wash less and weave more mats. Even men who cared little for visible prowess in these matters tended to admire and emulate monks famous for asceticism—to feel that they must be the best soldiers in the army of Christ. Basil was among the eminent churchmen who knew in middle life that they had seriously damaged their health and strength by youthful excesses in self-discipline. Gregory Nazianzen was another—and Chrysostom, and Gregory the Great.

In his own monasteries Basil laid it down that the Rule he drew up was enough—no one might exceed it without permission, and such permission was not to be lightly given. The common life, with its daily round of prayer and work, was the ideal: individual exaggeration might easily destroy the common life.

Basil's ideas about the common life developed as he lived
it. On his return from his grand tour of monasticism his
thoughts turned to the companionship he had first desired.
Gregory had hesitated to leave his father, the aged Bishop of
Nazianzus, and Basil first experimented with a place near
Nazianzus for his monastery. But he abandoned it as too
cold and damp. "O clean-footed, tip-toeing, capering man,"
says Gregory, reproaching him, "you are gentlemanlike and
wealthy and a man of the world; I cannot praise it. Say not
a word more against our mud. . .or I will match our wading
with your trading and all the wretched things which are
found in cities."

Finally Basil decided on a site across the river Iris opposite
his home, and there he remained. Newman in his *Church
of the Fathers* has painted pleasantly the friendship with
Gregory, his long visits to Basil and their opposite opinions
of Basil's idyllic dwelling.

Basil says:

> There is a lofty mountain covered with thick woods,
> watered towards the north with cool and transparent
> streams. A plain lies beneath, enriched by the waters
> which are ever draining off upon it; and skirted by a spon-
> taneous profusion of trees almost thick enough to be a
> fence; so as even to surpass Calypso's Island, which Homer
> seems to have considered the most beautiful spot on
> earth. . . . Does it not strike you what a foolish mistake I
> was near making when I was eager to change this spot for
> your Tiberina, the very pit of the whole earth? Pardon me,
> then, if I am now set upon it; for not Alcmaeon himself, I
> suppose, would endure to wander further when he had
> found the Echinades. (*Ep. XIV.*)

Gregory, after a visit to his friend, retorts on

> . . .the dwelling without roof and without door—the
> hearth without fire and smoke—walls, however, baked
> enough, lest the mud should trickle on us, while we suffer

Tantalus' penalty, thirst in the midst of wet.... I have remembrance of the bread and of the broth—so they were named—and shall remember them: how my teeth got stuck in your hunches, and next lifted and heaved themselves as out of paste. You, indeed, will set it out in tragic style yourself, taking a sublime tone from your own sufferings. But for me, unless that true Lady Bountiful, your mother, had rescued me quickly, showing herself in need, like a haven to the tempest-tossed, I had been dead long ago, getting myself little honor, though much pity, from Pontic hospitality.... (*Ep. V.*)

But now he had hurt Basil's feelings, so he hastens to write again of "the luxury of suffering hardship with you":

...Who shall restore me to those psalmodies, and vigils, and departures to God through prayer, and that (as it were) immaterial and incorporeal life? or to that union of brethren, in nature and soul, who are made gods by you, and carried on high? or to that rivalry in virtue and sharpening of heart which we consigned to written decrees and canons? or to that loving study of divine oracles, and the light we found in them, with the guidance of the Spirit? or, to speak of lesser and lower things, to the bodily labors of the day, the wood-drawing and the stone-hewing, the planting and the draining; or to that golden plane, more honorable than that of Xerxes, under which, not a jaded king, but a weary monk did sit?... (*Ep. VI.*)[2]

During this long visit the two friends collected the passages from Origen known as the *Philocalia*. Gregory, after leaving his friend, asks to hear more of his life among the men he has gathered around him, and Basil is nothing loath to write of their prayers and labors, their studies of the inspired Scriptures, their night vigils and "variety of psalmody," one choir answering another. He writes at some length on conversation, showing that social life within the monastery was in his eyes an important part of the common life: "To question without over-eagerness, to answer without desire of display, not to interrupt a profitable speaker," to study for a tone of voice pleasantly modulated, to be courteous and amiable. "Harshness is ever to be avoided, even when censuring."

Basil had at first been drawn to the solitary life—he came to feel that the monastic was both higher and safer. We get a hint of one of his reasons when we learn that his decision was partly based on reluctance to give up his books. And this was not only because the monastic movement under Basil was recruited from a different and more educated world. Basil saw that Christianity is an intellectual religion—Christians are "People of the Book." If a Basilian monk did not know how to read he would need to learn—unless, like the great Anthony, he could accomplish immense feats of memory. In the *Moralia* every admonition is supported with a dozen Scripture references, and Basil was the first man to organize the seven hours of daily and nightly recitation of the Psalms in all his monasteries.

"I think," he says, "it is advantageous to have diversity and variety in the prayers and Psalms at the fixed hours because when there is monotony the soul often gets weary and is a prey to distraction; but when the Psalms of each hour change and are variable, the desire of the soul is renewed and attention is restored."

Next in his remedies for extravagance, we may put the great stress laid on obedience. Basil's monasteries were of a moderate size, probably thirty to forty monks. Sometimes small village groups amalgamated—he points out the advantages of one fire, one lamp, fewer messengers to market their goods. And the phrasing of his views on authority seems to suggest that the heads of these groups formed something like a council of superiors. Basil also lays enormous stress on the value of frequent confession—and this more as consulting a soul-doctor than as sacramental. Confession was often made to monks who were not priests.

The third and highest safeguard against excess was the common life—and this involved not only prayer but work. Often there were two monasteries—of men and of women—under the one Abbot. The two together could be totally self-supporting, the women weaving and making the men's clothes, bed-coverings, etc., the men building, carpentering and doing the heavier field work. "Generally speaking," Basil says, "one may recommend the choice of such arts as preserve the peaceable and untroubled nature of our lives, needing neither much trouble to get the requisite material nor much anxiety to sell what has been made...preferring those arts which preserve for us a life undistracted and waiting continually on the Lord.... Of them agriculture is the best."

Sometimes their products must be sold at "the functions designated fairs" and then several brethren should go together. But selling and buying at martyrs' tombs is not suitable, and it is better to get a lower price for goods than to make use (as so many do) of a saint's feast and burial place "as a market and fair, and common emporium."

Every man should learn a skill, he who has one should stick to it, for "to gain a mastery of one skill is more useful than to dabble in a number." The care of tools must be "a special consideration to the workman in each occupation."

In his treatment of the details of daily life, one is especially struck by Basil's common sense, and his determination that details should not be made of undue importance. Food is to be simple and cheap; imported goods are only to be bought if essential for living (e.g., oil), the monks should buy the simplest (mainly bread and vegetables) of what is there for the public. There is an agreement here between the rules of Basil and Benedict, one saying of food, the other of material for clothes, that the cheapest and easiest to procure is to be preferred in any district. The extra hard worker can have extra food. (So, too, says St. Benedict.) Doctors should be called in for the sick, but a man must never allow the question of his health to fill his thoughts—must never fuss unduly over it.

Avoidance of fuss is a keynote in Basil's teaching. It is good to offer hospitality, but not to alter the daily simplicity of your life—you accuse your visitor of greed by "piling up the food and fussing over it." Our Lord told Martha not to fuss, He fed the five thousand with simple food. It is good to choose the lowest place, but bad to scramble for it—and perhaps a greater sign of pride. The shorter rules are answers to questions, and to the question, "What are the cares of this life?" Basil answers, "Every care is a care of this life, even if it seems to involve nothing forbidden, unless it contribute to godliness." The test of a man's rebuke of his neighbor's sin is to be "that which is most important, that of sympathy." If all else fails, "let us use at the proper occasion strong indignation with sympathy, in order to benefit and reform the sinners." The question, "Who is the meek?" receives the unusual reply: "He who is unalterable in his decisions upon the things that are done to please God."

Basil chose the life of the monastery with a conviction that it was more perfect than that of the hermitage. Obviously, he says, in the search for perfection, "it is impossible for a man to succeed if he lives in promiscuous intercourse." But if altogether alone he "will not recognize his defects, not having anyone to reprove him and to set him right with mercy and compassion." How can a man show humility with none to compare with, compassion when cut off from other men, long-suffering when no one withstands his wishes? Christ washed the feet of His disciples. Basil says to the solitary: "Whose feet wilt thou wash?"

And how is the complex of all good works to be achieved by one man alone? While we visit a sick man we cannot be receiving a stranger, while distributing alms we neglect work, work not done means we can no longer feed the hungry and clothe the naked. But by men living in community "many commandments are easily performed.... Who then would choose the idle and fruitless life in preference to the fruitful life which is lived in accordance with the commandment of the Lord?"

Basil, like most of the Fathers, thought of the early Christians as practicing the first form of the religious life— having all things in common, having on conversion laid all their goods at the feet of the Apostles for distribution to the needy.[3] And all solitaries as well as all monasteries held it a duty to give alms from the fruits of their labors.

Priest in Caesarea

Basil, with all his social sense, all his keen awareness of the value of the common life, had conceived of the monastery as its fulfillment, as the place for his life's work and his soul's perfection. But he was too great as thinker, organizer, and leader to be left in such times as these in the woods of Pontus. The Council of Rimini, at which Dianius, Bishop of Caesarea, had signed a semi-Arian formula, had caused Basil to break off relations with him, but it was Basil who received the assurance of Dianius' orthodoxy and assisted him in his dying hours. The new bishop, Eusebius, kept Basil in Caesarea and ordained him priest, probably in the year 362, Basil being then thirty-three. Before long, however, he began to be jealous of his popularity, and Basil went back to his monastery.

He could ill be spared by Caesarea. Incapable men tend to be jealous of the capable; Eusebius could not handle his important job unaided, and the threats of the Arian Emperor Valens led Basil's friends to make efforts for his recall. Gregory, himself in favor with Eusebius, wrote begging for him:

...Proud as I am of your notice (for I am a man, as someone says before me), and of your invitations to religious consultations and meetings, yet I cannot bear Your Holi-

ness' past and present slight of my most honored brother
Basil, whom I selected from the first and still possess as my
friend, to live with me and study with me, and search with
me into the deepest wisdom.... If there is anything you
will grant me, let it be this; and I trust you will, for really
it is equitable. He will certainly defer to you, if you do but
pay a reasonable respect to him. For myself, I shall come
after him as shadows follow bodies, being small, and a
lover of quiet... (*Ep. XVI.*)

Before long Eusebius sent for Basil, who became, says
Gregory, "his good counselor, his able auxiliary, his teacher
in the things of God, his guide in action, the staff of his old
age, the support of his faith. Most active in outside works,
most faithful at home, he showed himself as full of good as he
had been imagined to be of ill will." (*Orat. XLIII.*)

Though he never abandoned his literary tastes and style,
which had in youth become a part of him, Basil's mightiest
achievements lay in three fields: his molding of eastern
monasticism, his theological teaching—especially of the doctrine of the Trinity—and his vast creation of social services.

Basil brought back, says Puech,[4] what Greek eloquence
had lost: its qualities of "elevation, happy choice and clear
development of an image, magnificence of phrase and strong
simplicity of style." Even in translation his sermons are aston-
ishing, especially if we remember that they were preached
not to an elite but to a crowd of artisans and laborers, to
the mixed population of a large city. In one respect Basil
could probably make contact with these minds more easily
because of his dislike of the allegorizing which marked the
Alexandrians. Belonging more to the school of Antioch—
"When I hear grass spoken of," says Basil in an early sermon,
"I take it to mean grass, the same with a fish, etc."

Always he spoke as one having authority. "You sit around
me as judges not disciples, but you shall listen, not to what
pleases you, but to the truth."

The revolt of Procopius occupied Valens and averted the threatened persecution for a time. The first great test of Basil's powers came with the famine which swept Caesarea in 368.

Those terrible days come alive for us as Basil describes in a sermon a father forcing himself to sell one child that the whole family may have bread. Would it not be better, he asks himself, for all to die together? Should the eldest be sacrificed, or the youngest? what will the other children feel towards their treacherous father? How can he sit down with them to eat a meal bought at such a price?

Yet it is better than the death of all. He steels himself, but the tears flow down as he takes to the market the best loved of his children—"And you," cried Basil addressing the rich purchaser, "you are unmoved by nature's reproaches. Hunger is driving this miserable wretch and you drag out the business, you bargain, you prolong his agony. He is offering you his heart in exchange for a little food. Your hand does not fall paralyzed as you stretch it out with the money, but you haggle with your fellow slave for a lower price."

This thought was familiar with Basil: we are all the slaves of God, fellow slaves with one another. The highly placed is God's steward over his fellow slaves and owes them their share in God's bounties. The very animals set man an example, pasturing together in the same field or on the slopes of the same mountain. You lie, he cries out to the rich young man of the Gospel, claiming to have loved your neighbor as yourself. Long ago the money of the rich would have been shared with others had they really loved their neighbors.

Pitilessly he chases the rich man from one excuse to another. You have not enough to help everybody?

Your tongue swears it but your hand betrays you, silently proclaiming you a liar with the sparkles of your jeweled ring. How many debtors could that ring alone set free? How many crumbling houses could it rebuild?

Your chest of clothes could cover a whole shivering populace, and you dare to send away the poor with empty hands, having no fear of the judge's just punishment.

You have shown no pity; there will be no pity for you.

Another claims that he must save for his children's future. "Begin," says Basil, "by giving your soul its rights as the first-born. After that you can divide your wealth among your children." The future is uncertain, says another. "Strange madness," cries Basil, "you dug your gold out of the mines and now you are going to hide it again. And when you have buried your fortune you will find you have buried your heart with it."

All this means that "the Lord is not your master, the Gospel does not rule your life." "But I," says another wealthy man, "will make the poor my heirs, setting them down in my will as masters of all I have."

"When you are far from men you will become their lover, so when I see you dead I will praise your humanity."

But what can dust and ashes do either by display of splendor or by generosity? "No, when the market is closed there can be no more trading. He who arrives after the contest wins no crown. When the war is over so is the time to show courage."

In his life of their sister Macrina, Basil's brother says, "His renunciation of property was complete." But since then his mother had died and we may conjecture that a fresh fortune had come to him from this land-owning family who had estates both in Pontus and Cappadocia. In his *Funeral Oration* Gregory of Nyssa says that during the famine Basil "sold his possessions and turned money into food." And Gregory Nazianzen, telling of Basil's skill in opening the purses of the obdurate rich, adds that "with his own slaves, call them if you will his companions in slavery, become in the circumstances his fellow workers," he waited on the needy, solacing body and soul alike. It was a fiercer famine in

Caesarea than it would have been in a maritime town, where food could be brought in and merchandise carried out in exchange. The whole countryside was stricken and there were more than enough profiteers buying wholesale and selling at fantastic retail prices.

Comparing him with Moses, Elias, Joseph, and Our Lord Himself, Nazianzen describes how Basil saved the city. There were men and women, children and the aged, almost dead from hunger. He got them together and collected "every sort of food...cauldrons filled with a purée of vegetables, the home-salted meats which are the food of the poor; and then, copying Christ the servant, who, girded with a towel, did not disdain to wash His disciples' feet," he served them.

BISHOP OF CAESAREA

The threats of Valens and the clamorous demand of his people, much more than Gregory's entreaties, had induced Bishop Eusebius to recall Basil. When Eusebius died in 370, Basil had been in fact governing the diocese for several years. But it was by no means certain that imperial disfavor and Arian intrigues would not prevent him or any other Catholic, from becoming bishop. Basil has been accused of intriguing from the first to get the vacant see. This is quite possible, but it seems more likely that he had another candidate in mind— probably, he felt, a reluctant one. Unfortunately we have not got the letter which he wrote to Gregory Nazianzen but only Gregory's angry answer.

> You pretended to be very ill, indeed at your last breath, and to long to see me and bid me a last farewell...I shed a fountain of tears and I wailed aloud, feeling myself for the first time unphilosophically disposed.... But as soon as I found that the bishops were in the city I stopped short in my course... (*Ep. XL.*)

Basil had not, he felt, treated him fairly, had not guarded

himself against evil gossip, had not "remembered that such nominations are deserved by the more religious, not the more powerful or those most in favor with the multitude." Later, when he sees him, Gregory will have "more and graver reproaches to make."

Gregory may have suspected his friend of wanting to make use of him for his own election, but as editors of both his and Basil's letters suggest, it seems far more likely that Basil was planning for Gregory's. As to the illness—his health was always wretched, and Gregory may have read the letter in an alarmist mood. The story, however, gives a strong impression of deceit—but of a kind not uncommon in those centuries, when tricking a man into a bishopric was deemed rather praiseworthy than otherwise. To get a first-rate man for Caesarea came before all other considerations.

Gregory, who would later reproach Basil even more bitterly for putting loyalty to a friend too low on his scale of values, did himself realize the importance of this election. He believed Basil the best man for the post and wrote several brilliant letters, supposedly from his father, entreating the support of friendly bishops.

Whether or not Basil had first desired the election of Gregory, he contrasts interestingly at this point with Ambrose, Augustine, and the rest who shrank from the episcopal office. In his own election now lay the best hope of victory for the Faith, and he did not hesitate to try to secure it. The younger Gregory refused to be present; but finally his father, though very ill, was, at the risk of his life, carried in a litter to Caesarea. The people were enthusiastic for Basil, and Gregory's support made the adverse bishops yield; the old man consecrated him and he received the joyful congratulations of Athanasius and the whole Catholic world of the East.

*   *   *   *   *   *

Every battle between bishop and emperor has something of the same color, though each has its own details. Valens sent his prefect Modestus to give Basil his choice between banishment or communion with the Arians. He found neither threats nor blandishments got him anywhere, and had to report his total failure to the Emperor.

The dialogue between prefect and bishop had been striking enough.

"You, Basil," Modestus began, "what do you mean by opposing so great a prince and not yielding to him as others do?" On Basil's asking where his fault lay, he was told that it was in his refusal to worship after the Emperor's fashion.

"I have a Sovereign," said Basil, "whose will is otherwise. I can worship no creature—I, the creature of God and called to be a god."

"What do you take me for?" exclaimed Modestus.

"For a thing of nought while you give me such orders."

On Modestus' proclaiming his own rank and position in tones very unlike his name, Basil acknowledged them, but urged the equal dignity of all Christians. Modestus, enraged, asked Basil if he had no fear of his power.

"Fear what?" asked Basil.

"Confiscation, exile, tortures, death."

"Think of something else. What is confiscation if one has nothing to lose—these garments and a few books?.... Home is everywhere for God's pilgrim.... Tortures cannot hurt a body so frail that one stroke would bring death. It would only send me sooner to Him for whom I live...to whom I have long been journeying."

"No one," said Modestus, "ever before spoke to me like this."

"Perhaps," Basil answered, "you have never met a bishop."

This famous phrase was followed by the assurance that in all temporal matters the prefect would find Christians humble and submissive. "But when God's honor is at stake...fire and sword, beasts of prey, irons tearing the flesh are an indulgence, not a terror for the Christian. Insult, threaten, do your worst.... Go tell your Emperor. You will not persuade or win me to an impious creed by menaces even more frightful." (Gregory Nazianzen, *Orat. XLIII.*)

On the feast of the Epiphany Valens himself entered the cathedral while Basil was celebrating Mass. The bishop stood facing the people, his ministers in a semi-circle around him. The thunder of the singing, the immense throng of worshippers totally oblivious of the Emperor and his train, "the unearthly majesty of the scene," a worship "more like that of angels than of men," as Gregory Nazianzen has described it, overwhelmed Valens. Almost fainting, he tried, at the Offertory, to present his gift. The ministers hesitated—for was he not a heretic?—but Basil came forward and took it from his trembling hands.

Valens lived henceforward in a state of perpetual vacillation towards Basil. On this occasion he gave him a splendid present for the hospital he was planning, but shortly after ordered his banishment. Before Basil could depart the Emperor's only son grew ill and he was hastily sent for to pray over the child. He prayed and the child grew better. But soon Valens, breaking a solemn promise, had him baptized by an Arian. The boy grew worse and died.

Presently Valens again yielded to Basil's enemies and tried to sign the decree of his banishment. Three pens split in his hand and he departed from Caesarea leaving the bishop master of the scene. Modestus became Basil's friend and a number of his letters are written to the prefect begging his help for people in distress.

Commenting on the command to love our neighbor, Basil said, "Man's neighbor is man." He preached and practiced a universal charity, but I wish we had more details concerning the Basileiad, as his great composite institute came to be called. Basil was, Ephrem of Syria said, "filled with compassion for the widow and the orphan"—two classes for which the Church from her beginnings had specially provided. There were probably buildings for these. Gregory Nazianzen mentions too Basil's care for children during the famine, and that it was extended to Jew as well as Christian. Basil invites a fellow bishop to visit his "refectory of the poor." He made a special point of himself waiting on lepers. He seems to have known something of medicine, and his own feeble health inspired him with special sympathy for the sick.

The swift energy with which he worked seems to have disturbed Elias, Governor of Cappadocia. Experts date Basil's letter to him in 373:

> Can it be said that it is against the people's good to have raised to our God a magnificently built house of prayer, with dwelling-houses around it, one of them specially for the bishop, other, lesser houses allotted according to rank to God's ministers, but suitable also for use by you magistrates and your attendants? Who is wronged by the shelters we have built for strangers, for travelers, for those with illnesses needing treatment, or by the necessary aids we have provided for them—nurses, doctors, pack animals and men to lead them?
>
> For these various institutions there must be tradesmen on the spot, supplying both the strict necessaries of life, and those other things which have been invented to make life more livable. There must be other buildings to house these industries—and all these things improve the appearance of the place and give glory to the Governor, on whom the credit naturally falls. (*Ep. XCIV.*)

That the whole thing was on a vast scale we may gather both from this description and from the Emperor's decision, recorded by Theodoret, to give Basil "some very fine lands that he owned in the area." We know it too in another way, for the Basileiad grew so large it became known as the "new city" and to it shifted Caesarea's center of gravity. "The new city of Basil," says Sir William Ramsay, "seems to have caused the gradual concentration of the entire population of Caesarea round the ecclesiastical center and the abandonment of the old city."

Eustathius had already done the same thing on a smaller scale at Sebaste; Basil may have got some helpful hints for his own vast scheme. He saw this not as a single effort. Round the central bishoprics of the big cities were villages with assistant bishops known as *chorepiscopi*. Basil had several of these and he wanted them all to establish similar smaller buildings with their assisting monks. He pleaded with the civil authorities that these be free from taxes.

Here was the perfect fulfillment of the common life—not stopping short in its own group of seekers for perfection, but poured out over a very imperfect world. Basil was the first bishop, Lowther Clarke says, who united episcopacy and monasticism in one social mission. Ramsay compares the Basileiad and other such buildings to the cities founded by the Greek kings, as centers from which the Christian ideal grew and radiated as had that of Greece from its cities. These buildings were becoming the center of social and municipal life. "The Greek conception of a free people governing itself without priestly interference was dying out and the Asiatic conception of a religion governing in theocratic fashion the entire life and conduct of men was reviving."

In the background of Basil's life as bishop we must see always the woods of Pontus where he had been born, where his sister and youngest brother still lived, ruling the monasteries he had founded. He kept in close touch with these monasteries: sending them vocations, going there to rest and to pray. The two monasteries were in the end one. The nuns had begun in Basil's ancestral home. But finally both men and women were established on the other side of the river under the rule of Peter.

THE YEARS OF TRIAL

Difficulties with the Emperor and his myrmidons were a small fraction of the heavy burden Basil had to bear during the ten years of his episcopate. Many of the surrounding bishops were jealous of his elevation. They were mostly tainted with Arianism and it was only, says Gregory Nazianzen, the pressure of the multitude, faithful alike to orthodoxy and to Basil, which forced them occasionally to make professions of the Catholic creed. Strangely enough Basil's own uncle, although orthodox, was one of the bishops who disapproved his election. I wish there were fewer Gregories in this story—he was another, and Basil's brother, Gregory of Nyssa, embroiled the matter still further. He twice forged letters of reconciliation from uncle to nephew, joyfully received by the one, indignantly repudiated by the other. This well-meant folly Basil felt keenly: his letter to the elder Gregory is curiously beautiful and did finally win him round.

But most of his troubles were less with the men concerned than with their ideas. Newman has called Basil the Job or the Jeremiah of the fourth century, and, writing to Eustathius of Sebaste, he says of himself that he had, like Job, kept a long silence in the midst of afflictions, that, like the prophet, he had for three years been "as one who heard not and in his mouth are no reproofs." He had loved and admired Eustathius, and it was only on conviction that he was heretical about the Trinity that he broke with him—with bitter grief, often expressed bitterly.

We see in his letters to St. Athanasius how heavily the troubles at Antioch weighed on Basil's mind, how keenly he felt the estrangement with Pope Damasus and with the western bishops.

The schism in Antioch began with the consecration of Meletius, suspected of some tinge of Arianism, as bishop in 361. Paulinus was also consecrated. There were still (and would be for the eight years of Basil's bishopric and for fifteen years after) two Catholic bishops at Antioch. Paulinus, because of Athanasius' support, was acknowledged by Rome; Basil upheld Meletius. It was to Athanasius that Basil looked to win from Rome a keener interest in the affairs of the East. It was Athanasius who, if he were convinced, would be able to convince Pope Damasus of the real state of things at Antioch. Basil felt bitterly that whereas the slightest sign of heresy among themselves agitated the western bishops, they were apt to be indifferent to the terrible storms shaking the East, yet as he wrote to Athanasius: "The one way of safety for the Churches of the East lies in their having the sympathy of the Churches of the West."

It was suspicion of heresy in Meletius and, as Basil believed, mis-information, that had caused Rome to support Paulinus. The immense distance made it difficult for Damasus and the West to judge an Eastern situation, but, says Basil to Athanasius: "What through all the West is more honored than your venerable grey hairs?...send men of sound doctrine to the bishops in the West.... Tell them the troubles that beset us. Suggest some mode of relief."

In another letter he tells him that he has written to Damasus asking him, if the calling of a synod is difficult, to exercise his own personal authority and send men able to undertake this laborious journey to examine matters on the spot. A new heretic is arising, Marcellus of Ancyra, who teaches that the Word comes indeed from the Father but "had no existence before His coming forth, nor hypostasis after His return." This was in fact to treat the word *persona* in its classical meaning of a mask and to destroy the reality of the Persons in the Godhead, making the Son only a manifestation of the Father. Basil begs the help of Athanasius lest Christians "struggle as in a night battle, without being able to distinguish between friends and foes."

Basil had a lack, curious in so immensely intelligent a man, of the most elementary psychology. The letters between him and the Pope are enough to make one weep—probably he himself wept often enough. But his optimism rose unreasonably at the slightest cause. His first attempts had been wholly unsuccessful—partly because Athanasius was supporting Paulinus against Basil's candidate Meletius, but partly also because Basil's own orthodoxy was half doubted in the West.

In his panegyric of St. Athanasius, Gregory Nazianzen makes clear how these doubts had arisen—just as Athanasius himself had shown at the Council of Alexandria that Greeks and Latins were trying to say the same thing in different languages.

> We asserted one essence and three hypostases (one of these terms expressing the nature, the other the properties of the three Persons). The Latins thought as we did; but because of the poverty of their language and the lack of vocabulary, they could not distinguish hypostasis from essence. Therefore, to avoid talking of three essences, they brought in the word *persona*. What is the result? An utterly ridiculous, indeed lamentable, disagreement. A trifling difference in terms is seen as a difference in faith: the three Persons have given rise to Sabellianism; the three hypostases to Arianism . . . and as new disputes arise daily, we see the whole world in danger of perishing for a few syllables.

Jerome was also writing from the East begging the Pope to intervene there: "From me, a Roman, the phrase 'three hypostases' is being asked by this Arian brood of rustics. . . . Settle the matter, I beg of you. . . . No school of secular learning knows any difference between *hypostasis* and *usia*. Who would be so sacrilegious as to speak openly of three substances?"

If, remarks Pere Lebreton, even men of learning felt such distrust of the eastern vocabulary, what would the ordinary faithful of the West feel? When Basil sent really intelligent messengers to Rome who could explain the meaning of his letters, he received at last a friendly reply from Pope St. Damasus. It was a situation of immense difficulty for the Pope, but Basil realized this so little that, on receiving a first sign of understanding, he wrote back eagerly asking Damasus to censure three eastern bishops—one of them being Paulinus of Antioch!

But another was Apollinaris of Laodicea. Basil in fact realized earlier than the bishops of the West that a new Christological heresy was arising in the East. Apollinaris is an interesting figure. During Julian's brief reign, when Catholics were forbidden to teach the Classics in the pagan schools, he and his father, another Apollinaris, set out to write Christian Classics. They rewrote the Bible in Homeric verse, most of which has disappeared. The version of the Psalms attributed to the son is dismissed by Puech[5] as of poor literary quality. Violently anti-Arian, Apollinaris stressed the divinity at the expense of the full humanity of Christ, declaring that the Godhead had taken the place of the human soul. The phrase in which the orthodox attacked this heresy was, "Nothing is healed that is not assumed;" if Christ had not a human soul, then man's soul would not be healed; but it precisely needs healing first, sin is no mere bodily act. Christ had taken our whole nature.

St. Basil might have been more speedily successful in drawing the Pope's attention to this heresy had the question of *usia* and *hypostasis* been clarified earlier, or had he been content to leave the matter of the Antioch schism alone until or unless he could convince St. Athanasius, the man most listened to by Rome, and thus the great link between East and West.

Pope Damasus did in the end condemn Apollinarianism, but not until 377.

*   *   *   *   *   *

Basil had written to Athanasius of all that a meeting would have meant to him: to be able to talk of the Church's necessities, just to see and know personally the man he so much admired. One feels in these letters something deeper than is spoken—the yearning of a lonely man for intercourse, of a man of tempered steel for one strong like himself. Strong men are few, and Basil lived the years of his bishopric in an increasing solitude.

At first he showed intense activity, visiting all whom he could help, counsel, direct into the right path, but illness increasingly confined him to Caesarea. His letters show how hard it was for him to travel even a short distance, especially in cold weather. To an irate functionary who threatened to tear out his liver, Basil remarked what a kindness this would be since, where it was, he had suffered from it for years. Youthful excesses catch up with some men in middle life; Basil was dying of his youthful austerities.

Duchesne sees in "the distrust and bitter tone of his correspondence" the effect of this diseased liver. Basil enlisted, he says, in the service of a campaign for peace "a temperament both too sensitive and too combative." The way he fought for peace is indeed sometimes disconcerting, but reading his letters as a whole, one is more struck by another element. True, many of them are combative, but even these are written in love for truth and for souls, while many others are solely letters of service. With his miserable health, the immense burdens he was carrying, the feebleness of his friends and the fierceness of his enemies, the wonder is that Basil could concentrate on letter after letter of simple charity: letters to tax assessors begging consideration, that monks and private people may "be relieved of this many-headed hydra;" letters to Modestus the prefect, now Basil's friend, begging his protection for the oppressed; letters of consolation in which Basil is weeping with the afflicted—a father whose son has died, a man widowed after "a wedded companionship blended in uttermost harmony, dissolved more quickly than a dream." Yet, writes Basil, all must die and grief at the ending of a perfect marriage "is itself no small gift among the gifts of God. . . . Thus therefore you should think of her as having gone her way by a certain road that we all must travel."

If his psychology sometimes failed with popes or statesmen, it was perfect with friends in distress: he never forgot that praise of the departed is what the mourner craves. He writes to a general's widow of "that noble and unconquerable soul" who had left her "in the full flower of his years and the splendor of his successes," and bids her "give thanks to the Lord that you have been thought worthy of living with such a man whose loss nearly the whole Roman Empire has felt," and in her children and her own eternal future he offers "a noble occupation for your thoughts."

Asking a favor of a functionary Basil is careful to say "that this affair will cross over to great Alexandria and supply admiration for Your Honor to the people there is clear even if I do not mention it." But there was little he forgot to mention that would be of service to "a friend," "a compatriot," a "son," or even "on behalf of a stranger"—for consolation "is due to strangers from Christians." With his intimates we get another Basil again: "Whether I write or not I bear you about with me enshrined within my heart, " he writes when, "fretful at the long waning of the winter," he has set his heart on getting a married couple "to spend the saving days of Easter with us."

A light-hearted correspondence, blending pleasure and charity, is that with his old pagan master Libanius, whose answers make him very attractive. Basil sends various young Cappadocians "to seek after eloquence and learning and to employ you as the master of their training." He is "conferring as great favor on them as do those who guide the thirsty to a spring." Libanius is delighted, especially when one of them arrives bringing "a letter from the admirable Basil." He was an expensive teacher but not for Basil's poorer friends. "Our services are not measured by money; it is enough that he who cannot give should be able to receive...if any man in poverty loves learning he is preferred to those who are wealthy."

Delighted to relive the past, Libanius and Basil revive the classical allusions and Libanius questions Basil about their common friends. Then begins what Basil calls a game that Libanius is playing with him. For the rhetorician declares himself vanquished by the greater eloquence of his friend's letters—he has taken a vote on the matter with a group of eminent men who all agreed with him. Basil retorts that Libanius is behaving like a father who encourages his child by pretending he has won a game. But there was "something indescribably delightful in the language you used in your game...as if Milo should beg to be excused from boxing against *me*." After all, in this matter of language Basil now associates with Moses and Elias, "who communicate their thoughts to me in a barbarian tongue.... Even if I did learn something from you, time has made me forget it."

This new letter, however, made those present with Libanius "leap to their feet" when read to them. Whatever Basil may say, "of that which has always been mine and was formerly yours, the roots not only remain but will remain as long as you live and no lapse of time could ever excise them, not even if you almost wholly neglect to water them."

* * * * * *

Valens seems to have feared two men only—Athanasius and Basil. The death of the former in 373 was the signal for a fierce persecution in Alexandria. Athanasius had desired for his successor his brother, Peter, and the Catholics ratified his choice. But the Emperor forced upon them the Arians' candidate, Lucius. His intrusion was marked by scenes such as the city had witnessed with George of Cappadocia. Consecrated virgins were violated, paraded naked through the town or put to death; priests, deacons and monks imprisoned, exiled, sent to work in the mines. A young man

dressed as a girl danced on the altar of the basilica while
another stood naked in the pulpit whence Athanasius had
preached, pouring out blasphemies and obscenities.

Lucius came in supported by an official and by the old
Euzoius, who fifty years previously had been expelled with
Arius from Alexandria by Bishop Alexander, and had come
from Antioch to celebrate his revenge. Peter could only
disappear. For a while he hid in the neighborhood; before
long he had fled to Rome. But he was not the man to govern a
diocese or carry on a fight after his brother's grand style. Nor
did he possess the patience and balance that made Athanasius
an ambassador of peace. As far as in him lay, he embroiled
the Antioch dispute still further, fiercely denouncing
Meletius to the council in Rome at which St. Basil's letter was
read, and complaining to Basil because Basil's own envoy
defended the bishop supported by him.

None of this was cheering for Basil, and his difficulties
nearer home were becoming more acute and pressing every
day. The vast province of Cappadocia, over which he was
Metropolitan, had been, in 371, divided by the government
into two, and Anthimus, Bishop of Tyana, claimed that the
civil elevation of his city into a metropolis extended its
episcopal authority also over the new province. He began to
ordain bishops, to act in general as Metropolitan and to
manifest complete disregard of Basil's authority.

What was to be done? No support could be hoped for from
the civil authorities, and Basil saw the only solution in a
multiplication of sees, not necessarily in large or important
cities, but at strategic points. Thus he chose Nyssa for his
brother Gregory and Sasima for his friend of Nazianzus. The
brother did his best and struggled for many years with
circumstances adverse enough. But the friend failed Basil
totally, and this incident led to the breaking of his closest tie,
to the crowning loneliness of his life.

Poor Basil; yet he should have known better. Almost
immediately after his consecration, he had begged for

Gregory's presence and help and the answer had been a definite refusal, both for Basil's sake and his own—"That you might not seem to be collecting your partisans about you with indecency and heat as your objectors would say; next, for my own peace and reputation." A poet, a thinker, a recluse, Gregory seems to have been curiously unfitted to deal with the strange, wild world of Asia Minor in the fourth century. Yet so too, by temperament, was Basil. It was only by heroic courage that he had overcome a natural shrinking from all the things his office involved: general society, public functions and disputations. A heretical opponent spoke with contempt of his "retired cottage and closely fastened door, his flustered manner when people came in, his voice and look, the expression of his countenance and other symptoms of fear." If *he* had had to overcome all this, it must have seemed to Basil that his friend could do the same. And lately Gregory had offered to come "if the sea needs water or you a counselor, at all events to gain benefits and act the philosopher, by bearing ill-usage in your company."

They had in fact traveled together to collect the produce of a farm situated in the Second Cappadocia which belonged to the Church of Caesarea. On their way back the retainers of Anthimus had blocked the pass and attacked them. Sasima was a village or small posting town—important by its position, because whoever held it could more or less assure safe passage for his convoys. But for the rest: very few houses, a jail—you could hear, says Gregory, the groans of the victims and their rattling chains. There was nothing green in Sasima, no water, nothing but dust.

Gregory never claimed his bishopric, never ordained a priest for it. When Anthimus put in a rival bishop, Gregory would not contest the see with him, but went back to Nazianzus, where his old father was still alive. "Give me," he wrote to Basil, "peace and quiet above all things. Why should I be fighting for sucklings and birds that are not mine as if in a matter of souls and canons? Well, play the man, be strong, turn everything to your own glory, as rivers suck up the mountain torrent...so much shall I gain from this your friendship, not to trust in friends, or to put anything above God." It was probably the heaviest disappointment of Basil's life.

Basil died on the first day of the eventful year 379. He was not quite fifty, though he looked an old man, and all his struggles seemed to have led nowhere. There was still schism in Antioch, Constantinople was in heretical hands, so was Alexandria. Arianism was still strong, though beginning to grow tired, and a whole crop of new heresies were flourishing. The Empire was in confusion after the victory of the Goths at Adrianople. The Church in the West still appeared remote and indifferent. But he never lost hope. "Many times," says his brother, "we saw that he [like Moses] was in a dark cloud wherein was God. For what was invisible to others, initiation into the mysteries of the spirit made visible to him, so that he seemed to be encompassed in the dark cloud wherein knowledge of God was concealed."

And now as he lay "hardly breathing, life almost utterly gone," his friend saw "a renewal of vigor, as he spoke his words of farewell, his words of prayer. He laid hands on the most generous of his servants, giving with his hand the Holy Spirit that the altar might not be robbed of those who had been his disciples, and had borne their part in his own priesthood."

As he lay there dying, Gregory Nazianzen saw him, like St. Paul, his course run; like Moses, having heard God's words, "Come up into this mountain." Not, says Gregory, as Moses was told, "to die there," but "to be with Us." But Moses was also told that from the mountain he should "see the land of Canaan which I will deliver to the children of Israel to possess." And it may be that as he laid his hands on his disciples with the sudden strength that appeared miraculous, Basil saw how the failure of his fight would after all issue in triumph. Not merely the momentary immediate triumph of the vast multitudes that thronged around the

body of the man they at once proclaimed saint; of the ora-
tions which already entitled him Basil the Great; of his feast
celebrated as less only than those of the Apostles. If indeed he
was less! For listen to his brother:

> If Paul preceded him in time and Basil was raised up many
> generations later this is the work of the Divine Dispensa-
> tion on behalf of men, not a proof of inferior excellence.
> Even Moses was born many ages after Abraham, and
> Samuel after Moses, and after him Elias, and after him the
> great John; after John, Paul, and after him, Basil.

Few saints have had so instantaneous a personal triumph, but
for that Basil would have cared little.

The triumph of the Faith was what mattered, and within
three weeks of his death Theodosius had become Emperor,
within four months the hesitating Gregory had left Nazianzus
and established a Catholic Church in heretical Constantinople. Basil had to wait for time's healing hand to bring the
Antioch schism to its end, but doubtless it is easy to wait
patiently in heaven. In 380 Theodosius gave his adhesion to
the creed of Nicaea and restored the churches of Constantinople to the Catholics, and the following year the Council of
Constantinople brought back at least for a time the always
precarious peace between East and West.

St. Gregory Nazianzen

Newman tells some of this story in his *Church of the
Fathers*, and he remarks quaintly that it appears impertinent
for him to be arbitrating between two saints, but that he does
feel, looking merely at the external facts of history, that a
saint and an ascetic should not have objected to be sent to
Sasima because "it was deficient in beauty and interest,"
although he will allow Gregory to object to the responsibilities involved in becoming the neighbor of Anthimus. But
Gregory himself almost saves the historian the need to
arbitrate, by his own oration on Basil from which I have

already quoted copiously. It was delivered three years after Basil's death. During those three years Gregory had gone through a greater variety of experience than in all his previous fifty.

Historians are puzzled as to how he got to Constantinople; he speaks himself of a call from "many pastors and sheep," which Tillemont reads as meaning the people and the neighboring bishops. Technically he was still Bishop of Sasima; actually he had even left Nazianzus on his father's death, and the Catholics of Constantinople dug him out of a monastery in Seleucia. Whether legally appointed or not, he poured new confidence into his discouraged flock. He was a brilliant preacher and the Arian population, which began by despising him, raged as his congregations grew too large for the chapel called by him Anastasis, or Resurrection, to express his hope of the resurrection of the Faith in Constantinople. He preached a series of magnificent sermons on the Trinity, which cannot have soothed Arian susceptibilities. During the Easter Vigil, as he celebrated the Mysteries, they broke in and drove out the congregation with a volley of stones. Then they brought Gregory into court with the charge of provoking a riot!

An attempt at introducing another bishop was crushed by Theodosius, who had Gregory solemnly installed in the Basilica of the Apostles. This was confirmed by the Council of Constantinople, and Gregory was enthroned by Meletius of Antioch, who very inconveniently died almost immediately afterwards. As Gregory struggles to end the schism, vainly entreating the followers of Meletius to accept Paulinus and bring peace to their Church, we feel, as we have through these three years, that the mantle of Basil had briefly fallen upon him. "Was it Gregory," asks Newman, "or was it Basil that blew the trumpet in Constantinople and waged a successful war in the very seat of the enemy?"

But alas, wars are long to wage and a defeat or two must not mean withdrawal if they are to be won. Gregory gives the impression of a man living always at fever point. He has none of the calm with which Basil confronted misfortune. He failed to win support for Paulinus. Flavian was consecrated as Meletius' successor, and Pope St. Damasus also expressed his doubts, not about the enthronement by Meletius, but about the canonicity of the transfer from Sasima. Such transfers, he said, "are not made without some degree of ambition, and are contrary to the tradition." The Egyptian bishops, on arrival at Constantinople, refused to take part in the liturgy celebrated by Gregory.

This was the last straw and Gregory saw the horrible specter of Sasima arising before him again. He threw in his hand and returned to his solitude. He bade farewell in a final and powerful discourse to the town of Constantinople, to the little Church of the Resurrection, to the great basilicas of Sancta Sophia and the Holy Apostles, to the East and West, for whom he was suffering persecution, to the guardian angel of his Church, and—very curiously—to the Trinity, whom he had untiringly made known to his people.

He was succeeded by Nectarius—an old senator, not baptized when he was chosen—and he, in due course, by the great John Chrysostom.

Before his total retirement, Gregory preached in Caesarea the eulogium of Basil which is so revealing about them both. And in it he defends Basil's action in creating new bishoprics when his province was divided. He speaks of the wild confusion that ensued, of the robberies committed, of the priests who upheld Basil being expelled. But Basil "made the dispute serve the Church's development and gave to evil the best possible result by adorning his fatherland with a greater number of bishops. What came of this? Three results, all excellent: greater care for souls, the possession by each town of its own bishop, hence the end of the war."

Even now, however, after so many years, he cannot wholly forgive Basil for making him a pawn in the game. "From this have arisen all the irregularities, the agitations of my life. This made it impossible for me to be a philosopher or to win the reputation of being one—not that this last matters very much." But while at the time he had blamed the pride and ambition of Basil, he can say today: "His thoughts were above the thoughts of men; detached from this world while still in it, he referred all things to the Holy Spirit, and knowing how to respect friendship he only despised it from the moment that he was obliged to put God's honor before all things and place our hopes of eternity above perishable things."

This was a generous judgment, and we may well ask whether Basil had perhaps, like many great men, forgotten that no man is expendable even in the service of others. But there seems to have been at this period the curious idea that one did nothing but good to a man by forcing him to accept the grace of ordination, and with it responsibilities for which he might well be unfitted. Although thousands were flying into the deserts to seek the life of contemplation, the principle that a man might have simply a contemplative vocation was often curiously ignored.

And it must be admitted that, in theory, both Gregories made this attitude easy for Basil. They both insisted that only the man who fears high office is worthy of it. Nazianzen especially, in his eulogy of Basil, descants at length on the damage to the Church wrought by ambitious men grasping at episcopacy. The humble must be exalted, not the proud. The elder Gregory of Nazianzus forced the younger to become a priest, Basil pushed him into being a bishop. They both claimed that the needs of the hour were urgent, that no man should put his own spiritual life above the general need of Christ's people for the Bread of Life, given in sacraments, given in teaching. But it looks as though for Gregory Nazianzen, the call of solitude was altogether too strong. He could leave it to meet an emergency, but he could not live in the series of emergencies through which the great Basil prayed and fought his way to the very end. He ends his eulogy:

> This, O Basil, to you from me: receive this offering from a tongue once very dear to you, your peer in honor and in age. Look upon me now from on high, divine and blessed man, and hold back by your intercession that thorn in the flesh given me by God for my discipline, or else gain for me the courage to endure it. Direct my whole life to my greater good, and when I die may you receive me where you are dwelling. Living thus together and contemplating ever more clearly and perfectly the holy and blessed Trinity whose faint reflection is all we have yet seen, may our desires be thereby sated and the reward bestowed for the fights we have waged or that others have waged against us. But when I die who will praise me as I have praised you?—always supposing he could find anything in me worthy of an oration, in Jesus Christ Our Lord, to whom be everlasting glory. Amen.

St. Macrina had been a second mother to all her brothers: Gregory of Nyssa wrote her life, describing her influence upon Basil, whom she converted, on Peter, whom she educated, and on himself, whom she described as naturally quite unfitted for the splendid position he attained after Basil's death. She told him this on his last visit to the monastery and he described himself in all simplicity as rejoicing at the wisdom and beauty of her words. But her death was very near and as the evening drew on, she tried with failing voice to repeat the prayer sung at the lighting of the lamps. When "her hand brought to her face to make the Sign had signified the end of the prayer, she drew a great deep breath and closed her life and prayer together."

Macrina died shortly after Basil; Gregory of Nyssa and Peter both outlived him for several years. Peter too was made a bishop, succeeding Eustathius at Sebaste. A man of great practical ability, he managed to secure a harvest even in the famine years, could do anything with his hands, and ruled his diocese most capably. Gregory, far less efficient, was great as preacher and as a profoundly mystical writer. Rufinus said of them that the two together were equal to Basil; Gregory in word and doctrine; Peter in works of faith. But saints though they both were it would, I think, take many Peters and even Gregories to equal Basil the Great.

NOTES

[1]Bull's translation, given in the *Dictionary of Christian Biography*, article on "Gregory Thaumaturgus."

[2]I have borrowed Newman's translation of these passages.

[3]For a discussion of the Apostolic life see Jacquier, *Les Actes des Apôtres*. He makes a strong case for the renunciation of goods not having been absolute, but only a total readiness to renounce when called upon.

[4]In *Histoire de la Littérature grecque chrétienne*.

[5]*Littérature grecque chrétienne*, vol. ii, p. 635.

BASIL'S BROTHER, GREGORY OF NYSSA

William Meninger, OCSO
(Monk of St. Josephs Abbey,
Spencer, Mass.)

It was the glory and the cross of Gregory of Nyssa to be the younger brother of Basil of Caesarea. Even the greatness of their common ancestry somehow seems to be attributed by biographers more to Basil than to Gregory! Unquestionably both were worthy sons of worthy parents. Their father, St. Basil the Elder, a well-known lawyer at Neocaesarea in Pontus was himself the son of St. Macrina the Elder. It was she who influenced Basil as a youth especially by teaching him a creed, drawn up for the use of the Church of Neo-caesarea, by Gregory the Wonderworker. During the persecution of Diocletian the grandparents were forced to flee to the mountains of Pontus where they suffered great hardships for the faith. Gregory's mother, Emmelia, was the daughter of a martyr from the same persecution. His father died while Gregory was quite young apparently after having restored much of the family fortune.

Gregory's eldest sister, St. Macrina the Younger, wielded considerable influence on the rest of the family (including Emmelia). A strong-minded woman, she seems single-handedly to have thwarted the efforts of her family to marry her off, after the untimely death of her betrothed, by the pretext of obediently remaining faithful to the husband her father chose for her—even though the chosen one was dead and her father was urging her on to a second betrothal. Gregory attributes to her influence Basil's conversion, their mother's embracing of the contemplative life and no little share in his own pursuit of Christian perfection. Gregory's biography of Macrina, written in the form of a letter to his friend, Olympius, is a splendid example of early Christian hagiography. The scene for his work *On the Soul and the Resurrection* is set at her death bed (380). Gregory assumes the role of antagonist and allows Macrina to defend the Christian doctrine on the soul and immortality.

Basil, born in 330 and five years older than Gregory, was the eldest of the five brothers. Another, Naucratius, "surpassing the others in the excellence of his nature and the beauty of his body and strength and swiftness and adaptability,"[1] at twenty-one years of age, retired to the monastic life at a remote location on the Iris River in Pontus. There he foraged for food in the woods and cared for a group of old people for five years until he was killed in a hunting accident.

Gregory was the third son, born about 335. There were also two other brothers: St. Peter of Sebaste (appointed to that see by Basil), and Nectarius, a rhetorician. The names of four other sisters are unknown.

It was St. Macrina the Younger who turned her property at Annesi on the Iris River into a monastery and who was responsible for St. Basil's decision to embrace monasticism and to settle nearby. In spite of statements of biographers to the contrary, there is no evidence that Gregory of Nyssa joined them at any time except for visits of varying length.[2] In his treatise *On Virginity* Gregory mourns his failure to respond to Basil's attempts to draw him to Annesi.

Like Basil, Gregory's baptism was deferred until he was an adult, a practice both of them subsequently deplored. During a visit to Annesi he was converted by a dream, baptized, and ordained lector. He soon abandoned his first fervor to take up the study of law for which he was taken to task by both Basil and his friend Gregory Nazianzus who charged him with being guilty of vanity and public display.[3] During this time it would seem that Gregory married (cf. treatise *On Virginity*) although nothing seems to be known about his wife's background or even her name.[4]

Little is known of Gregory's education. Basil was educated first by his father and then in schools in Caesarea, Constantinople, and Athens (where he met Gregory Nazianzus, the third of the great Cappadocians, in 351). Gregory, it seems, received his education in Caesarea. To what extent Basil had a hand in educating him is questionable, given, among other things, the closeness of their ages. It is true that Gregory makes many references to Basil as "his teacher," "his master," and even "his father" (especially in his *Books Against Eunomius*) but, clearly, these are to be seen as rhetorical exaggerations. In the introduction to the *Hexaemeron* Gregory claims that anything of note in that treatise will be due to Basil and what is of lesser value will be "the pupil's." This statement, however, stems from the fact that Gregory was there completing an unfinished work of his brother. Indeed, in a letter written early in his adult life to Libanius, Gregory attributes some of his ability in regard to style and oratory to St. Basil but insists, at the same time, that his pedagogical influence was limited because he had enjoyed his brother's company only for a short time.

Both of the brothers had a good background in Greek philosophy which they utilized extensively in their theological works. Nonetheless, both agreed in expressing extreme caution in regard to profane education. Gregory warns about the dangers of this in his *Life of St. Macrina* and especially in his magnificent treatise on the *Life of Moses*. In the latter work, Gregory refers to the Pharoah's daughter who adopted Moses as an allegory of profane philosophy: "For truly barren is profane education, which is always in labor but never gives birth."[5] Yet a bit later Moses' Midianite wife assumes the same role but in a more affirmative sense, as she follows Moses back to Egypt.

The foreign wife will follow him for there are certain things derived from profane education which should not be rejected when we propose to give birth to virtue. Indeed, moral and natural philosophy may become at certain times a comrade, friend, and companion of life to the higher way, provided that the offspring of this union introduce nothing of a foreign defilement.[6]

Gregory admits that in his youthful years, which coincided with the last revival of pagan culture, he was completely won over to the pagan humanistic ideal especially as he read it in the writings of Libanius (Epis., 13. P.G. 46.1049A). As for Basil, he admits when he describes his spiritual awakening (Epis. 223, 2) that he had wasted a great deal of time on foolishness and had dedicated most of his youth laboring in vain after "a wisdom that God had made foolish."[7]

Nonetheless it remains true that Gregory's works are permeated by his extensive knowledge of Greek philosophy. However, he avoids referring to pagan authors as authorities and claims to be a disciple of Basil and St. Paul with the Scriptures as his norm of truth and chief authority. Basil, on the other hand, was more immediately dependent on the Scriptures and, of course, much less speculative, a characteristic which tended to preserve his orthodoxy. Almost inevitably Gregory's speculations would lead to ideas not accepted by later theologians (especially concerning the afterlife). Theological speculation influenced by Greek philosophy is not absent in Basil, of course, as we can see from the obvious influence of Platonism in his *Treatise on the Holy Spirit* (possibly by way of Gregory Nazianzus or Eustathius).[8]

At Basil's insistence (possibly over-insistence) Gregory was consecrated as Bishop of Nyssa in 371, a small suffragan of Basil's See of Caesarea in Cappadocia. It was at this time also that Basil appointed his hitherto devoted friend, Gregory Nazianzus, to the episcopate of Sasima, a city so mean and impoverished that their friendship terminated from that day. Obviously, Basil's intentions were good. He was attempting to provide a bulwark of orthodox bishops to withstand the almost overwhelming (and emperor-supported) advances of the Arians. Yet in his administrative zeal he seems to have "bulldozed" over his brother and his friend to such a degree as to have greatly disappointed the former and to earn the lifetime anger of the latter.[9] At any rate, Gregory Nazianzus later allowed himself to be divested of his see without any effort to resist. Gregory of Nyssa had to be constantly supported by Basil to retain his episcopal seat and even then was exiled from it from 374-378. When a friend showed surprise that Basil had chosen so obscure a place for such a man as his brother, Basil replied (somewhat paternally?) that he did not desire his brother to receive distinction from the name of his see but rather to confer distinction upon it![10]

Basil and his brother, Gregory, both experienced conversions as adults (indeed, Gregory had two of them). Basil, as we have seen, received his at the hands of his sister Macrina. As Gregory describes it in his *Life of St. Macrina*

> ...the distinguished Basil came home from school where he had practiced in rhetoric for a long time. He was excessively puffed up by his rhetorical abilities and disdainful of all great reputations, and considered himself better than the leading men of the district, but Macrina took him over and lured him so quickly to the goal of philosophy that he withdrew from the worldly show and began to look down upon acclaim through oratory and went over to this life full of labor for one's own hand to perform, providing for himself, through his complete poverty, a mode of living that would, without impediment, lead to virtue.[11]

We have seen Gregory's first conversion after his dream at Annesi. His second one probably occurred after his banishment from Nyssa in 374. It was at this time that he was won over to Basil's ideas on reform and began to help Basil in this great work of bringing monasticism to Cappadocia. It was for this purpose that he wrote his first treatise *On Virginity*.[12]

Gregory was deposed from his episcopate by an Arian-dominated synod in 376 for negligence in financial matters. Judging from his subsequent lack of administrative success, it would seem likely, in spite of Basil's vigorous denials, that

the Arian accusation had some substance to it. Gregory was
also charged with canonical irregularities regarding his ordination, again, not an unlikely charge given even Basil's
admission that Gregory received Holy Orders under a certain
constraint from him.[13] For this he was summoned to a synod
at Ancyra where Demosthenes, a member of the Arian
Emperor Valen's court, also levied the charges of misuse of
Church funds.

Claiming illness, Gregory did not attend the synod. Basil,
meanwhile, summoned a synod of orthodox bishops who
wrote to the Synod of Ancyra denying the charges of embez-
zlement. Basil also wrote to Astorgas, a person of influence
at court, to save his brother the indignity of a secular tri-
bunal, but to no avail. Gregory was finally called to appear
at a synod held in his very own See of Nyssa. He refused to
attend, was deposed and banished. He was not able to return
until the grip of Arianism was loosened by the death of
Valens in 378. He gives a description of his triumphal return
in Letter 3 (to Basil?).[14]

A strain in the relationship between the two brothers is
clearly shown in Basil's letter (100) to Eusebius, Bishop of
Samosata, where he writes "I am compassioned with anxi-
eties. . .in the consideration of the trouble caused me by the
simplicity of Gregory of Nyssa who is summoning a synod at
Ancyra and leaving nothing undone to counteract me."[15]
Gregory's attitude is said by some to stem not "from want of
affection but from want of tact" (cf. footnote 15).

A situation even more incomprehensible is found in Basil's
Letters 58, 59, and 60. Here it seems that Gregory actually
forged letters to his uncle, Bishop Gregory, in order to
smooth over some difficulties Basil was having with his
uncle. This was done not once, not twice, but three times!
Basil writes to his brother:

How can I upbraid, as it deserves, your simplicity in all
matters? Who, tell me, ever falls a third time into the same

snares?... Even a brute beast would scarcely suffer that to happen to it. You forged a letter and brought it to me as from the most revered bishop, our common uncle, deceiving me, for I know not what purpose. I received it as sent by the bishop through you. Why should I not?... The forgery was exposed, since the bishop himself denied it with his own voice. We were put to shame because of it. Involved in the disgrace of fraud, falsehood, and deceit, we prayed that the earth might open for us.... I have written this to upbraid you for your simplicity—which I consider not only unbecoming in a Christian, but especially inappropriate at the present time...you are untrustworthy as a messenger in such matters.[16]

It might be appropriate to repeat here what was said at the beginning of this article, only reversing the names: "It was the glory and the cross of *Basil of Caesarea* to be the older brother of *Gregory of Nyssa.*"

It must be admitted that the repeated evidence in Gregory's writings does attest mightily to the love and respect he had for his brother, even granted the penchant of the Eastern mind for hyperbole. This regard is seen in an especially touching way in his earliest ascetic treatise *De Virginitate*. He promises in the introduction of this work to present Basil as the ideal ascetic: "The examples we have in biographies cannot stimulate to the attainment of excellence, as much as a living voice and an example which is still working for good; and so we have alluded to that most godly bishop, our father in God, who himself alone could be the master in such instructions."[17]

St. Basil died January 1, 379, and Gregory inherited much of his extensive activity—theological, monastic, and ecclesiastical.

It may well have been that Basil's dominant personality had, up till then, prevented Gregory from expressing himself. For, despite Basil's affection for his brother, he had no true notion of Gregory's worth. Their characters were too essentially opposed for that. But now, with Basil's death, Gregory was forced to stand on his own and thus, in the years that followed, he was able to reveal himself as he really was.[18]

It was only now that Gregory's reputation really grew. He took part in the Council of Antioch in 379 and in 381 he was one of the 150 bishops summoned by Theodosius to the Second Ecumenical Council at Constantinople where he was accepted as a veritable pillar of orthodoxy and a kind of extension of the thought of Basil. Here also he read to the assembled Fathers a first installment of his great work—itself a defense of Basil—*Against Eunomius,* one of the most significant treatises ever written in refutation of Arianism. This council was to result in a complete victory of those doctrines for which Basil had fought for so many years.

After the Council of Constantinople Gregory made some attempts at administrative reform in behalf of the bishops, but without much success. He attended the Synod of Antioch, convoked to heal a long lasting schism in that see. By that same synod he was given an important role in attempting to reform the churches of Arabia and Babylon. These, along with the Church of Jerusalem, he found to be beyond all his powers of reform.

After this, his influence in external affairs waned considerably. However, now that he was less burdened with administrative duties and dogmatic controversy, Gregory turned wholeheartedly to matters of the spirit. Most of his works belong to this period of his relative leisure and maturity (382-394), especially his mystical writings.

In contrast to Basil who is authoritative, frank, and realistic to the point of harshness, Gregory is emotional, mystical, and enthusiastic. Basil, in his writings, deliberately chooses scriptural expressions in preference to philosophical terminology. This can be clearly seen in his *Rules*. On this basis Basil refrains from a favorite expression of Gregory's, and never calls monks "philosophers" or refers to the ascetic life as the "philosophic life."

In a sense, however, Gregory did shift more and more to Basil's approach in his use of Scripture. *De Instituto Christiano* is one of the works of his maturity and in it one can see a marked difference in this area from his earlier writings (e.g. *De Virginitate*). He is writing to ascetics who he feels have given up, not only worldly values, but also their secular, intellectual life. Thus he cannot base his argumentation on Platonic principles but rather must find his roots in the revealed word.

Basil, in his treatise *On Faith*, had clearly indicated the necessity of giving biblical evidence and as a matter of course in his ascetical treatises concentrated on biblical language. In his dogmatic treatises he was more apt to resort to philosophical concepts. Gregory eventually had to be very careful in expressing his mystical theology in terminology that resembled either Origenistic or Neoplatonic sources. We can see this carefulness to a marked degree in that splendid work of Gregory's later years *The Life of Moses*. Here we can easily see the influence of both Origen and Plotinus but entirely expressed in a scriptural ambience.

Basil's influence on Gregory is perhaps more in direction than in content even though we do find specific ideas, such as Gregory's all important *Synergia*, taken directly from Basil's works. Werner Jaeger points out that many of Gregory's ideas "received their first coinage from his brother Basil." He also indicates many points of congruity between Basil's *Rules* and Gregory's *De Instituto Christiano*. Gregory leaves the routine details of daily monastic living up to Basil, but does parallel his framework of ideas. Both works were written for the same purpose but use different approaches—Basil using the popular question and answer form, Gregory favoring the exhortatory treatise. The *Rules* regulate minutiae of monastic

living, the treatise is concerned with the spirit behind them.
Both begin by describing the goal of Christian life with a
view towards directing the ascetical life to it. Both take as a
point of departure the natural tendency man has to strive for
the good which includes his desire for purification of the
soul. Both also derive this theory from the Genesis account of
man created in the image of God. Indeed Jaeger goes so far as
to say that Gregory's authorship of the treatise could be
discovered, were it not known from other sources, merely by
the "exact shade of its agreement with Basil's thought."

Gregory had to bring much of Basil's work to completion.
As an organizer and man of action Basil touched upon many
areas without going into them too deeply. For this reason
Gregory wrote his *Hexaemeron*. As he says in the introduction, it was his intention to complete the sermons Basil had
begun several years before. Where Basil had simply set forth
the facts, Gregory tried to reveal the underlying causes and
effects. Basil had ended on the fifth day of creation and
Gregory added the sermon on the *Creation of Man*.

Jaeger points out that all of Gregory's ascetical works form
an important complement to Basil's fundamental codification
of the *Rules*.[19] This is as true of his earliest ascetical work *De
Virginitate* as well as of his last word on the nature of the
ascetic life, *De Instituto Christiano*.[20] This is the case even in
his *Life of St. Macrina* where Gregory presents a concrete
embodiment of the *Rules* in the person of his saintly sister.
Gregory's intention in the *Life of Moses* was to give a mystical orientation to the monastic establishment organized and
lived by Basil. In *De Instituto Christiano*, which treats of the
goal of Christian monasticism, he gives in a rather complete
outline the fundamental spiritual doctrine of St. Basil. The
very essence of Gregory's own spiritual message is likewise
contained in these works.[21]

(*Special thanks to Father Jean Gribomont for reading and
correcting this article. -- Wm. M.*)

NOTES

[1]Callahan, V.W., trans., "Life of St. Macrina," *Gregory of Nyssa Ascetical Works*, Fathers of the Church Series, Vol. 58. Washington, D.C.: Catholic University Press, 1967, p. 168.

[2]Musurillo, Herbert, S.J., trans. and ed., *From Glory to Glory: Texts from Gregory of Nyssa's Mystical Writings*, (selected and an introduction by Jean Daniélou, S.J.). New York: Charles Scribner's Sons, 1961, pp. 3ff.

[3]*Nicene and Post-Nicene Fathers*, Second Series, Vol. 5: Gregory of Nyssa. Grand Rapids, Michigan: Wm. B. Eerdmans Publishing Co., 1974, p. 3.

[4]Some claim she was Theosebeia, sister of Gregory Nazianzus, cf. *Nicene and Post-Nicene Fathers*, Vol. 5, p. 3. Also Vol. 7, pp. 461-462.

[5]Gregory of Nyssa, *Life of Moses*. New York: Paulist Press, 1978, p. 57.

[6]Ibid., pp. 62-63. Also Daniélou, J., *Platonisme et Théologie Mystique*. Aubier: Editions Montaigne, 1944.

[7]Quasten, J., *Patrology*, Vol. 3. Antwerp: Spectrum Publishers, 1960, pp. 204ff.

[8]Cf. "Gregory of Nyssa, St.," *New Catholic Encyclopedia*, Vol. 6, p. 795. One author (H.F. Cherniss) even goes so far as to claim that Gregory's doctrine was only superficially Christian and essentially Neoplatonist, a problem some Greek Orthodox theologians tried to resolve centuries later by "purging" Plotinus from Gregory's writings.

[9]There are few pieces of literature from any age expressive of such disappointment, personal chagrin, and anger as Gregory of Nazianzus' letter to Basil expressing his reaction to the Sasima appointment. Indeed Jerome, at his very best (worst) is mild compared to it! Even in writing Basil's praises some time after his death, Gregory does not forgive him Sasima. Cf. Ruether, Rosemary, *Gregory of Nazianzus*, Oxford: Clarendon Press, 1969.

[10]Cf. *Nicene and Post-Nicene Fathers*, (supra n. 3), Vol. 3, pp. 4-5.

[11]Callahan, *Gregory of Nyssa Ascetical Works*, (supra n. 1), pp. 168-169.

[12]Cf. Musurillo, *From Glory to Glory*, (supra n. 2), pp. 4ff. During his exile Gregory did not visit Annesi at all.

[13]Cf. Basil's Letter 225, *Nicene and Post-Nicene Fathers*, (supra n. 3), Vol. 8, p. 267.

[14]Ibid., Vol. 5, p. 5.

[15]Ibid., Vol. 8, p. 184.

[16]Basil's Letter 58, *St. Basil Letters 1-185*, Vol. 1. New York: Fathers of the Church, Inc., 1951, pp. 148-149.

[17]*Nicene and Post-Nicene Fathers*, (supra n. 3), Vol. 5, p. 343.

[18]Musurillo, *From Glory to Glory*, (supra n. 2), pp. 4-5.

[19]Jaeger, Werner, *Two Recently Discovered Works of Ancient Christian Literature*. Leiden: E. J. Brill, 1965, pp. 83ff.

[20]Ibid., pp. 19ff.

[21]Ibid., pp. 133-142.

THE GREATER RULES OF
SAINT BASIL — A SURVEY*

Adalbert de Vogüé, OSB
(*Monk of the Abbey of
La-Pierre-Qui-Vire, France*)

The quick growth of Christian monachism in the fourth century is marked by the appearance of three cenobitic rules. Destined to exert a permanent influence on the long chain of legislative documents which will follow them, these first three texts appear successively in Upper Egypt, in Asia Minor, and in Africa. The languages used and the environments differ as much as the regions: Pachomius wrote in Coptic, Basil in Greek, Augustine in Latin. The intervals are regular: thirty or forty years—the space of a generation—separate the Pachomian (about 320-346), Basilian (about 361-378), and Augustinian (about 394-397) legislations. In spite of this chronological gap, which ought to have allowed each work to influence the one following, it does not seem that Basil had read Pachomius, nor Augustine his two predecessors. They are original productions which appear thus one after the other in the three corners of Christendom.

The extreme diversity of content and form confirms this independence. All through the four collections which are attributed to him, Pachomius set up by means of small juxtaposed articles a meticulous community rule where Scriptural foundations, reasoned motivations and spiritual advice are almost entirely lacking. With Basil, on the contrary, Bible quotations, theoretical considerations, and developments of spirituality superabound, relegating to a secondary plane practical norms which are neither numerous nor detailed. As for Augustine's Rule (the *Ordo monasterii* followed by the *Praeceptum*), it holds a middle course between these two extremes, while its trifling dimensions place it in marked contrast with the Pachomian work, almost three times its size in length, and especially with the very large *Regula Basilii* which, even in its primitive and short form, is nearly ten

times longer.[1] Besides, Augustine's continuous redaction has
no relation with the broken-up and disconnected state of the
greater part of Basil's Questions, to say nothing of
Pachomius' articles.

Other resemblances and dissimilarities should be noticed—
we will return to them—but these are sufficient to place
quickly our subject, the Basilian rule, between its two sister
rules. For the present, it is this rule itself which has to be considered in its complexity, in order to make intelligible the
purpose of the present study and its title.

Recent works, those of Jean Gribomont in particular,[2]
have brought to light the genesis and the relations of the
different parts, recensions, and versions, the whole of which
constitutes what we (very improperly) call today the
"Monastic Rules" of Saint Basil. These do not seem to belong
to the first period when Basil led a monastic life at Annesi
(359-361), when he traced the still generic program of the
"Moral Rules" and poetically described his retreat in his
second Letter, but rather to the following period, in the
course of which he visited, as a priest-ascetic, brotherhoods
not founded by him, and answered various questions that
were put to him. Once written down, these questions and
answers were first collected into a body of 203 Questions, the
Small Asketicon, which has only survived in a Latin and a
Syriac translation. The Latin version made by Rufinus,
probably in 397, is particularly important, not only because
of its accuracy, but also because of the influence it exerted on
Latin monachism.[3] It is the *Regula sancti Patris nostri Basilii*
mentioned by Saint Benedict.[4]

Shortly after this first collection, Basil wrote his Letter 22,
which condenses, under the deliberately dry format of nearly
fifty maxims, the substance of the Small Asketicon. But the
rounds of visits begin again, provoking new questions and
answers. From these continuous exchanges, as well as from
the more mature reflections which follow them, proceed an
ample supplement of Questions, which Basil later completed

and joined to the primitive work only when he became bishop (370). This Large Asketicon he edited under several forms, which are the origin of the multiple recensions which we know, thanks to Greek manuscripts and versions in different languages.

Of these recensions, the most important for us is the "Vulgate," constituted about the end of the fifth century, for it alone was printed and is now accessible to all.[5] It presents two series of Questions, arranged under two distinct numberings: first, there are 55 long Questions (the "Great Rules"), and then 313 short Questions (the "Small Rules"). If the first category, that of the long or "expanded"[6] Questions, owes its origin certainly to Basil himself, we cannot say as much of their fragmentation into 55 numbers. In fact, it seems that there were originally only 18 Great Rules, which roughly corresponded to the 20 of some recensions which have reached us. It is to this primitive distribution that we must go back, if we wish to restore to the first part of the work its true aspect.[7]

Another indispensable consideration is that of the relations between the Great and the Small Asketicons. Of the 203 primitive Questions, the first 11 are relocated, amplified to twice their size, in the Great Rules 1-23, whereas the 192 remaining ones, not lengthened but redistributed, have found their way into the Small Rules. The rest of the Great Asketicon is entirely original, i.e., both the Great Rules 24-55 and the 121 new Small Rules which are mixed with the old ones. In its totality, the Great Asketicon must be at least twice as long as the Small one.

This sketch of the history of the Basilian Rules shows up the fragmentary character of the research we are undertaking here. If we content ourselves with a survey of the Great Rules, we not only isolate a part of the whole by neglecting the Small Rules, but we also prescind from the evolution of the work, such as we may reconstitute it by taking account of the Small Asketicon.

In spite of this twofold lacuna, the investigation seems to us both legitimate and useful. For a first contact with Basil's monastic thought, the analysis of the Great Rules alone is doubtless more profitable, by its very limitation, than a complete survey which might attempt to embrace the detailed multiplicity of the Small Rules. Concerning these, it is enough to know, in order to find one's way around at least summarily, that they are distributed over a dozen series.[8] Moreover, we shall appeal to them in order to illustrate certain Great Rules. The more methodical organization of these facilitates the entry of the modern reader into the Basilian world. Our wish is to bring out the structure of this discourse, such as it is presented in its last stage. As for its prehistory and its genesis, already well brought to light by other works,[9] they will not be ignored, but most often taken for granted.

*   *   *   *   *   *

After careful reflection, it seems to us that the Great Rules are best distributed into seven sections. The first of these (Prol.-7) treats of obedience to the commandments and of the two fundamental precepts: love of God and love of neighbor. Then come renunciation (8-15), mastery over the appetites (16-23), good order in the community (24-36), work (37-42), the duties of superiors (43-54), the use of medicine (55). Let us run through these seven steps before taking some general views.

I.   Separation from the World and Common Life (Prol.-7)

The purpose of this initial discourse is to place the setting where all the further elements are going to take place. This setting is a community of men separated from the world. The two aspects—separation and community—are successively described and connected to the two great precepts of the love of God and neighbor.

To love God is to do his will, to fulfill his commandments. Being a true labor, a profession which absorbs all one's energies, this fulfillment of the divine will requires an undivided attention. Whence the opportunity of separating oneself from sinful men, from the secular society which does not care for God. Love of God leads, then, to living apart (*idiazein*).

On its side, love of neighbor requires the common life. By separating from the world, the Christian ought not to isolate himself from those who have the same purpose to obey God. Required as it is in the name of charity which "does not seek its own interest," social life is also indispensable if we wish to put into practice the doctrine of the Body of Christ, the individuals finding their fulfillment only by their interaction as members within this body. The personal charisms, granted for the good of all, are only developed within the community. For their exercise or their control, the virtues also require a communal environment. The latter also allows, collegially, so to speak, the fulfillment of all the commandments, even those which the isolated individual cannot practice simultaneously.

In short, everything militates in favor of the common life. Announced by the *Ecce quam bonum* of the Psalmist (Ps. 132:1), given as a model by the primitive Church when the crowd of believers was but one heart and one soul (Acts 2:44 and 4:32), this fraternal communion imposes itself so rigorously that any solitary existence—"monastic," evidently in the strictest sense, as Basil says—seemingly ought to be excluded. So categoric a communal option, which will be renewed several times,[10] stands in vivid contrast, it goes without saying, with that openness to the anchoretic life which, following Cassian, both the Master and Benedict will maintain.

Love of God and of neighbor, then, leads to living away from the world, in community. Afterwards, Basil will constantly rely on this twofold exigency of separation and union,

whether in the general disposition of the Great Rules—to
a first part based on renunciation succeeds, beginning with
GR 24, a second part which treats especially of the common
life—or in the detail of the Questions, especially with regard
to the habit. Thus, it is certainly the main structure of his
work which is foundationed right at the beginning in this first
section, in reference to the first two precepts of the divine
law.

But this structure itself rests on a fundamental principle,
fully brought to light here and continually recalled afterwards: that of obedience to the commandments. Before
discoursing on the love of God and of men, Basil answers the
question of order and succession of the divine precepts. And
this beginning, which was already that of the Small
Asketicon, in turn is prepared by a Prologue, almost entirely
proper to the Great Asketicon, in which the necessity of
accomplishing *all* the commandments is inculcated at great
length.[11] Thus it is obvious from the outset that the very
purpose of the new existence is to labor at doing what God
wants, without neglecting any of his precepts; and this will
be reiterated by the doctrine—analyzed above—of withdrawal from the world.

Such is the essential proceeding of this section. Many
secondary elements in it require attention, like the beautiful
enumeration of the motives for loving the Lord, the recipro-
cal bond established between the two great commandments,
the affirmation of the natural character of such a love of God
and of men. But what is especially to be kept in mind is the
powerful way the main lines of the religious life are inferred—
starting from the very center of the revealed teaching.

In this respect, one must regret the fact that the Greek text
of the "Vulgate" breaks up into seven segments a statement,
the simplicity of which appeared much better in the primitive
division of the Small Asketicon, into three Questions only:
order of the commandments (GR 1), twofold commandment
of love leading to separation (GR 2-6), necessity of the

common life (GR 7). In particular, it was an evident mistake to have erected into a distinct Question (GR 4) a small passage on the fear of God in which this sentiment is mentioned only as a disposition little worthy of the aspirants after perfection whom Basil was addressing. This contrast between the fear of the beginners and the love of the perfect is moreover to be found, with the same accessory character, in the middle of the Prologue.[12]

II. Renunciation (GR 8-15)

In order to enter this community separated from the world, the first step to be accomplished is to *renounce*. The present section occupies, then, a necessary place, and in some way initial also.

In fact, the question of renunciation will be the occasion of treating of the beginnings in the religious life, that is, of the recruitment of communities and of the probation of postulants. Besides the ordinary vocations of adults, whose desire for humility is tested by imposing on them lowly tasks, Basil considers several particular cases: slaves, married people, and especially children. The oblation of the latter by their parents, their life apart from the adults, their education entrusted to a competent master, the profession of virginity freely made by them when they have reached sufficient maturity, all this is regulated with care. As will be done later by Cassian, Cesarius, and many legislators following them,[13] Basil then places toward the beginning of his large exposition on the monastic life what is effectively, in the existential order, the beginning of that life. Others, like the Master and Benedict, will follow a different order.[14]

Moreover, these directives for the admission and the formation of recruits only come in the present section, after a more general statement on renunciation (*apotagè*). The notion is taken from the synoptic Gospels, where Jesus proposes to whoever wishes to follow him to "deny himself"

(Matt. 16:24) and to "renounce" all (Luke 14:33). Basil's analysis does not neglect any of the objects of renunciation enumerated by Christ: material goods, family affections, worldly appetites and cares, attachment to life itself. If the first point—the forsaking of property—receives a particular, though rather imprecise treatment,[15] it is specified that this material deprivation is but a beginning.[16]

Being a prefatory step, an entrance into the service of Christ, renunciation in religious life is, however, not an absolute beginning. Discreetly, Basil puts it in relation to the primordial renunciation of the devil, which baptism is.[17] Within the Asketicon itself, the present statement about the *apotagè* is manifestly connected to the program of retreat and of separation developed in the preceding section. Renouncing everything in the world is the consummation of the rupture already virtually achieved by the *idiazein*. The continuity of the motion is underscored by the fact that Basil invokes on both sides the same appeal of Christ for "denying oneself" and for "taking up one's cross and following him."[18]

Another very evident link connects these first two sections. When, in the beginning of the second one, Basil prescribes that we should consider as our true parents those who begot us through the Gospel, and as our brothers those who received the same Spirit of adoption,[19] this positive counterpart to renunciation of family according to the flesh brings the mind back to the fraternal community extolled just before (GR 7). Besides, the whole system of admission of postulants implies there are communities to welcome them; and it is even here that the latter receive for the first time their proper name of "brotherhoods."[20]

Besides these connections with what precedes it, this second section presents more than one characteristic which announces the following ones. The program for the education of children contains a method of correction by contraries which will be resumed, in relation to the reforming of adults, in the second-to-last section of the Great Rules.[21]

The latter will, moreover, return to the subject of the correction of children and will substitute for the master who, in this section, corrects them, the superior himself.[22] On the other hand, the profession (*homologia*), which is treated here, will reappear in the section about the order of the community, not without a significant difference: defined in the present section as a commitment to God and a "profession of virginity" which "consecrates" the person, it will reappear in the latter section as a "mutual commitment," a promise to "live together."[23] Considered by both sides as indissoluble, the relation is here rather theological and vertical; there, fraternal and horizontal.

The renunciation of family instituted here is also the basis for the rules governing the associations with relatives which will be formulated in the same section on good order.[24] But the most visible of these anticipatory pointers is an announcement of the section which will follow immediately, that on *egkrateia*. Among his admonitions for the formation of novices, Basil inserts a paragraph concerning the ascetic practice of silence. Convinced for a long time that the perfect "Christian" has a characteristic way of speaking and of being silent,[25] he wishes that the newcomers would first unlearn the manner of the world by practicing complete silence.[26] This reserve of the tongue will manifest, in one point, that they possess the general and great virtue of discipline and of self-mastery (*egkrateia*), about which Basil will soon treat.

III.   Mastery of the Appetites (GR 16-23)

Egkrateia is in fact the theme of the following section. As in the case of renunciation, the subject is a New Testament virtue, which is especially found at the end of the list of the "fruits of the Spirit" (Gal. 5:23) and—in its verbal form—in the famous passage in which Paul compares the life of the Christian to that of the athlete who "abstains from everything" (1 Cor. 9:25).[27] To bridle one's desires, to deny them what they crave, to abstain from coveted objects, such is the continence or mastery of the appetites called *egkrateia*.

Like renunciation also, *egkrateia* has an unlimited field of application. Doubtless, it applies before all else to the primordial appetite, that of eating. But this continence in the matter of food is but the most obvious part of a general ascesis which embraces all desires. Thus it is not surprising that the present section coincides with the previous one in many respects. Among the objects of abstention, Basil mentions not only speech—already included, as we just saw, in the training of novices—but also pride, so abused in the probation of new recruits, and even property, the forsaking of which constituted the first and most typical of "renunciations."

As for the lived reality, then, *egkrateia* coincides in a large measure with *apotagè*. The two attitudes have a resemblance in their negative turn and their universality. They are two ways of turning one's back on all the visible. From the notional point of view, however, *egkrateia* places greater emphasis on dominion over oneself, the control exerted by the mind on sense appetite. Less evangelical than Pauline, less scriptural than philosophical, this new concept enables one to push the moral analysis and the ascetic effort farther ahead.

Among the instinctive motions to be governed, Basil names in particular laughter, which our "Vulgate" presents even as the subject of a distinct question (GR 17). However, he does not mention here another one, which a short Question that goes back to the Small Asketicon gives formally as the object "par excellence" of *egkrateia*: "self-will."[28] If we take notice of it here, it is because, together with speech and pride, self-will constitutes a familiar trilogy for any reader of the Benedictine Rule. Obedience, silence, humility: these three fundamental virtues of the monk, according to the Master and Benedict, depend, then, in the Basilian system, on the general virtue of *egkrateia*. If our author were to treat of them *ex professo*, it is doubtless here, in this third section, that he would speak of them.

But the emphasis given by Benedict to these three virtues comes from another of his predecessors: Cassian. As for Basil, what he gives preferential treatment to in this section, in spite of his efforts to generalize, is the discipline of food, to which he joins that of dress. Just as renunciation, in spite of its generality by right, was particularly developed in the line of dispossession, so is continence especially considered in the domain of food. On both sides, attention is directed by priority to the primordial material goods.

In the matter of food, in order to exorcize the ghost of Gnosticism, Basil wishes that one should taste of everything, and yet strictly limit oneself to what is necessary. Necessity, not pleasure: this must be the criterion of a wholesome and Christian diet. Needs vary from one person to another; it is impossible to fix a common measure, whether for quantity, quality, or the time of meals. It is for the superiors to "give to everyone according to his needs."[29]

To our modern ears, this program seems to be reasonable, moderate, liberal. But the concrete reality that Basil and his readers have in mind is very far from our comfortable menus and timetables. To convince ourselves of this, it is sufficient to read, at the end of the Great Rule 17, the contrasted description of the Christian and of the athlete. Pale, thin, almost fainting, the former is the living antithesis of the latter. According to this picture, confirmed by several of Basil's letters,[30] it is clear that "need" and "necessity" are for him reduced to very little.

The impossibility of setting up norms for food is also due to the diversity of places. Basil wants, in fact, account to be taken of the region where one lives, in order to buy only foods easy to find on the spot and inexpensive. This simplicity of the table should be maintained when guests are received. Nothing is more injurious for the latter than to assume that they have artificial needs, vicious demands, sophisticated desires. Nothing, moreover, is more contrary to the Christian spirit than to be ashamed of one's poverty and to present to the visitor a false appearance, a little luxury for show. The Christian is essentially a "monotrope," that is, simple in his manners, unchanging in his behavior, homogeneous. Basil, who otherwise avoids the monastic vocabulary, here slips in a term approaching very closely this vocabulary and very characteristic of the spirit of monachism.

The same principles rule the question of dress. Like food, it must be poor, simple, made of material easy to find where one lives. It must also strictly respond to the needs for which it is intended (decency, heat, protection) without any concession to aesthetics and elegance. In every circumstance, it must remain the same. Each individual has only one habit, and this one habit is used both inside the monastery, and for going out, by day and night. This polyvalence, which is difficult to imagine,[31] linked with a contempt for all that is not strictly functional, will evidently give the habit of our "Christians" a very original look. The habit in question will then be distinctive, visibly separating the religious from the secular. At the same time it will be communal, constituting for all the members of the brotherhood a kind of uniform. Thus we find again the two essential elements of the religious life, as Basil has defined them in the first section: *idiazein* and *koinônia*, separation and community.[32]

With this reminder comes an announcement. By requiring that the habit be suitable for work, Basil brings our attention to what will be the object of a subsequent section, that of the *ergasiai* (GR 37-42). This orientation towards work appears especially at the end, when he treats of the belt, one of whose main functions is to draw in the habit against the body in order to allow one to work.

But before the section on work, we shall meet the long treatise on good order in the community (GR 24-36). The latter is also announced, in this section on *egkrateia*, when

Basil, just before speaking of dress, treats of a final question relative to food: that of places at table. The Gospel no doubt recommends to take the last place, but all cannot aspire to it simultaneously. Within the brotherhood, humility practically consists in taking the place assigned to you. Being humble is not a question of exterior rank, but of submission. These instructions on order and obedience, as well as the quotation from 1 Cor. 14:40 on which they are founded ("Do everything decently and with order") lead us to the heart of the section on *eutaxia* with which we are now going to deal.

IV.   Good Order in the Community (GR 24-36)

From here on, the Great Asketicon presents entirely new texts. Only the emphasis placed on obedience and correction, especially in the beginning, recalls Questions 12-28 of the Small Asketicon, which already studied these matters in a rather systematic way.

These pages are distinguished from the previous ones by the nature of the subject treated, as much as by the full originality of their redaction. Henceforth, Basil's attention will be focused on the relations between the members of the community. He will not treat any longer of the manner of entering religion, of food and of dress—which are all questions regarding primarily, although not exclusively, each individual—but of the manner of living together in brotherhood. If the sections on renunciation and continence exemplified the "separated" aspect of religious life (GR 6), the second part of the Great Rules which begins here will mainly develop its communal aspect (GR 7).

The present section originally began with a long Question, which the Vulgate divides into nine segments (GR 24-32). Our analysis will consider these as a whole. From the beginning, the tone is given by a characteristic Pauline quotation: "Let all be done decently and with order" (1 Cor. 14:40). This notion of order (*taxis*) or of good order (*eutaxia*), which we have already met in passing,[33] will serve as an axis for Basil's thought throughout the second part. Sometimes founded on the same word of the Apostle,[34] sometimes proposed without reference to him,[35] it will recur several times in the Great Rules as well as in the Small ones. It is by this notion, in particular, it seems to us, that the section we are about to study is best summarized.

In what, then, does the "good order" of the community consist for Basil? We are not surprised to learn that this order should reproduce the model of the body and the members, according to Saint Paul's metaphor. Already Great Rule 7 proposed such an image. What surprises us more is the promptness and the resoluteness with which Basil fixes his attention on the relation superior-subjects, in other words, on authority and obedience. While Great Rule 7 considered the members of the social body as all equally interdependent and capable of exercising certain charisms, Great Rule 24 immediately sets apart the privileged organ which is the eye, taken as symbol for the superior, and makes "order" to consist in the subordination of all to this sovereign: the eye directs, the other members obey.

Thus involved at once in a clearly authoritarian perspective, the treatise holds on to it with persistence. In these pages about the common life, the main subject is the superior. His first duty is to correct faults, and Basil insists that he must fulfill it without slackening, in the very name of that charity which particularly one responsible for souls must have,[36] while reflecting on the account he will have to render for each one of these.[37] This duty to correct is imperative especially toward the brothers who disobey or work with pride or with murmuring. These painful cases furnish Basil with the occasion to examine more deeply the doctrine of obedience, by leaning especially upon the example of Christ "obedient unto death," and they force him at the same time to foresee measures of excommunication and expulsion. It is also the duty of the superior to control the relations of the religious with his family, either by prohibiting the individual from going out to visit them, or by taking care, in the name of the brotherhood, of the parents who live according to God—the others are simply rejected—or by strictly limiting the conversations of the brothers with their relatives to what is able to edify.

Though predominant, this role of the superior does not exclude certain collaborations, which go beyond simple obedience. The whole community is invited to take part either in the pressures exerted on the unruly brother, or in the solicitude shown to parents who deserve it, the latter becoming, without distinction, relatives of all the members of the brotherhood. But especially, it is certain particularly qualified brothers that Basil entrusts with functions which complete or even counterbalance that of the superior.

The care of addressing remonstrances to the latter is not left to all but reserved to "those who are distinguished by age and intelligence." It is also to "those who are entrusted with the charge of taking care of the sick brothers with kindness and sympathy" that everyone must open his heart to receive spiritual direction. Likewise, only "those who have been entrusted with the charism of the word" may converse with outsiders for their edification. And it is also in the plural that "distinguished" members of the brotherhood are referred to as rendering corporal services to the brothers out of humility. We will encounter more than once this care on Saint Basil's part to bring out an elite, upon whom would devolve an important part of the direction of the brotherhoods.

Besides this corrective, the rule of the superior is tempered by appeals to humility, which begin to be heard towards the end of these Questions.[38] After having underscored his duty to correct and the rigor with which he must discharge it, Basil puts him on guard against self-exaltation and inculcates in him the spirit of service. Although these considerations are in part addressed to subjects, who are invited to accept with humility lowly material services of their superiors—here we find again the theme already developed about seating at table—it is no less remarkable that hierarchy begins to be considered here under a new aspect, which will be powerfully emphasized in the second-to-last section.

This is, in broad outlines, the content of the Great Rules 24-32, originally united, let us repeat, in a simple Question. As to the last four pieces of this section, originally grouped two by two (GR 33-34 and 35-36) they first treat of relations with the sisters and of the procurators of the brotherhood, then of the preservation of unity against any separation, either collective or individual. If we include them in the present section, it is because they are connected with the preceding ones and are united among themselves by means of several common traits, which will gradually appear as we run through them.

The relations with female communities are considered by Basil as a matter of *eutaxia*, submitted to the Pauline principle of decency and order (1 Cor. 14:40). In addition to this reminiscence of a familiar theme, the continuity with what preceded is recognized by the conjunction of subjects: we had just dealt with the theme of relations with the family, and now we consider those other outsiders: the sisters. However, Basil likens the relations with these to the relations of the brothers among themselves, so that the exposition deviates less than it seems from the fundamental subject of the Great Rules 24-32: the relations within the community. Finally these conversations with the sisters or between brothers are regulated in the same manner as those of the religious with their relatives. Like the one preceding it, the Great Rule 33 reserves the conversations to specialists. "Those who have received the charism of the word" were then designated; now, "ancient" brothers and sisters inspiring confidence are referred to. However, in dealing here with consecrated men and women, Basil takes special precautions: there will be two or three on either side.[39]

Having mentioned in conclusion the brothers charged with

supplying for the material needs of the sisters, the document passes on to those who fulfill the same office within the brotherhood. This task of distributing the necessary objects occasions some considerations that are interesting in more ways than one. Urged to the strictest impartiality, showing neither favor nor disfavor to anyone, the procurators are held responsible for fraternal harmony, which would be seriously threatened if they were to let themselves be influenced by their personal attractions and aversions. The Great Rule 34 thus plays with Basil a role similar to that of the chapter on the cellarer with Benedict. Within an authoritarian system, where the relation of hierarchical obedience is primordial, it introduces solicitude for good fraternal relations in concord and charity. When, on the other hand, Basil proposes to the procurators the model of the primitive Church—"They gave to everyone according to his needs" (Acts 4:35)—it is less the figure of the cellarer than that of the Benedictine abbot which comes to mind;[40] and this appeal made to the ideal of the apostolic community—as will be the case later with Augustine and Benedict—establishes the respect for persons in the community of goods which, in turn, is the sign of the union of souls and hearts.

This reference to the first chapters of Acts is one of the characteristic traits which unite the Great Rule 34 to the following one, where Basil fights separatist projects which tend to divide certain brotherhoods. If the Church of Jerusalem gathered about five thousand believers under the collegial authority of the Apostles, why should not a handful of brothers remain united, even if it includes more than one "eye" capable of directing? Another hyphen between the two neighboring Questions is the fear of that opposition (*philoneikia*) which is liable to break out as much within the communities, due to the partial conduct of the procurators, as between two brotherhoods established in the same place, thanks to the spirit of rivalry which subtly takes hold of them.

This new Question remains then within the perspective of unity opened out by the previous one. By resuming, besides, the metaphor of body and members—especially the "eye"—it reverts to the beginning of the section which is thus circumscribed in a sort of inclusion. To this concluding role some strokes are annexed which announce the sequel. By commending the preservation of communal unity, and the harmonious collaboration within its bosom of personalities endowed with charism of leadership, Basil prepares his future directives for the establishment of a second-in-charge who would replace a sick or absent superior. On the other hand, his reaction against separatism goes so far as to make him wish that, far from establishing several brotherhoods in the same locality, all the communities dispersed in various places might be assembled under a single direction. This desire which—unconsciously, without doubt—tends towards the centralized Congregation of Pachomius, will, later on, quietly begin to be realized when the superiors will be invited to meet periodically for conferences.

Basil reproves individuals who leave their community as severely as the brotherhoods which split up. In this regard, he recalls the "mutual promise to live together," uttered by all those who entered. Thus, the communal import of the profession is made manifest, while the section about renunciation had only indicated its aspect as commitment to God and as consecration.[41] The religious does not bind himself only to the Lord, but also to that brotherhood of which he becomes a member both stable, as Benedict will put it, and normally inseparable. At the same time, this last Rule of the section resumes the problem of correction, which occupied so much space in the preceding ones.

V.   Work (GR 37-42)

This section appears as a very homogeneous and clearly delineated whole, although intimately connected, as we shall see, to what precedes and what follows it. From beginning to end it treats of work; and the Messalian objections which moved Basil to treat of this subject stand out, at the end, just as they do at the beginning.

For the Messalians, to work with one's hands is neither compatible with the requirements of continual prayer to which spiritual people are called, nor consonant with the evangelical confidence towards our Father in heaven, who nourishes us provided we look for the Kingdom. The first of these arguments is refuted by Basil in the Great Rule 37, where he endeavors to conciliate work and constant prayer, while maintaining—always against the Messalians—the necessity of common Offices celebrated at certain hours of the day and of the night. As to the second argument, it is in the background of Great Rule 42, which treats of the motives of work. Conceding the Messalian argument and at the same time correcting it, Basil sets aside any interested motive. We do not work for ourselves, out of solicitude for our own preservation and mistrust of Providence, but in order to obey the divine commandment and do good to our needy neighbor.[42]

Between this beginning and this conclusion, the exposition first treats of the crafts befitting religious, then of the trips these have to make to sell the products of their work; finally, with regard to the duties they perform, of their entire and constant subordination to the superior and to the community. Each one of these points brings out correspondences with other sections. To conciliate prayer and work, Basil suggests seeking in the work itself incessant motives to return thanks and to invoke the divine help. "The soul," he says, "thereby obtains the absence of distraction (*ameteôris-ton*),"[43] according to the ideal of continual attention to God and to his wishes, which has been proposed in the first section. However, it is the second section that comes back to mind when Basil requires that everyone should "deny himself" and "renounce" all in order to fulfill the tasks assigned to him.[44] At the same time, this requirement of obedience harks back to the fourth section, although the one here vested with authority is less an individual—the superior—than the whole community and its responsible officers, to whom Basil seems to entrust as a body, the discernment of the task befitting everyone.[45]

The same section about good order is also evoked by several traits. The term *eutaxia* itself recurs under Basil's pen when he tries to define the appropriate crafts; they must be compatible with "the psalmody, prayer, and the rest of regular observance (*eutaxias*)."[46] In other words, they must not hurt the Pauline ideal of a "life without distraction, all attentive to the Lord," which Basil was already striving to defend, in the preceding section, against the disturbances provoked by the family.[47] Likewise, the image of the members of the body comes up anew to illustrate the duty of mutual help, even to abandoning if need be one's particular work in order to assist a neighbor in distress.[48] But while the fourth section applied this metaphor to the relations of the members with the "eye," that is, to hierarchical obedience, the image applies here to the horizontal relations between brothers, in the primitive line of the Great Rule 7.

More discreetly, the section on continence is represented here by at least two details. Under its aspect of corporal ascesis, work is connected to this ascetic self-mastery called *egkrateia*; and this is underlined by the reference made in both places to the saying of Saint Paul: "I chastise my body and reduce it to servitude."[49] In both places also, Basil wishes that local conditions be taken into account. Like the diet and the dress code, the choice of crafts to be practiced depends on the places and the regions.[50]

Provided with references to the preceding sections, this treatise on monastic work looks also towards the sequel. Its final appeal not to expect one's daily bread from human labor, but from God's Providence, ushers in the last Great Rule, which will apply the same principle to the use of medicine. And the theme of trips outside, brought in at this place by the question of selling manufactured objects, will reappear within the coming section.

VI. The Duties of Superiors (GR 43-54)

Treating again of the superiors' functions, already described with care in the section about order, Basil does not hide the fact that he is back-tracking. This repetition is justified, he says, by the extreme importance of the subject. As is the leader, so are the subordinates. It is not a waste of time to model the one who will serve as model for all.

In fact, this second directory for the superior will insist on humility and kindness in the line of the recommendations of the Great Rule 30. We remember that after having exhorted the superior to correct without weakness all the shortcomings, Basil had marked there, as a counterpart, the necessity of avoiding all pride and fulfilling the duty of correction like an infirmarian who humbly nurses his sick. Here, similarly, humility is presented as the major virtue of which the superior has to give an example. Basil joins kindness to it, since Christ, the model of all, is at the same time "kind and humble of heart" (Matt. 11:29). This new recommendation is especially necessary for the ministry of correction. At present, it is no longer the duty of severity which is underscored, but that of patience and clemency.

Beside these traits which complete and balance the character of the leader, Basil gives two important indications concerning his function. First of all we learn how he comes to office. He does not seize the power, we are told and, we may add, he is not put in by the election of the brothers either. It is his colleagues, the superiors of the other brotherhoods, who designate him.[51]

As soon as this non-democratic manner of choosing has been indicated, Basil sketches the role of this personage: to assure the good order of the brotherhood and to distribute

the tasks according to the various capacities.[52] While bringing back to the fore the concept of *eutaxia* which governed
the fourth section, this definition recalls what had been more
recently said about work. According to the second-to-last
Rule which dealt with it (GR 41), it was apparently to the
entire community or to a plurality of responsible brethren
that the assigning of tasks belonged. Here, it is the superior
alone who seems to distribute them. By doing this, he emerges from the role of correction to which Basil had so far
almost exclusively confined him.

Without entering into the details of organization which
this notice gave us to expect, Basil mentions only two cases in
which the superior must choose fitting persons: the designa-
tion of the brothers sent outside on mission, and that of a
lieutenant capable of replacing him. Already the object of
repeated preoccupations in the preceding pages,[53] the trips
outside the monastery are thus put back on the carpet. It is
clear that they inspire much anxiety, an anxiety which is at
the same time the cause and effect of the severe requirements
placed on the traveling brothers. The latter will be submitted,
on their return, to an interrogatory which brings to mind
certain parts of the education of children and of the spiritual
formation of adults.[54]

As for the nomination of the substitute, it brings into full
light certain prominent traits of the social thought of Basil: a
horror of "democracy"—the very word is used—of which he
fears "the pernicious effect for the rule and the established
order;" an ideal of order (*eutaxia*) affirmed in opposition to
it, in relation with a rule (*kanôn*) and a tradition;[55] a will
to reserve the word, considered as a sacred ministry, to
competent and responsible men, whether in the case of
addresses to the community or conversations with visitors.
Previously, as we remember, the latter had already been
exclusively reserved to "those who have received the charism
of the word." Now, it comes out that only the superior and

his assistant are considered such, any infringement on their exclusive right being considered as a disorder (*ataxia*).

However, the choice of an assistant is not made without the cooperation of "men capable of testing," who would help the superior in discovering the appropriate person. This note on the subject of an elite which helps the superior relates to those which we have already noticed in the section on order. Much as Basil mistrusts democracy, so much also does he incline to surround authority with a group of selected counselors. No less typical are the precautions taken for the eventual correction of the assistant. Like the superior himself, he may be reproved by a subordinate, but only privately, again for fear of disorder (*ataxia*).

The nine remaining Rules, which originally formed only one Question (GR 46-54) treat especially of correction. Already predominant in the section on order, this theme invades in turn the statement on authority. As was done in the beginning of the section, kindness is especially recommended for the superior when he is correcting. Not only must he avoid anger then, but also he must take care not to react with more vehemence to the offences which regard him personally. The absence of personal interest (*philautia*) thus demonstrated is not without analogy with the detachment which Basil previously prescribed while analyzing the motives for work. Total self-renunciation, in line with the second section, dictates these similar attitudes.

Administered out of pure charity, correction must be accepted by all as a benefaction.[56] Its beneficial character foundations the strict obligation which is incumbent on everyone to procure it for delinquents by denouncing any fault committed, if it has not been confessed by the culprit himself.[57] In the case of children working with adult masters, the latter themselves correct the professional faults, but they refer to the superior the moral deficiencies, which he alone can competently redress.[58]

Another particular case, and one of peculiar importance, is

the correction of the superior. Basil returns to it by almost repeating what he has said in the section about order,[59] but this time the text specifies that the religious who are "closer to the superior by their rank and intelligence," to whom control over his acts is reserved, form a permanent council which helps him in all his decisions. Nevertheless, this return to the superior's failings is especially meant to forbid the generality of the brothers to concern themselves with it. Basil quotes in this regard a saying of Saint Paul which he will invoke several times in the Small Rules: "Let everyone stay where God has called him."[60] In this instruction of the First Letter to the Corinthians, he rediscovers the demand for respect for the various competencies and for the hierarchy which he had drawn from the other quote from this Epistle: "Let all be done decently and with order."

In the midst of these paragraphs on correction, two connected questions are approached: that of questioning what the superior has decided and that of settling the controversies which arise in the brotherhood. The one who questions must liberate himself from his negative sentiments by making them known to the superior himself, whether in private, in public, or by intermediaries—the sovereign authority of the Scriptures serving, as always, as arbiter in the discussion.[61] As for the controversies between brothers, they are settled by a procedure typical of the Basilian manner. To avert any dispute (*philoneikia*) the judgment is entrusted to those "more capable" of it, and to avoid everyone asking questions at every moment, to the great detriment of "order," a responsible person, duly "tried," is charged with submitting the question either to a common discussion, or to the examination of the superior. Once more, Basil reserves to a very small number of competent men the exercise of the word, considered as the most sublime and the most difficult of all crafts.[62]

Finally, the section ends with a short paragraph on the meetings of superiors, which begins to fulfill the hope expressed formerly, when Basil was opposing the breaking up of the brotherhoods.[63] Besides, we see, once more in this, the intention of submitting the thought and the conduct of each individual to the control of the neighbor. Just as the brothers must open their hearts and manifest their thoughts,[64] in like manner the superiors must confer among themselves at regular intervals and put their problems in common.

VII.   The Good Use of Medicine (GR 55)

After this section on the duties of superiors, one does not at all expect a last Rule, one of the longest, on the medical art. This unexpected conclusion is, nevertheless, not so out of place as it would seem. Doubtless it has its specific object, which is to clear up the delicate question of the use by Christians of such an art. But the answer which Basil gives to this question recalls in more ways than one the preceding sections of the Great Rules and thereby proves itself apt to conclude them.[65]

First of all, as a human art, medicine is comparable to the crafts practiced by the brothers. The section concerning the work had defined the conditions required for these crafts to be suitable to religious. While laying down similar conditions for the use of medicine—it must not hurt the life of the soul, but serve it—Basil brings out here in a new and useful way the profound meaning of all techniques. They are helps given by God to make up for the consequences of original sin. From this theology of productive activity an attitude proceeds which is at the same time positive and reserved. The providential help afforded by techniques is neither to be despised nor idolized. They must be used courageously and intelligently, and we must neither shrink before the effort they require, nor, on the other hand, put our trust in them; this we must constantly direct towards God.

To this elucidation of the meaning of work are added comparisons with continence, soul curing, and correction. Like *egkrateia*, medicine compels the removal of luxury and satiety, refined and superfluous foods; it invites hunger, the mother of health. But its chief merit is to offer a model for the cure of the soul: to eliminate what is superfluous and add what is lacking, to abstain from what is harmful and choose what is beneficial. These general maxims of medicine are valid for the spiritual being as well as for the body. More precisely, the behavior of the sick man brings to mind that of the sinner who is subject to ascesis and correction. To persevere in prayer, penance, and effort, to bear with reproaches and punishment, to follow the advice of superiors, all this very much resembles what the doctor requires of his patients, who are subject to long and painful treatments, obliged to many curtailments, compelled to observe his prescriptions.

Finally, Basil considers that certain illnesses are providential chastisements, inviting the soul to conversion and thus procuring health for it. These mysterious ailments, against which it is useless and even dangerous to have recourse to human solicitude, are kinds of corrections inflicted by God, similar to those administered by superiors. Here also the question of medicine emerges into the spiritual life, and the teaching of this last Great Rule crowns what was said in the fourth and sixth sections on the preeminence of the process of correction.

CONCLUSION

This cursive review of the seven sections into which the Great Rules are distributed allows us now to take a general view of the work. Placed at once under the sign of obedience to the divine precepts, it proceeds from the two most general commandments—love of God and of men—to very particular considerations on sickness and medicine. These are nevertheless not so distant from the point of departure as may appear.

Love of God and of neighbor generates in fact a kind of life separated from the world and, at the same time, communal,[66] which we enter by renunciation and in which we exercise ourselves in a permanent way to the mastery of every desire. Body of Christ, this fraternal community is directed by one of its members, the "eye," to which all owe obedience and which provides for all the benefit of correction, being himself maintained in the right way by means of the advice of some, more capable, religious. Such a life of work and common prayer, with its trips outside and its relations with the sisters, its reception of the families of the religious and of visitors, its requirement of perfect equity towards all the brothers and of concord safeguarded among them in spite of every controversy—such a life remains continually under the influx of the inspired word and of the divine will by the mediation of the men whom this will uses to direct it, whether it be the superior, or the subordinate established by him, or the ancients surrounding him. To him whom it touches, sickness is a reminder of this sovereign mastery of the Lord over all and over everyone, and at the same time a particular invitation to straighten out his course and to recommend himself entirely to God.

Thus, once the community of those separated from the world (which serves as a framework for it) has been established, the individual existence of the "Christian" unfolds before our eyes, from the initial renunciation to the approaches of death. A scheme both logical and chronological orders with great flexibility the sequence of the diverse treatises. The primacy of the two great commandments causes them to be placed at the starting-point of the work, where they raise up a brotherhood, established out of the world. Immediately after this rings out Christ's call to renunciation, and this primordial condition for his service leads to the treatment of the modalities of admission. From this preliminary and mostly external stripping, we pass to a continuous ascesis which penetrates, starting from its corporeal elements (food, clothes) to the very depths of the soul.

Once these big lines of each person's behavior towards

things are traced, there remains to order the persons among themselves, and that is what the second part, starting with the Great Rule 24 undertakes. Beginning with a section on the order of the community, which treats in principle of the "manner of living together" in all its generality, it continues, beyond instructions on work, with a directory for superiors where we meet again, under a form hardly more particular, with that which already constituted in fact the main topic of the initial treatise: the relations of the brothers with their head, obedience and correction. This fundamental theme holds also an important place in the intermediary survey on work, which survey is prolonged, in certain respects, by the ultimate considerations on the medical art. Except for these, which recapitulate at the same time the theme of continence and that of correction, the whole of the second part is dominated by the Pauline ideal of the good order of the community and the no less Pauline image of the body and the members both mainly interpreted in an authoritarian and hierarchical sense, where the function of the "eye" and the "charism of the word," which tend to fuse into one, are supremely important.

Order of the commandments, order of the community: is it accidental that this word, *taxis*, appears in the beginning of the second part as well as of the first? In any case, it is clear that the model of the body and the members inspires the initial option for community, with its decided rejection of the anchoretic life, as well as the subsequent modeling of this common life according to the relation of the eye with the other organs.

Such a strongly marked vertical structure makes these Cappadocian brotherhoods look like the communities of Pachomius, in which even the centralized direction and the union into a congregation are, as we have seen, not foreign to the aspirations of Basil. But the enormous difference of level and of kind renders difficult a more extended comparison between the two "rules."

With Augustine's "rule," which is much closer, a twofold contrast is noticeable. First of all, on the formal plane, the embryonic dialogue which consists of the brothers' questions and Basil's answers, and corresponds to an initial situation of advisor rather than that of founder and superior, is replaced with Augustine by the imperative address of a superior who simply "enjoins"—*motu proprio* and with full authority— what must be "observed."

As for the content, on the contrary, the Augustinian Rule insists less on authority and more on the relations of the brothers among themselves. If the superior appears here and there from the beginning, it is only at the end that his relations with his subjects are briefly studied in themselves. Antecedently, the dominant theme is that of mutual relations. Respective needs of the rich and the poor, of the healthy and the infirm, respect for the brothers who wish to pray by themselves, and corrective solicitude for those who commit some fault, care for the sick and care of the vestry, labors for the community and mutual forgiveness of offences, all is mainly considered from the point of view of charity which must unite souls and hearts after the pattern of the first believers. In this realization of the model of Acts, the accent is placed, more than with Basil, on what everyone must do and think to remain in communion with his brothers in unity.[67]

Finally, beyond Augustine, we cannot refrain from making a parallel with Benedict. The Prologue of the Benedictine Rule has many a reminder of that of Basil. On both sides, there is the same pressing exhortation to work for God, in obedience to his commandments and the expectancy of his imminent judgment. In turn, the first chapter of Benedict, with its definition of cenobitism, recalls the first Great Rules and their option for a community separated from the world, although a rejection of the anchoretic life does not appear there in conjunction with the praise of the "very strong race of cenobites."

If we omit the following chapter, on the abbot, whose equivalent appears with Basil only much later, the spiritual part of the Benedictine Rule, which opens here, is not without analogy with the first part of the Great Rules. Doubtless, the modalities of admission and the probation of the postulants are relegated by Benedict to the end of his Rule, but the Basilian themes of renunciation and of self-mastery correspond broadly, it will be remembered, to the large exposition on ascesis, articulated into obedience, silence, and humility, which our Rule makes at this point, following that of the Master.

And when Benedict moves on to a more practical second part—the *ordo monasterii*, as the Master used to say—where he will treat of the divine office, of the correction of faults, of the cellarer, and of the other servants of the community, we think of the second half of the Great Rules, which also treats of these various themes, united under the rubric of good order and of the common life. On both sides, a first part, rather theoretical, spiritual, and regarding the individuals, is followed by a second part which is more directly interested in the communal organization and in the relations between persons.

In spite of numerous and important differences,[68] a certain similitude is therefore observable between the two structures. We should not, on that account, make of Basil in this particular regard, the "father" of Benedict. That would be to add a new misinterpretation to those which the reference in the epilogue of the Benedictine Rule to "our holy Father Basil" usually creates.[69] The analogy which we have just made note of can, however, help us to investigate more thoroughly the relation which, directly or through Evagrius, Cassian, and the Master, links together these two men who have been, whether rightly or wrongly, considered the patriarchs of Eastern and Western monachism.

NOTES

*French text in *Collectanea Cisterciensia*.

[1]See our comparative survey of the ancient rules in *La Règle de saint Benoît*, I. (Sources Chrétiennes, 181). Paris, 1972, p. 29, n. 1, as well as the developments of our article *Regole cenobitiche d'Occidente*, to be published in the *Dizionario degli Istituti di perfezione*. Reproduced in French in *Autour de Saint Benoît*, (Vie monastique, 4). Bellefontaine, 1975, pp. 15-29, and in English in *Cistercian Studies*, 12, (1977), pp. 175-183.

[2]See especially his *Histoire du texte des Ascétiques de saint Basile*, (Bibliothèque du Muséon, 32). Louvain, 1953, fundamental work whose conclusions we summarize hereafter.

[3]It is printed, as a section of the *Codex Regularum* of Benedict of Aniane, in Migne, PL 103, 487-554.

[4]RB 73, 5. On the meaning of this quote, see below n. 69.

[5]In Migne, PG 31, 889-1306.

[6]Basil himself refers us to it by the expressions *en tè platutera apokrisei* (SR 103) and *en tois kata platos* (SR 74 and 174, to which are added SR 314, GR 54bis and 48bis, edited by J. Gribomont, *Histoire du texte*, pp. 183-184).

[7]Here is, according to J. Gribomont, op. cit., pp. 172-173, the correspondence between the Great Rules of the Vulgate (V) and the primitive Questions preserved by the Oriental and South Italian recensions (O and N): GR 1, Q 1; GR 2-6, Q 2; GR 7, Q 3; GR 8-9, Q 4-5; GR 10-14, Q 6; GR 15, Q 7; GR 16-18, Q 8; GR 19-21, Q 9-11; GR 22-23, Q 12; GR 24-32, Q 13; GR 33-34, Q 14; GR 35-36, Q 15; GR 37, Q 16; GR 38-42, Q 17; GR 43-45, Q 18; GR 46-54, Q 19; GR 55, Q 20.

[8]That is, according to J. Gribomont, op. cit., pp. 205-207: 1) Penance and conversion, SR 3-20; 2) Sins, SR 21-84; 3) Poverty, SR 85-95; 4) The duties of superiors, SR 96-113; 5) Obedience, SR 114-125; 6) Fasting, SR 126-140; 7) Manual

labor, SR 141-156; 8) Interior dispositions, SR 157-186; 9) The family, SR 187-190, and the virtues recommended by Scripture, SR 191-238; 10) Moral exegesis of Scriptural texts, SR 239-278; 11) Series without internal unity, SR 279-286; 12) Supplement, SR 287-313, with the SR 314-318 added by Gribomont (see above, n. 6).

[9] We shall cite at least J. Gribomont's first study "Obéissance et Evangile selon saint Basile le Grand," in *Supplément de la Vie spirituelle*, n. 21, (1952), pp. 192-215, and one of his latest, "Saint Basile" in *Commandements du Seigneur et libération évangélique*, (Studia Anselmiana, 70). Rome, 1977, pp. 81-101.

[10] See GR 36 and SR 74. The first of these texts reproves only the brothers who are separated from the community, without specifying, as the second one does, that they do it in order to live a solitary life or in small groups.

[11] GR, Prol., 2-4. cf. SR 83 and 233, which quote the same saying of Jesus to Peter (John 13:8).

[12] GR, Prol. 3 (896B). These three attitudes—servile, mercenary, and filial—evidently bring to mind Cassian, *Conf.* 11, 6-8, but instead of a scale of perfection, we find only an argument to prove that it is indispensable to obey *all* the divine commandments, whatever may be the attitude adopted towards God.

[13] Cassian, *Inst.* 4, 3-9 (cf. 4, 39, 1 and 4, 43). If we consider the whole of *Inst.* 1-4, it is clear that the habit and the office precede the formation of postulants. — Cesarius, *Reg. virg.* 2-6; *Reg. mon.* 1.

[14] Admission of the newcomers is relegated by them to the end. See RM 87-91, RB 58-61.

[15] GR 9, Reg. 5. cf. SR 187, Reg. 31; Ep. 150, 3, which recommend to entrust to ecclesiastical administrators the use of renounced goods. These should go to the poor, but not necessarily all at a time and immediately. In GR 9, 1 Basil insists on the responsibility that the renouncer has with regard to the good use of his goods.

[16]GR 8, 1 (936C), text proper to the Great Asketicon.

[17]GR 8, 1 (936A), text already present in the Small Asketicon (Reg. 4, PL 103, 496C). cf. SR 234, which speaks expressly of baptism.

[18]Matt. 16:24, quoted in GR 6, 1 (925C) and GR 8, 1 (936A).

[19]GR 8, 1 (936B), Reg. 4 (496C).

[20] GR 10, 2 (945B): *tè adelphotèti*; GR 11 (948A): *tais adelphotèsi*; GR 14 (949C): *tèn adelphotèta*; GR 15, 4 (956CD): *tè adelphotèti*. We find also *tô sômati...tôn adelphôn* (GR 15, 1), to which corresponds in Rufinus, in a different place *corpori fraternitatis* (Reg. 6).

[21]Compare GR 15, 2 and GR 51.

[22]Compare GR 15, 2 and GR 53. On both sides (GR 15, 4 and GR 53) the subject of the relations between children and craftsmen also comes up.

[23]Compare GR 14 and 15, 4 with GR 36. Apostasy is considered in both cases.

[24]Compare GR 8, 1-2 and GR 32, 1-2.

[25]See Ep. 2, 5 and 22, 1.

[26]GR 13, cf. SR 208, Reg. 136.

[27]GR 16, 1. Moreover, the contrary vice (*akrateia*) is mentioned by 2 Tim. 3:3 (GR 16, 2). Same quotes in Reg. 8.

[28]SR 128, Reg. 88 (the Latin is less clear than the Greek, because of the confusion between *voluntas* and *voluptas*).

[29]Acts 4:35, quoted in GR 19, 1 (the quote is missing in Reg. 9).

[30]See Ep. 46, 2 and 284. However, Basil does not admit that fasting hinders one from working (SR 128, Reg. 88; SR 139, cf. SR 135, Reg. 94).

[31]See GR 22, 2, Reg. 11, which is confirmed, in what concerns the absence of special night clothing, by SR 90, Reg. 129. However, SR 210, Reg. 143 admits differences for winter and summer, for work and rest, and this according to the principle of decency (*kosmiotès*; cf. 1 Tim. 2:9 and 3:2), which GR 22, 3 also appeals to.

[32]See our detailed analysis in *La Règle de saint Benoît*, VII. *Commentaire doctrinal et spirituel*, Paris, 1977, pp. 375-381.

[33]In GR 21 (976C), Reg. 10, with quotation from 1 Cor. 14:40.

[34]GR 24; 33, 1; 45, 2. cf. SR 72; 108, Reg. 197; 238; 266; 276.

[35]*Eutaxia*, GR 27; 33, 2; 38; 43, 2; 45, 1-2; 53 (cf. SR 100, Reg. 98; 136, Reg. 97; 141, Reg. 101; 156; 173, Reg. 137; 303; 307). We also find *eutacton*: GR 24 and 45, 2. *Taxis*: GR 49. We will also meet with *ataxia* in GR 45, 1-2 (cf. SR 303).

[36]GR 25, 2, quoting 1 Thess. 2:7-8.

[37]See especially GR 25, 2 (985B), where Basil is obviously thinking of Heb. 13:17. cf. GR 25, 1 (984C) and GR 30. This "account to be given" will be found again in GR 48.

[38]GR 30, cf. GR 31 (service rendered by the *leaders* of the brotherhood, in the plural).

[39]GR 33, 1. cf. SR 220, Reg. 174, with reference to GR 33. (About the problem created by this reference, see J. Gribomont, *Histoire du texte*, p. 253).

[40]See RB 55, 20. cf. RB 34, 1.

[41]Compare GR 36 with GR 14 and 15, 4 (cf. supra, n. 23). The communal import of the profession reappears in SR 2, entitled: "What profession should those who wish to lead together a life according to God require of one another?"

[42]Cf. SR 207, Reg. 127; SR 252, Reg. 173; SR 272.

[43]GR 37, 3. cf. GR 5.

[44]GR 41, 1. cf. GR 8.

[45]All the expressions designating authority, in GR 41, are in the plural. The *proestôs* (singular) shows up only at the end (GR 41, 2), in reference to the use of tools.

[46]GR 38, (1017B). Conversely SR 238 invokes "order" (1 Cor. 14:40: *kata taxin*) to set aside the obligation of praying and reading continually. This "order" or "good order" includes then the use of time and the choice of occupations, as well as the subordination of the subjects to their head.

⁴⁷ Compare GR 38 (1017B: *tèn aperispaston zôèn kai euparedron tô Kuriô*) and GR 32, 1 (996B: *to euschèmon kai euparedron tô Kuriô aperispatôs*), both alluding to 1 Cor. 7:35. To the subject of the crafts, considered in themselves, Basil will return in reference to medicine (GR 55, 1).

⁴⁸GR 41, 2. cf. Ep. 22, 2.

⁴⁹ GR 16, 1 (*ho hupôpiasmos tou sômatos kai hè doulagôgia*) and GR 37, 1 (*dia ton hupôpiasmon tou sômatos*), alluding to 1 Cor. 9:27.

⁵⁰Compare GR 38 with GR 19, 2; 20, 3; 22, 1. Moreover, the products that are made and sold by the brothers should be similar to those they use themselves—plain, cheap, practical, healthy for body and soul.

⁵¹ GR 43, 2 (1029A): *egkrithenta tôn en tais allais adelphotèsi proechontôn*. The expression seems to point to "those who are at the head of the other brotherhoods...the neighboring superiors" (J. Gribomont, "Obéissance et Evangile," p. 210), while previously (GR 27 and 31) the *proechontes* seem to be the group of the directors in each brotherhood.

⁵²GR 43, 2. The adaptation of tasks to capabilities is again recommended in SR 149, Reg. 112, as well as in SR 303 (1297B), in which Basil recommends the careful testing of the superior who will be responsible for this distribution of tasks (cf. 1 Tim. 3:10, quoted in GR 43, 2: *dokimazesthôsan*).

⁵³See GR 35, 2 (the disadvantages of repeated trips outside the monastery are one of the arguments invoked to forbid the breaking up of a brotherhood) and GR 39-40.

⁵⁴Compare GR 44, 1 with GR 15, 3 and GR 26 (control of thoughts; cf. SR 227).

⁵⁵ GR 45, 1 (1032C): *epi dialusei tou kanonos kai tès paradedomenès eutaxias*. cf. SR 303: it would be a disorder (*ataxia*) to let everyone speak.

⁵⁶GR 52, cf. SR 158, Reg. 24.

⁵⁷GR 46, cf. GR 26 (confession of thoughts) and Augustine, *Praec.* 4, 8-10 (informing out of charity).

⁵⁸GR 53, cf. GR 15, 2 (correction of children by their

master, according to a method restated in GR 51; cf. n. 22) and 4 (956D-957A: children entrusted to master craftsmen).

[59]Compare GR 48 with GR 27. Appearing here for the first time, the quote from Ecclesiasticus (Sir. 32:24) will be found again in SR 104 (nomination to offices). The reasoning which follows (when we entrust our soul to the superior, it is illogical to mistrust him for some details) has already been used in GR 28, 2. As to the name "brother" applied to the superior, see GR 27.

[60]GR 48, alluding to 1 Cor. 7:24, cf. SR 91; 98; 125; 303.

[61]GR 47. On the liberation of the *diakrisis*, see already GR 27, end. As for the supremacy of Scripture, see SR 114, Reg. 13 and SR 303.

[62]GR 49, cf. GR 32, 2; 33, 1; 45, 2.

[63]GR 54, compare with GR 35, 3 (1007B).

[64]GR 26 (cf. SR 227): the double effect of the correction of evil and of confirmation of the goods found again in GR 54.

[65]The doctrine of GR 55 is found again in a shorter form in SR 314, edited by J. Gribomont, *Histoire du texte*, pp. 180-183.

[66]Earlier, we connected separation with the love of God and community with the love of neighbor. To be absolutely exact, we must note that Basil does not separate the two commandments, but treats of the second before he even considers retreat from the world and invokes considerations depending rather on the first (practice of the commandments, correction,...) in order to found community life.

[67]As for the particular points of contact of Augustine with Basil and Pachomius, see R. Lorenz, "Die Anfänge des abendländischen Mönchtums im 4. Jahrhundert," in ZKG 77 (1966), pp. 1-61, mainly pp. 46-56.

[68]Besides the difference in place taken by the treatise on the admission of postulants and that on the duties of the superior, let us point out that obedience is studied by Benedict toward the beginning (RB 5) and by Basil in his second part (GR 24, etc.); that continence in the matter of food and cloth-

ing, of which Benedict treats rather late (RB 39-41 and 55), are the subject of one of the first sections of Basil (GR 16-23); that the love of God, placed by Basil at the beginning (GR 2), appears as a term at the end of RB 7, etc.

[69]See once more A. Wathen, "Methodological Considerations of the Sources of the Regula Benedicti as Instruments of Historical Interpretations," in *Regulae Benedicti Studia*, 5, (1976), pp. 101-117: "Benedict specifically calls him (Basil) our holy father" (p. 116; cf. p. 107). In fact, this title given to Basil by Benedict (RB 73, 5) is not more "specific" than the mention of "our holy fathers" which may be read elsewhere in the Rule about two monks of Egypt made famous by the *Vitae Patrum* (RB 18, 25; cf. VP 5, 4, 57). It is a generic appellation (cf. RB 48, 8; 73, 2 and 4), which in the present case indicates no special filiation of Benedict with respect to Basil, as we already pointed out in *La Règle de saint Benoît*, I, p. 147.

WORKING WITH SAINT BASIL

Basil Pennington, OCSO
(Monk of St. Joseph's Abbey,
Spencer, Mass.)

It seems to me inevitable that when a monk of the West
begins to read what has commonly and popularly been called
the *Rule* or *Rules of Saint Basil* he is drawn to make comparisons with his own *Rule for Monasteries*. The humble
legislator of Monte Cassino, in concluding his rule for beginners, points his disciple toward the great Master of Eastern
Christian monasticism:

> Now we have written this Rule in order that by its
> observance in monasteries we may show that we have
> attained some degree of virtue and the rudiments of the
> religious life.
> But for him who would hasten to the perfection of that
> life there are the teachings of the holy Fathers, the observ-
> ance of which leads a person to the height of perfection...
> What book of the holy Catholic Fathers does not loudly
> proclaim how we may come by a straight course to our
> Creator? Then the Conferences and the Institutes and the
> Lives of the Fathers, as also the Rule of our holy Father,
> Basil—what else are they but tools of virtue for right-living
> and obedient monks?...
> Whoever you are, therefore, who are hastening to the
> heavenly homeland, fulfill with the help of Christ this
> minimum Rule which we have written for beginners; and
> then at length under God's protection you will attain to the
> loftier heights of doctrine and virtue which we have
> mentioned above.

With some expectations then does the disciple of Saint
Benedict turn to the *Rules of Saint Basil.* He hopes perhaps to

find there some "high-powered" teaching that will propel him into lofty mystic states or at least set him on the way of the proficients. He or she may be disappointed. Comparisons are generally odious. Any attempt to compare these two documents to decide which is the greatest, deepest, most profound, and so forth, would indeed be odious. But a complementary comparison of their teaching can be enlightening and bring out facets of the richness of them both.

In a short paper a general study of the *Rules of Saint Basil* could only be quite superficial, a skimming across the surface. So I would prefer here to concentrate on one particular theme or area. The one I have chosen is that of work.

Saint Basil, in preparing his text, remained in the mainstream of the tradition which sees monastic formation to lie essentially in the relation of the disciple with the Spiritual Father. And so, like the profession of the vows of the monastic formation and like the Desert literature, his legislation adopts the format of a dialogue, the disciple questioning the holy Father. The generic: "Father, give me a word of life," expresses itself in a series of particular questions, some fifty-five in all. This perspective of a Spiritual Father imparting wise teaching to the disciple is certainly not absent from Benedict's *Rule for Monasteries*. In fact we might say it remains primary, for his *Rule* opens:

> Listen, my son, to your master's precepts, and incline the ear of your heart. Receive willingly and carry out effectively your loving father's advice, that by the labor of obedience you may return to Him from whom you had departed by the sloth of disobedience (*Prologue*).

But after a very paternal *Prologue* Saint Benedict goes on through seventy-three chapters to lay out his teaching in a rather formal and legislative way. There is a definite order in his Rule, yet it is also quite evident that he was open to a certain evolution coming out of his experience and his contact with the sources and witnesses of the Christian monastic tradition, including Saint Basil. There are many references to work woven through the *Rule for Monasteries.* The Legislator even speaks of the Divine Office as "the Work of God" (Cc. 7, 19, 22, 43...). But in this paper we are concerned more specifically with the kind of work he provides for in Chapter 48: "On the Daily Manual Labor."

When we think of work in a monastic context we quite spontaneously think in terms of manual labor. However, when we think of Saint Basil we think of student, scholar, theologian, hierarch, contemplative, but hardly of the laborer and of manual labor. Yet as one reads his chapters on work it is immediately evident that we are hearing from a Father who knows a great deal about work, who has worked, and has guided the work of others.

Saint Basil's teaching on work is contained substantially in six chapters or the responses to six questions. The first, Question 37, lays the solid theological foundations for his teaching on work. Much of it is applicable to all Christians, based as it is on the teaching of the Sacred Scriptures, yet it has specifically monastic dimensions placing the monk's work squarely in the context of his life of prayer. The following chapters display Basil's practicality and wisdom, and address themselves more specifically to the monastic: the sort of work suitable for a monk, how he should act in the business world (Questions 38-40). His final question (42) on the dispositions of the laborer can be readily applied to any Christian life, as can much of the preceding chapter (41) which, nonetheless, underlines what is the primary virtue and concern of monastic labor—obedience.

Obedience to the superior and community in this matter of one's work is absolutely fundamental for Saint Basil, yet this is ultimately only a concrete expression of one's obedience to God's will as expressed in the Scriptures. In the course of these six chapters we find forty-four Scripture quotations.

The Saint's exegesis is sometimes surprising. His main base is no particular text but the example of Christ. And that is as it should be for all who call themselves Christians, His followers, and for the monks who are to find their primary Spiritual Father in this Father of the World to Come (Is. 9:6). Saint Paul is also a model, he who so forcefully proclaimed himself a Spiritual Father (1 Cor. 4:14-16), because he is such a wholehearted follower and imitator of Christ, our Master.

Surprisingly, although Saint Basil does not neglect the important ascetical and penitential aspects of work—for him it involves struggle and great endeavor, fostering the growth of patience and bringing the body into subjection—he nowhere in these chapters alludes to the primal text of Genesis: "By the sweat of your brow you will earn your bread" (Gen. 3:19). Rather, when he comes to speak of the aims and dispositions that should motivate the Christian and monk in his labor (Q. 42), he downplays this role of earning one's own bread. Paul's classic text: "...working they would eat their own bread" (2 Thess. 3:12), Basil insists is directed toward the unruly. And in their case, to work for their own food is better than their general uselessness; at least, they will not be a burden to others. The emphasis for this very community-minded Father is on the other. Paul prided himself on his own manual labor in that it freed him from being a burden to others. We are not to seek our own—"Be not solicitous for your life, what you shall eat, nor for your body, what you shall put on" (Matt. 6:25). The Christian works that he might have to give to others (Eph. 4:28), for the other is Christ (Matt. 25:35). To trust in one's own work, or even in that of others of the brotherhood, is forbidden (Jn. 15:5). Basil does not forbid monks to work to support themselves— he expects them to do it—but in their labors they are to seek to earn, not to make themselves comfortable, but to keep themselves from being a burden to others and to have something to help others. All selfishness and self-reliance is set aside. Depending on the Lord, the Christian works for Him, in Him, and in those with whom He identifies Himself.

The Apostle's command "to pray without ceasing" (1 Thess. 5:17) and the monk's communal responsibility to gather repeatedly for prayer are not to be used as excuses for holding back from work. The monk, the Christian, is to pray while he works. As he expands on this, Saint Basil gives us some of the most precious teaching to be found in these chapters.

First of all the Saint is very realistic. Sometimes the monks can pray and recite psalms while they work. Saint Pachomius, with whom Basil was surely familiar, made elaborate provisions for this. But Basil recognizes that sometimes this is not possible, or it is not conducive to edification, to building up. It would be forced. In such circumstances the monk could at least seek to praise God in his heart with psalms, hymns, and spiritual canticles (Col. 3:16). Yet he goes further. Conscious of how God is at every moment truly present in his creative love, bringing forth all that is, Basil notes that we can praise God by being in touch with the reality that it is God who is at each moment of our labor (as I write this paper and as you read it) giving to our hands the strength to do the task and to our minds the knowledge and insight to inspire and direct it. Furthermore, it is He, present and active, who is providing the materials—keeping also them in being in His creative love—that we are using: both the instruments (the pen in my hand, the chisel or shovel or computer in my brother's) and the matter (my paper, his wood, or earth, or ticker tape). The fully responsive use of these, of our own activity, and the ordination of it all to "the good pleasure of God," is the practical way in which we do pray constantly.

Saint Basil's attitude toward tools flows from this theological attitude. While we do not find in his *Rule* any statement quite so striking as Benedict's "the tools of the monastery are to be treated as the vessels of the altar" (C. 31)—a statement that invites us to think of our daily labor as the celebration of the Mass of the Universe, a eucharistic transformation of the creation—his teaching is as full and as practical. It flows from basic monastic values and principles.

The care of the tools devolves first of all on the worker who uses them. But if he should be negligent, since the tools are for the good of all, anyone aware of the neglect should remedy it. A shovel left out in the path in the rain is everyone's care. Even if it be the tool of another's trade, no one can be indifferent about it. At the same time, the user himself is not to assume a proprietor's attitude toward the tools of his craft. He must allow the Superior to use them in any way he wishes. He may not sell or exchange them, or dispose of them in any other way, or acquire others without the Superior's blessing. Basil's appeal here reminds us again of Benedict: "How could he who has irrevocably chosen not to be master even of his own hands and who has consigned to another the direction of his activity, how could he be consistent in maintaining full authority over the tools of his trade, arrogating to himself the dignity of mastership over them?" (Q. 41). This readily brings to mind Saint Benedict's statement that the monk is no longer master even of his own body (C. 58).

Saint Basil's lively and insightful faith readily reconciles the monk's (and Christian's) call to constant prayer with responsible labor. This carries over into his provisions for the Hours of Services or the Office. Here he may be a source for Saint Benedict, or they are giving unified witness to a common monastic tradition and practice. Saint Basil first gives a very beautiful and meaningful explanation of the significance of the respective Hours of Service and then he approaches the practical question of reconciling this call to prayer with the daily labor.

At the Third Hour—this would be around 9:00 a.m.—the brethren are to gather together "even if they may have dispersed to the various employments" (Q. 37). At this Hour they are to recall the gift the Spirit bestowed on the Apostles and so worship that they might be worthy of such sanctity. They are also to implore the guidance and instruction of the Holy Spirit so that all that they do will be good and useful.

Then Saint Basil's moderation and practicality come into

play. He realizes that distance or the nature of the work the monks are doing may make it difficult to drop everything and come to the community assembly. In such cases the monks are to consider it a strict obligation to carry out the Service where they are and as promptly as they can. The Saint reminds the monks that the Lord is equally present wherever they gather in His Name (Matt. 18:20).

Obedience to the Lord, a constant attentiveness to His Presence in all, in the full responsiveness of the obedience, this is fundamental in Saint Basil's attitude toward work. Given this, the other attitudes he would have enliven this obedience—the labor of the monk—are not surprising. The monk is to go to his work with enthusiasm, a ready zeal, and yet he is to give it careful attention. He is to strive to work blamelessly because he knows that his true, ever-present overseer is none other than the Lord Himself.

This is the simplicity we see prevailing in Saint Basil, and indeed it is an essential quality of monastic life— monk = *monos*. The monk is one whose eyes are set blamelessly on the Lord. Saint Basil's simplicity is reflected here in another way. He counsels the laborer to set himself with constancy to one task and not be moving about, now busy at one kind of task, now at another. "We are incapable by nature of following successfully a number of pursuits at the same time; to finish one task with diligent care is more beneficial than to undertake many..." (Q. 41). But as always, Saint Basil's moderation prevails. If necessity requires it and one has the ability, he can lend his brother a hand. The Saint encourages this with the concrete and meaningful analogy of the body: "...just as, in the case of our bodily members, we support ourselves with the hand when the foot is limping" (Q. 41).

Saint Basil is simple, simple as a dove, yet wise as a serpent. In the course of three chapters he lays down many wise provisions in regard to the monk's work.

In Question 38 he asks: What sort of trades are suitable to

the monastic profession. His principles here are excellent and equally valid for our times.

A monk wants to live a recollected life, one that is in constant attendance on the Lord. Therefore, in choosing his work he will seek that which allows him a tranquil and undisturbed life, a livelihood marked with simplicity and frugality. It will be an employment for which he will be able to get the necessary materials and tools without great difficulty, he will be able to sell the products readily, and he will not have to get involved in unsuitable or harmful relations. His product will not pamper the foolish and harmful desires of men. Basil suggests such crafts as weaving, shoemaking, construction, carpentry, and metal work. He illustrates his last point from these trades. The weaver should make things that will serve daily life and not fancy things to trap and ensnare the young. The shoemaker should seek to satisfy real needs.

The employment of predilection for Saint Basil is farming. It deals immediately with procuring necessities and responds well to the other conditions he has laid down. Farmers do not have to go about much. And it is good for monks to stay in one place. Such stability is seeming and beneficial; it is productive of mutual edification; it fosters faithful observance.

Saint Basil is concerned about the monks' travel just as was Saint Benedict, who wanted all necessities to be as much as possible within the enclosure (C. 66). But here again Basil shows his moderation and wisdom. It would be better to stay home and lower prices to attract customers to the monastery. But he realizes this cannot always be done. He allows, then, that monks will have to go out to the market—they are not to go about as peddlers. When they go out he urges them to travel in groups, to go to places that are not far distant where they can stay with devout people, and to stay together. This not only helps their spiritual life by providing mutual edification and support and an opportunity to pray the Hours together. It also provides mutual protection: difficult and avaricious men will be slow to take advantage of one in the presence of others. Saint Basil also notes that the monks should not try to sell their wares at shrines. Undoubtedly there would be a temptation to capitalize on the piety of the pilgrim. Shrines are for pilgrimage and prayer only, not for trafficking. Christ's action in the Temple is proof enough for this.

Basically, Basil opposes traveling, or anything else that can weaken or rupture the unity among the brethren. He does want men to use their talents, but only in the context of the blessing of the community. Saint Benedict was also strong on this (C. 57). One should not exercise a craft, or learn a new one, without a blessing, nor should he refuse to learn one when asked.

For Saint Basil, community, unity in fraternity, is of primal import. But Christian community can only be founded on obedience, obedience to the Gospels, to God, and to the legitimate authority, the expression of God's direction, at the center of the community.

Next year the Christian world will celebrate the centenary of Saint Benedict of Nursia, the great monastic Legislator of the West. His own statement establishes this Father's great reverence for the Legislator of the East. There are grounds for arguing that Benedict drew a great deal from Saint Basil's *Rules*, some of his most significant communitarian attitudes and provisions. The very least we can affirm is that they give a common witness to many of the same values of the monastic tradition. Especially is this so in regard to Christian and monastic labor. What Saint Benedict sacrificed to gain conciseness and precision in the treatment of his matter, Basil has in many cases retained for us, giving the matter a certain enfleshment which enables us to appreciate more the full significance of the statements in the Western monastic code. It is providential then that the sixteenth centenary of Saint Basil invites us to consider again his teaching as we in the West move toward the Benedictine commemoration.

THE FATHERS AND CHRISTIAN UNITY[1]

Jean Daniélou, SJ

*(Late Cardinal, well-known
theologian and patristics scholar)*

I would like to begin at the outset of this communication by getting rid of one ambiguity, namely the somewhat doubtful value of any attempt to make us represent the age of the Fathers as a golden age in which Christians lived together in unshadowed harmony. I suggest myself, that if this were indeed the picture they give us, then they would only aggravate our sufferings by giving us a nostalgic longing for the early years of the infant Church, which has ever since been inexorably compromised by the destructive processes of time. If indeed the Fathers of the Church can assist this process of bringing Christians together, it is on account of the very fact that we find that they experienced the same problems that we face ourselves. "It is true," writes Prestige, "the modern reunion problem is immensely complicated by vital questions of Church and Institutions, which did not arise in the fifth century. This makes the problem more difficult, but does not make it essentially different."[2] The Fathers, then, give us cause to fear, for they show us that the tragedy of division is as ancient as the Church itself—I would say, as old as the people of God. But they also give us reasons for hope, because they show us that in the course of history, divisions have been overcome—and that therefore they always can be overcome.

It is difficult for men of different mentalities to live together in a harmony of faith and charity. From the very beginning, we observe that this difficulty was experienced by Christians of Jewish origin, and by those coming from the Gentile world. The first threat of schism was the first schism of Antioch (the distant ancestor of the Antiochene schism of the fourth century) which nearly separated St. Peter from St. Paul. In fact the entire history of the beginnings of Christi-

anity is overshadowed by conflict. Jewish Christianity at an
early period in its history was to have great difficulty in not
setting itself up to be Christianity pure and simple, while
conceding to the appearance of a hellenistic Christianity
which taught the same faith, side by side with itself. And
hellenistic Christianity, triumphing over this, was to have
great difficulty in not condemning Jewish Christianity, both
for its ascetic practices and for its theological modes of expression.

Besides these racial differences, there were also intellectual
differences. The age of the Fathers is spanned by great
currents of thought, both literary and philosophical, which
consequently had their effect on exegetical methods and
theological systems. There was a Platonic tradition, which
stressed above all the ordering of the human spirit to the
intelligible world, and exalted the greatness of this human
spirit; and there was the Stoic tradition, more concerned with
the importance of the mission of the spirit in relation to the
cosmos. These two anthropologies were to give rise to two
different Christologies, the one at Antioch and the other at
Alexandria; and these different Christologies were in turn to
become the source of disagreements which were finally to
result in the dividing of the Church. Hence, this multiplicity
of theologies which should have been the outward expression
of the wealth of the Church, was eventually to bring about its
division.

Then there is the question of different customs. One of the
first schisms which nearly rent the Church had to do with the
different dates for the observance of the Easter festival—a
difference, which in my opinion, reaches back right into the
apostolic age—and on this occasion, Victor almost succeeded
in severing the Quartodecimans from the Church. To take a
less familiar example, the introduction into Cappadocia at
the end of the fourth century of the Syrian practice of singing
the psalms antiphonally during the vigils, was nearly the
source of another schism. (Thus music, which should have

created harmony between human souls, is capable sometimes of creating discord.) This is in fact one of the reasons for which Atarbius, the irritable bishop of Neo-Caesarea, claimed the right to reject St. Basil from his communion. "These practices," he wrote, "were not even in existence in the days of Gregory" (Thaumaturgus). "But then, those litanies you sing now," replied St. Basil, "did not exist then either." (*Epist.* 207, 4.) "Nevertheless," he added, "on this matter, we shall give way to you entirely. We are only concerned that the essential teachings should remain authoritative. Do not on any account dispense with the doctrine of the hypostases."

The important statement here is made by St. Basil. In matters on which diversity is permissible, agreement can be reached on all sides. But the essential teachings, the *prohegoumena*, must be preserved, for questions of custom are only of importance when they concern matters of faith. "Church order," Prestige has rightly said, "is relevant to Church union only in so far as it is relevant to the doctrine of the Church." (*Fathers and Heretics*, p. 177.) The tragedy is that both are so often inextricably confused with one another, so that the precise difficulty is to delineate the dividing line between two opposed and wholly irreconcilable spheres of theology. There is that of lawful diversity, which must be accepted and itself constitutes in fact the very richness of the treasures of Catholicity. But there are also the *prohegoumena* which constitute a part of the very essence of the message of the Church, and are an integral part in its foundation. It is on a basis of these alone that we must make our way towards unity.

These *prohegoumena* then, these are the articles of faith which have been derived from the Apostles themselves, enshrined in Holy Scripture, and handed down by the Fathers. They are the common possession of the whole Church. This, as it is well known, is a theme dear to the heart of St. Irenaeus of Lyons:

The Church which fills the whole world and which guards securely the traditions of the Apostles, offers to all but a single faith. All confess their faith in the same God, all believe in the same economy of salvation by the Incarnation of the Son of God, and in recognition of the identical gifts they have received from the one Spirit, endeavor to follow the same precepts. The same form of organization is preserved among them, and all are looking for the same Coming of the Lord, and earning a salvation which is the same for all men. (*Adv. Haer.* III, 2, 1.)

This unity on matters of faith, however, is accompanied by certain cultural differences. Hence, there may well be differences between the languages spoken in different parts of the world, but the teachings of the Church have the same effect everywhere. "For the churches situated in Germany," writes St. Irenaeus, "neither hold nor teach a different faith from that believed in and taught by the churches located in Spain, Gaul, the East, Lybia, and at the very center of the world." (*Adv. Haer.* I, 10, 2.) Basil speaks in the same vein. "There is no such thing," he writes, "as the faith of Seleucia, the faith of Constantinople, the faith of Zela, the faith of Lampsacus, and the faith of Rome. The faith that is taught today is no different from that taught yesterday, for it is one and the same faith. We have been baptized into the faith which we received from the Savior; and we still believe in the faith of our baptism." (*Epist.* 251, 4.) "What our Fathers taught," he adds elsewhere, "we also teach." (*Spir. Sanct.* 7.)

I must emphasize these words of St. Basil. The one faith in its many different modes of expression, is the faith which we have received from the Fathers, and in this we see a primary aspect of the contribution the Fathers have to make towards Christian unity. They are not as yet the primary witnesses to the faith; but they are, however, those who in each local church have instilled the life of Christ into us, for this is how St. Basil understands it. "For my part," he writes in the *Trea-*

tise on the Holy Spirit, "if you want me to give a personal
testimony, then I hold to the phrase 'with the Spirit' as
something I have had handed down to me by a man who has
lived a long time in the service of God, who baptized me and
introduced me into the life and organization of the Church."
(*Spir. Sanct.* 27.)[3]

The same teaching is found again in Gregory of Nyssa.
"Let no one," he writes in the *Contra Eunomium*, "make the
suggestion that it is necessary to substantiate what we teach
by means of some sort of proof. We have already sufficient
proof for our statements in that we possess the traditions
delivered to us by the Fathers, an inheritance in fact which
has been transmitted in unbroken line of succession since the
time of the Apostles themselves by the saints who followed
them." (III, 2, 98, Jaeger, 84.) And in the *Letter to Eustathia,
Ambrosia and Basilissa* (382), he writes,

> Have in remembrance always the holy Fathers, in whose
> hands you yourself were placed by your own good father,
> for by the grace of God it is we who have been judged
> worthy to be the guardians of their inheritance. Do not go
> beyond the limits set by your fathers, and do not despise
> the common language of the simple Kerygma. . . . Do not
> on any account pick and choose among a variety of dif-
> ferent doctrines, but walk according to the ancient rule of
> faith. (*Epist.* III, Pasquali 27.)

If, however, this question of disunity were only the result
of certain differences in outlook, which in turn had degen-
erated into the formation of a number of rival groups, then
its solution would be comparatively easy. The real tragedy in
this issue occurs when one is no longer dealing with questions
of mere "diversity" but with fundamentally opposed points
of view as to how Scripture and Tradition should be interpreted. Scripture and Tradition have to be interpreted, and
hence if there are different interpretations, it is understand-
able that they are opposed to one another. It is not easy to

trace the dividing line between issues raised simply over the multiple forms in which the faith is expressed, and those which are the result of major divergences from the faith itself. The confusion that ensues is agonizing. Christians grow perceptibly more suspicious of one another, and then they treat one another as heretics.

This situation has been encountered since the very beginnings of the Church. We come across it at the beginning of the third century in the discussions on the subjects of the unity of God and on the nature of the Son and of the Holy Spirit. We are faced with a strange confusion in the controversies between Hippolytus and Tertullian on the one hand, and between Callixtus and Praxeas on the other, in which it is difficult indeed to discern what in fact is the result of two different theological systems, and what in fact reaches down into the very heart of the faith itself. At the end of the third century, the great trinitarian debate opened between Dionysius of Rome and Dionysius of Alexandria, which heralded in the conflicts of the fourth century.

Here I would like to pause a moment at what seems to me the most dramatic point in these controversies—for two reasons. First because the situation at this point is most difficult to elucidate, and second, because the greatest of the Church's Fathers were involved in it: St. Athanasius, St. Basil, the two Gregories, Damasus, and Meletius. Here we see the Fathers confronted in the fullest sense of the word with our problem. It was at a time when Damasus of Rome and Peter II of Alexandria were in communion with the schismatic bishop of Antioch, Paulinus; whereas Basil of Caesarea and Gregory of Nazianzen were in communion with Meletius. It was at the time when Basil was forced to break off communion with men to whom he had been very close, Eustathius of Sebaste, on account of his doctrine of the Holy Spirit, and Apollinaris of Laodicea, on account of his Christology. In this sort of confusion, no one was able to tell where exactly was the dividing line between heterodoxy and mere "diversity," and no one could escape being suspected of heresy.

In the midst of this obscure situation, people entered into communion with one another and left in the most arbitrary fashion. To use the language of the time, "Altar was set up against altar" in the same town. In 382, St. Gregory of Nyssa, writing to Eustathia, Ambrosia, and Basilissa, asked, "What have we done wrong and why do people make us the objects of their hatred? What is the meaning of these new altars set up in opposition to ours? Is it that we are the expositors of another set of Scriptures?" (*Epist.* 3, Pasquali, 26.) Basil also denounced these "tricks" played at the expense of the Church.

> These are the sort of tricks they play against the Church of God, leveling their accusations at people, or showing their approval of them as they think fit. On his way through Paphlagonia, Eustathius overturned the altars of Basilides the Paphlagonian, and celebrated on tables of his own. And now he is asking Basilides to allow him to enter into communion with him. He has excommunicated the saintly Elpidius of Satala because he was in communion with the bishop of Amasia, and now he is asking the bishop of Amasia to receive him into communion. (*Epist.* 251.)

The result of all this was that discredit was brought to the Church in the face of the pagan world. John Chrysostom wrote:

> How are we going to stand up to the mockery of the pagans? We have the same faith, the same sacraments. Why then does another leader set himself up as the head of another church? Can't you see, now, say the pagans, how Christians are motivated in everything by nothing but the desire for their own advancement? (*In Ep. ad. Eph.* XI, 5.)

What is one to do in the midst of all this? Basil's example is typical. He was trapped between the danger of intransigence which would make him separate from his communion those who in reality were orthodox, and the danger of an attitude of appeasement, which would force him to admit those of heterodox beliefs into his communion and thus in other words, add to the confusion. For the peace of the Church had to be sought for, but it could only be found when she was united on matters of faith. But what was it in this problem which concerned matters of faith, and what was it that concerned but a difference in theological approach. For Basil was ready to welcome the Galatians, the disciples of Marcellus of Ancyra, into this communion, in order to please Damasus. But if he did this, he would be suspected of heresy by the followers of Eustathius of Sebaste. Contrariwise, his unswerving loyalty to Meletius made Peter of Alexandria suspect him of Arianism right in front of Damasus. So he sat down and courteously, but firmly, wrote to Peter.

In this situation, it appears that there are two necessary things that have to be done, and it is imperative that they are done in any search for Christian unity. The first is to go as far as one can to interpret the other's opinion in the most favorable light. Athanasius gives us an example of this attitude when he offered to shake hands with the *homoeousians*, Basil of Ancyra and Meletius of Antioch, in recognition that the faith which they held was sound, even if the manner in which it was expressed tended to stress the side of it which was somewhat contrary to the aspect of this faith that he himself regarded as more important.

The other side to this question, however, is that one must make no concession whatsoever on matters of truth, i.e. one must believe that there is one true interpretation of the word, and in consequence, since unity must be reached on a basis of this true interpretation, then one must not adopt any position as would prevent this happening. For if it is possible to sin through pride and intransigence, then it is also possible to sin by being careless and conceding on matters of principle. For there are not only differences of theological approach; there are also questions in which the faith itself is involved. There is indeed a quest for truth, but this research can be carried out within the compass of unity itself.

There is in Gregory of Nazianzen an excellent text on this subject:

> Let no one be under the impression that I am saying that we must always look for peace. I know in fact that just as it is sometimes better to have disagreement, so on occasions, agreement can be worse than discord. In short, it is my opinion that one should adjust one's degrees of flexibility and rigidity so as not to give way to all and sundry simply through cowardice, nor to cut oneself off from others by being foolhardy. For weakness does not achieve much; and one does not make much contact with other people by being over-enthusiastic. When, therefore, we are only upset by suspicions and unfounded fears, it is more useful to be patient than to precipitate ourselves headlong into it, and better to give way a little than to be arrogant. And further since we are in the same body, it is better and of more use to adapt ourselves to one another, than to begin by condemning one another, then breaking off from one another, then destroying our confidence in one another by living in separation from one another, and then in the long run ordering things to be put right, after the manner of tyrants and not that of brothers. (*Orat.* VI, 20. PG 35, 748-749.)

The Fathers of the Church, then, are in the fullest sense of the word those who have faced up to these battles, and have come out of them victorious; and it is for this reason that they will always remain as our examples. It is in fact for the very reason that they have first of all suffered for the sake of the unity of the Church that they have earned for themselves the title of witnesses *par excellence* to the common faith. It is in this respect that they constitute for us a particular authority and equally in this respect that from the beginning of the fifth century, they were to be quoted in the Councils. Theodoret, according to Cyril of Alexandria, writes in their honor:

> It is true that mountains and seas separate them widely from one another, but the distance between them does not prevent them being in agreement with one another. All in fact have been carried along by the grace of the same Spirit. Were I to bring to you once more the words of the victorious defenders of the faith, Diodore and Theodore, then you would know that these too have written in a manner that is wholly in agreement with that of their predecessors.

And in another place he adds: "Differences in language did not cause them to hold a number of different beliefs, for they were themselves the very fountains of the grace of the Holy Spirit, and they drew their waters from a single source." (*Epist.* 151, PG 83, 1141 D.)

                    *   *   *   *   *   *

If, however, the unity of the Church consists, so far as the Fathers are concerned, in a unitedness on matters of faith, then there must also be charitable relationships between the churches which are in themselves an expression of this unity. Certainly, it is true that each local church which possesses the apostolic succession is in itself a true church. But no such church can do without actual communion with other churches. Basil insists on this point in his *Letter to the Bishops by the Sea* (i.e. the bishops of the islands in the Aegean Sea), who argued in this way. "We live surrounded by sea, we are out of reach of the sufferings that others are undergoing; what advantage therefore could we possibly gain from being in communion with them?" (*Epist.* 203, 3.) In short, these communities, thinking themselves capable of existing on their own, had the idea that they would in this way be able to escape contamination from recent errors, and held fast to the ancient traditions. Basil answered them:

> The Lord himself has cut off the islands from the mainland by sea, but he has united in charity those who live on the islands to those who live on the mainland. We have but one Lord, one faith, one hope; and even if you do consider yourselves to be the head of the Universal Church, the head cannot say to the feet, "I have no need of you.".... So far as we are concerned, in consideration of our own weakness, we are seeking to be united in a living union with you. We realize that even if you are not present in the body, yet the assistance that you obtain for us by means of your prayers will, in these most difficult circumstances, be of the greatest use to us.... For how can we, the sons of those fathers who ensured by a number of small indications that the signs of our relatedness to one another were to be circulated from one end of the world to the other... how should we now cut ourselves off from the world, how can we possibly fail to be ashamed of keeping ourselves to ourselves, and how indeed can we fail to consider this breach in our unity as nothing less than a disaster. (*Epist.* 203, 3.)

Basil has used a word here whose depth of meaning I want to bring out—*sumpnoia*. It is a medical term, derived from the language of Hippocratic medicine, where it signifies a "living organic harmony" (i.e. of the parts of the body) and has a deeper meaning than just *sympatheia*. Gregory of Nyssa develops this idea admirably. "Those," he writes, "who are aware that Christ is the head of the body, should consider also that first and foremost, the head is of the same nature (*homorphues*) and of the same substance (*homoousios*) as the body which it controls, and that all the parts of the body work together in harmony with all the other parts, effecting by a single organic harmony the solidarity of the

parts of the body in respect of the whole." (*Perfect. Christ.*
Jaeger 197.) The word *sumpnoia* expresses here the necessity
of a lively cooperation of head and members in order to
ensure the health of the whole body.

However, this unity must have some concrete form of
expression. Basil calls to mind the custom amongst the early
Christians of distributing small "tickets" in time of persecution as a means of calling the community together, and thus
signifying their union with one another. In another place, he
defines more clearly what is meant by communication
between the churches:

> Ask your fathers, and they will inform you that even if the
> various local churches were geographically separated from
> one another, they were at least at one in their feelings for
> one another, and ruled by a common mind. Again and
> again the people of these churches were in contact with one
> another; again and again their clergy visited one another,
> and the pastors themselves were inspired by such charity
> for one another that each looked upon his colleague as
> master and guide in the service of his Lord. (*Epist.* 204.)

Basil recalls that he himself is in the habit of receiving letters
from Armenia, Achaia, Illyria, Gaul, Spain, Italy, and
Africa. All over the world, great numbers of bishops are
united. Why then should he separate himself from this
communion? So precious in fact does this unity seem to St.
Basil, that if he himself were liable in any way to impede or
disrupt this unity, then he would prefer to be out of it altogether. (*Epist.* 204, 7.)

The outstanding feature of St. Basil's thought in this text is
the importance of communion between the churches. Basil is
in the habit of running to other churches to help him in his
own difficulties and it is well known how he intervened in the
controversy between St. Athanasius and Peter of Alexandria.
All this is but the expression of a deep consciousness of the
solidarity of the episcopate of the Universal Church, in which

the bishops are bound to help and sustain those who find themselves in difficulties. Thus St. Basil shows himself to be the true inheritor of the traditions of the first centuries. We know already how the Paschal controversy of the second century gave rise to a number of exchanges between the churches. Eusebius has preserved for us the correspondence between Dionysius of Alexandria and the bishops of Crete and Pontus at the end of the second century on issues such as encratism. And we are acquainted with the correspondence between Dionysius of Rome and Dionysius of Alexandria at the end of the third century. The Council of Antioch of 262 resulted in a number of exchanges between the churches in order to give a ruling on the question of Paul of Samosata. Episcopal collegiality in fact seems to have been one of the most lively features of the Church of the first centuries, and that is why St. Basil constantly makes appeal to this aspect of the Church's life.

He reminds Damasus that this mutual assistance of one another is but a matter of tradition.

> We are not asking you for anything out of the ordinary, only that which good and religious men of an earlier generation regarded as a matter of course, and in particular is something which you yourself are quite used to. For we know from the memories that have been preserved of him, and thanks to the letters that we still possess, that the saintly bishop Dionysius wrote to our church of Caesarea in order to help it and sent it something to ransom those of our fraternity who had been taken captive by the Persians. That is why we do not hesitate to write to you to ask your protection, asking you to send us help, to send us a few people from among you who share the same spirit as we do, in order to gather together the dissentient parties, and revive the spirit of friendship between the churches of God. (*Epist.* 70.)

*   *   *   *   *   *

Thus the great cavalcade of the Fathers of the Church is there to teach us that by means of a cheerful acceptance of differences, by an honest searching together for the truth, and by the preservation of brotherly and charitable relationships with one another, the divisions which could have shattered the Church have in the long run been conquered. It is true to say, as we mentioned at the beginning of this communication in quoting Prestige, the situation today is more difficult. But the example of the Fathers of the Church rouses in us the hope that one day, the world will look in amazement on the wonderful scene of a rediscovered unity, and will recognize in all this the seal of the living God.

NOTES

[1] A lecture given to the Fourth International Conference on Patristic Studies, Oxford, September 1963.

[2] *Fathers and Heretics*, p. 177.

[3] He is comparing the two phrases "in the Spirit" and "with the Spirit." — Editor.

INTRANSIGENCE AND IRENICISM IN SAINT BASIL'S "De Spiritu Sancto"*

Jean Gribomont, OSB
(*Monk of the Abbey of
Clervaux, Luxembourg and
of St. Jerome's Abbey, Rome*)

I. Historical Setting of the Treatise

The threat of Arianism which troubled the major part of the fourth century must be considered one of the greatest crises which threatened the Christian faith. This is so not only because the dogma it imperiled touches upon the very nature of God and conditions the salvation brought by Christ, but also because from an ecclesiological point of view the whole hierarchy seemed at one point to have succumbed. In 359, "the world awoke to find itself Arian," according to St. Jerome's saying,[1] when the two Councils of Rimini and Seleucia forced both the West and the East to subscribe to compromising formulae; and the titulars of the great sees, even including Pope Liberius, bowed to the imperial policy.

Twenty years later, however, Arianism was fully defeated. It is one of the rare heresies which disappeared without leaving any schism behind it. Indeed, from the crisis there came forth a formidable Trinitarian affirmation, still proclaimed by Christian churches today in the *Credo*, the *Gloria*, the *Te Deum*. How did such a turnabout happen?

To be sure, it did not come about suddenly; barbarian Vandals and Goths helped the heresy to survive for centuries. But it is in the 370s that the decisive battle was waged when all the forces that stood for the traditional faith were gathered together against the heresy. The man who brought about this gathering was Basil the Great.

At the beginning of the quarrel, attention had focused on the eternity of the Word and his equality with the Father. But the period which concerns us found itself forced to bring about a confrontation of the traditions of the different churches with regard to the Holy Spirit, thus completing the circle of the Trinitarian doctrine. This shift of emphasis is perhaps not unrelated to the development of monasticism and of its charismatic experience in Egypt and Syria and Cappadocia, the most active centers of theological activity.

When Basil fashioned his first tools in a juvenile polemic against the rationalist Eunomius shortly after 360, the question of the Spirit was scarcely raised; it was treated in an appendix of a few pages.[2] During his episcopacy, on the contrary, from 370 on, his preaching and his rich correspondence testify to ever tenser controversies concerning the veneration of the Spirit. Here lies the crux of the whole policy of peace and union which, in spite of the storm, his common sense and his strong charity meant to pursue. How reduced, however, was his activity! Out of ten years of an all too short episcopacy, the last years of suffering and of sickness allowed him only an extremely limited production: only ten letters can be traced to the year 377,[3] two to 378;[4] one wonders what part of the oratorical[5] or administrative, ascetical,[6] dogmatic, or political work should be assigned to this period. On the other hand, the beginning of his episcopacy must have been spent establishing the personal authority of the bishop-elect, whose ascetic style and popular support had met with a strong opposition on the part of the episcopacy of the region,[7] and no doubt also of the majority of the ruling class. Finally, even the years 373-375 were, as we shall see, a time of mortification and of silence.

The only writing of notable size in the period of Basil's episcopacy is the treatise on the Holy Spirit,[8] completed in 375. Even then, it was discreetly addressed to a trustworthy disciple, Amphilochius of Iconium. The conclusion[9] notes that, given the times, the intelligent man should remain silent (Amos 5:13), since only in silence can the voice of the wise be heard (Eccles. 9:17). It was the trust and the zeal of Amphilochius that forced Basil to open his heart to him; but he should avoid divulging the book out of season. This was the sowing-time; the harvest would bear fruit right after the saint's death, at the Council of Constantinople, in 381.

II. Bibliographical Clarifications

Lately, some excellent works have paid homage to the importance of the treatise. An *Abhandlung*[10] of 200 large pages was presented in the year 1956 to the Academy of Göttingen by the late H. Dörries: *De Spiritu Sancto. Der Beitrag des Basilius zum Abschluss des trinitarischen Dogmas.* With a remarkable delicacy of interpretation, the author analyzes, chronologically, the entire work of Basil. He deliberately abstains from recourse to the sources, in order not to trace the history of the previous controversies, but to concentrate only on the spiritual and intellectual portrait of the bishop of Caesarea; in conclusion, however, he places the latter in a perspective which leads from the Council of Nicaea to that of Constantinople. It is the *economy* of Basil, that is, his reserve and his silences, then the interpersonal dialogue which he held with his friends and his adversaries, and finally the function of charismatic monachism, which attract above all the interest of this very ecumenical theologian.

In the same year, in the *Lutherische Rundschau*, Dörries summarized the same theses in an article free of every apparatus of erudition;[11] this text was resumed and slightly added to in Volume I of *Wort und Stunde*,[12] miscellanies offered to the Master in honor of his seventieth birthday.

In the same line of scientific research, we can mention the two monographs of H. Dehnhard, *Das Problem der Abhängigkeit des Basilius von Plotin*,[13]and of A. M. Ritter, *Das Konzil von Konstantinopel und sein Symbol*,[14] which, respectively, clarify Chapter 9 of the treatise, and its immediate influence on oriental orthodoxy. We can also mention an article by A. Heising, whose object is restricted, but which touches on one of the characteristic points of the Basilian

112 *Word and Spirit*

argumentation: *Der hl. Geist und die Heiligung der Engel in der Pneumatologie des Basilius von Cäsarea. Ein Beitrag zum Verständnis der theologischen Arbeitsweise in der griechischen Patristik.*[15]

On the other hand, we must mention an important edition, given by B. Pruche to the Sources Chrétiennes.[16] I am not speaking only of the first edition, that of 1945; another edition issued in 1968, with a double introduction, a translation and annotation totally reworked and improved, does not seem to have received the attention it deserved. We notice in it a polemic against Dörries (already announced in an article of Pruche in the *Recherches de Science Religieuse*[17]), but this is far from being the only point revised in the second edition.

To tell the truth, Pruche's objections are especially opposed to many articles in which I had taken up and completed the theses of the professor from Göttingen. Apart from a book review in the *Byzantinische Zeitschrift*,[18] this involves two articles on *Eustathe de Sébaste*, published in the *Dictionnaire de Spiritualité*[19] and in the *Dictionnaire d'Histoire et de Géographie Ecclésiastique;*[20] and also various Basilian studies, in particular *Esotérisme et Tradition dans le Traité du Saint Esprit.*[21] Without being able to present again all the argumentation of Dörries, I used his discoveries, and it was my more accessible formulae which jarred Father Pruche. The late professor from Göttingen, in a few discreet lines,[22] was unwilling to recognize himself in the summary that Pruche made of his theses, and in a peace-making gesture, he blamed the misunderstandings on his difficult German. In fact, one does not get the impression that Pruche had carefully read the German work and its solid argumentation. It might be good to go back over the question in order to elucidate the misunderstandings as courteously and peaceably as possible, and to try to formulate a synthesis which would do justice, at varying levels, to all the positive observations.

III. The Basilian Economy

Basil's friends were often stupefied at the reserve with which he abstained from proclaiming the divinity of the Spirit, or from declaring him *homoousios* with the Father and the Son—he who named him at their side in the profession of faith and the doxology. Beginning with letters 113 and 114 (dated 372), he rejected from his communion those who blasphemed the Spirit by calling him a creature; but he stopped there, and did not think it necessary to require a positive formula of profession of faith of any kind, for he did not link the orthodox faith to a verbal definition. Others, much more affirmative, criticized this reserve which, they felt, was the outcome of an exaggerated prudence which was surnamed *economy*.

Already during Basil's lifetime, two first-class authorities had to intervene to make an apology of his orthodoxy and his intentions. At an uncertain date, probably in 372, the monks John, Antiochus, and Palladius, had appealed to St. Athanasius. The latter answered most nobly,[23] giving full confidence from a great distance to the bishop of Caesarea, the glory of the churches, the fighter for the truth, "who makes himself weak with the weak, in order to win them" (1 Cor. 9:22); he should be obeyed like a father! At about the same period, after a homily of Basil, another monk was scandalized by the adroitness with which the orator had succeeded in not taking very clear positions on the problem of the divinity of the Spirit, and this "with more politics than piety." Gregory Nazianzen, alerted, defended as best he could the reputation of his friend. He appealed to diplomatic considerations, explaining that the position of the champion of orthodoxy being extremely precarious, Basil had to avoid any provocation in order to keep his influential post. Gregory did not fail, nonetheless, to make everything known to Basil, thereby inviting him to clarify his own position. He would have liked on his part a precise commitment, but he did not press him without the most emphatic oratorical precautions:

I have always seen in you the master of my life, the doctor of my faith...and if anyone extols your merits, he certainly does so either with me or after me.... In this life, the greatest good for me is your friendship and your intimacy.... It is not with a joyful heart that I write now what I am about to write; nevertheless, I will write it. Do not be upset with me or I would be quite upset myself, if I were not to find in you the belief that I tell you all this and write it out of sheer affection.[24]

The writings of Gregory continue to explain with the same reasons of prudence Basil's doctrinal economy even after the latter's death, as, for example, in a famous discourse about the Holy Spirit[25] on Pentecost in 379, and in the funeral eulogy[26] that he pronounced in honor of Basil (380). The economy is always explained by means of the threat of banishment that came from Valens and from the Arian party.

Pruche is fully satisfied with this interpretation[27] which has the authority of Basil's own friend. According to him, Basil would willingly admit in private that the Spirit was God, *homoousios* with the Father and the Son; for tactical reasons, however, he would have agreed in public to replace the *consubstantial* with the word *homotimos*, "identical in honor," which would not subject him to State interference as the other would have.

It is right to underscore Basil's interest in the *homotimos*, although the epithet does not constitute for him a password, a dogmatic formula. But how would the accusers have been deceived by such a ruse of vocabulary? Basil is not without foreseeing the implacable war which was going to be waged against his argumentation[28] with shouts, a summary stoning,[29] the sword, the axe, fire, the whole apparatus of torture.[30] This myth of martyrdom has a strong rhetorical tinge, but it remains clear that the adversary is not naive enough to let himself be duped by the *homotimos*.

There is a more serious objection against the Gregorian interpretation: it is that Basil refused it. We have mentioned the oratorical precautions with which his friend had trans-mitted to him the difficulties of the "right wing" theologians, and tried to obtain from him, at least in private, an agree-ment with certain more "integrist" formulae. The reply was sharp, more so than Gregory had feared.

> I received the letter of your piety through the intermediary of the venerable brother, Helladios, who has moreover expounded very clearly the criticisms which you suggested. You should have no difficulty in imagining our reaction! Nonetheless, we decided to place the love we owe you ahead of every sort of conflict and we welcomed, as was befitting, even this sort of news. We pray the all-Holy God that the days and times to come shall be the same for you as in the past wherein we ourselves are aware not to have been wanting in anything, either little or much.[31]

This expression of gratitude to a friend who had been trying to be his advocate does not look like much of an approbation.

> The monk whose criticisms you quoted is but a new-comer who has barely taken the trouble to take a look at the ascetic life, hoping to obtain a good reputation for having shared our fellowship. That he enlarges on what he did not hear and makes comments on what he did not understand does not surprise me in the least. But what does surprise and upset me is that he could find from among the most intimate of your brothers someone who would listen to him; and not only listen to him, but it would seem, be willing to be persuaded by him.[32]

After this "estoppel" Basil pushes aside the "gossips and calumnies" reported by his correspondent, and thoroughly refrains from any explanation concerning the motives of his economy: "I have no time to give an answer on this sub-ject."[33]

Pruche makes no allusion to this categorical refusal which Dörries brings out with great emphasis,[34] but it is not possible, when one knows Basil, to reduce such an answer to wounded sensitivity.[35] It has a well thought-out doctrinal foundation, as is clearly brought out by his letters to the church of Tarsus.

IV. Integrism and Economy at Tarsus

Sylvanus, the bishop of Tarsus, was part of that group of numerous Oriental bishops in the 350s who were of basically sound faith but very distrustful of Marcellus of Ancyra, an acknowledged Sabellian, and therefore distrustful of Athanasius, too, and of the Occidentals who supported him. They rejected the term *homoousios*, which did not sufficiently express the distinctness of the person of the Son. Later on, facing the affirmation of Arianism at the Councils of Seleucia and Constantinople (359-360), this group was forced toward the right, and when at the death of the Emperor Julian (363) it was able to assert itself, a council was held at Lampsacus, and a delegation was sent to Rome. It was made up of the same Sylvanus with Eustathius of Sebaste and Theophilus of Castabala. These three bishops, agreeing henceforth to subscribe to the Nicene formula, received letters of communion from Pope Liberius and from the episcopate of Italy, thus enlarging considerably the homoousian front, but introducing into it troops of a mentality quite different from that of the old Nicaeans.[36] It is, moreover, in this milieu that Basil first makes his appearance, even though he immediately showed personal convictions which were much more decided than this whole group of Neo-Nicaeans.[37]

After the death of Sylvanus, about the beginning of 372, the church of Tarsus was divided into many segments. The majority, guided by Cyriacus, held on to the "moderate" line of the deceased bishop. To the left, there were Arian tendencies. To the right, on the contrary, an anxious group, more demanding on the subject of Trinitarian orthodoxy, threatened to go into schism, somewhat as the small church of

Paulinus had done in Antioch. But this group, as well as the majority group, respected Basil; both sides sought his advice. Basil's answers to both are equally friendly and respectful. To the *Zelanti*, he speaks of edifying the Church, of repairing false moves (very moderate terms indeed!), of sympathy towards the sick, as well as of protection for the brethren of sound faith;[38] he complains of the rarity of such dispositions, which ought to cure the already propagated evil, and prevent the threatening one. He invites these faithful, therefore, to look with the greatest zeal after the union of the scattered sheep, a union which requires that one allow oneself to be carried along (*symperipherô!*) with the weakest ones, in all questions which would bring no harm to souls.[39] Having thus focused not on integrism but on ecumenism, he specifies how to apply these principles: to be content with subscribing to the Nicene faith, adding only one stipulation—an altogether negative one: to receive those who *do not* say that the Spirit is a creature.[40] The end of the letter reveals that this is not a vague "greatest common denominator," insufficient no doubt, but imposed by circumstances:

> Nothing should be added beyond these conditions, for I am convinced that the protracted practice of a common Christian life and a fraternal exercise duly purified of all evil zeal will also bring about what would be necessary in order to see more clearly. It is the Lord who will give it, he who makes all things to cooperate for the good of those who love him (Rom. 8:28).[41]

These words one also finds at the end of the treatise on the Holy Spirit: "Either through us, or through others, the Lord will bring to fulfillment what is still lacking, according to the knowledge given by the Spirit (Gal. 3:5) to those who are worthy of it."[42]

It is not, therefore, a human controversy which may succeed in exposing in a convincing manner the contents of the faith. Confronted with hesitations, like those which con-

cern the divinity of the Spirit, one ought to be satisfied with
the traditional faith which precedes the difficulties—such as
the faith of Nicaea, so vague as to the third article, but
positive, nevertheless, so as to enumerate the Spirit after the
Father and the Son. Let there be added an explicit refusal of
the scandalous novelties of error. Such an economy does not
intend to minimize anything essential.

The following letter (114), addressed to Cyriacus' group
also deserves an analysis. After a eulogy of irenicism, Basil
praises the charity he found in the "Integrist" party: love of
the brethren at the same time as zeal for Christ, scrupulous
and conscientious care with regard to the faith.[43] He then
assumes his role of conciliator,

> I have gone so far as to be answerable to them for your
> rectitude, and I assured them that you also, by the zeal for
> the truth that you owe to the grace of God, stand ready for
> the battle in order to suffer when necessary for the doctrine
> of the truth.[44]

After the episcopate of Sylvanus, the community sided easily
with the confession of the 318 Fathers "who were assembled
with no mind to quarrel and did not speak without the action
of the Holy Spirit."[45] After this tranquillizing presentation of
the *Nicaenum*, which belongs to none of the parties, Basil
added that we cannot profess that the Spirit is a creature—a
new and blasphemous formula, which must have been offen-
sive to the bulk of the community. If these points are accepted
as basis for discussion, Basil makes commitments in the name
of the minority: "It will manifest the necessary submission,"
even "a superabundance (*hyperbolè*) of discipline."[46] This
solution sacrifices the scruples of the dissidents of the right
wing to the habits of the majority; a Gregory Nazianzen, an
Athanasius, would no doubt have been more supportive of
the intransigents.

At any rate, the Basilian economy does not seem to be
conditioned here by fear of the police; the explanation of it

that Gregory proposes (elsewhere) does not account for the nobility of the motives involved. Athanasius who valued condescension toward the weak and gave evidence of having full confidence in Basil was closer to reality in spite of his militant past. Nevertheless, the bishop of Alexandria takes for mere apostolic condescension what with Basil is also the discernment of a theologian who does not identify the verbal formulation received at a given moment with the essence of the spiritual faith. It is just in this sense that Paul wanted to be Greek with the Greeks. We must examine this point in greater detail.

V. Dogma and Kerygma

In order to distinguish between the inner and spiritual substance of the faith and its verbal formulation, Basil has recourse to the two words *dogma* and *kèrygma*, derived from the verbs *dokeô* (believe, judge, think) and *kèryssô* (proclaim). *Kèrygma* is practically equivalent to what present-day theology calls *defined dogma*. *Dogma*, antecedent to *kèrygma*, is also its spiritual fruit; it is revealed truth, present and active in the mind. Dörries has consecrated many pages to this distinction,[47] analyzing the texts, and perhaps introducing into them sometimes, without meaning to, a problematic more elaborate than that of the fourth century. After E. Amand de Mendieta,[48] I myself have consecrated a study to this question[49] which I will not consider here in detail, even though more remains to be said about it. I only remind the reader that, more than Athanasius and more than Gregory, Basil values especially this almost ineffable content of revelation and of the spiritual knowledge of God; in this he is no doubt a disciple of Origen. In this perspective, the economy is not explained merely by the people's intellectual deficiency or their ineradicable mental habits; it results from the scale of values. What is essential is the sharing in the reality of the faith: the apostle must sow, and then he lets prayer, the charisms, the living unity in charity bring about the indispensable growth.[50]

The conception that Pruche has of theology makes it particularly difficult for him to understand such a point of view as though this economy minimized the value of the truth.

VI.   The Doctrinal Exigencies of Gregory Nazianzen

We must concede to Father Pruche that at least one, and not the least, of Basil's familiars, Gregory Nazianzen, upholds and guarantees his interpretation. But the funeral oration, first declaimed, then published by Nazianzen, has for centuries commanded the hagiographic stylization of Basil; it is not surprising that history, basing itself on the saint's own work, finds it hard to free itself from legend.

It is important to take into account what distinguishes the two friends.[51] The doctrinal conception of Gregory is much more demanding not only than that of Basil, but than that of the Church, at least such as it was expressed in the Council of Constantinople and its Creed. No one is unaware that Gregory had to abandon with bitter disappointment the presidency of this assembly.[52] We also notice that he systematically passed over in silence the formula of faith promulgated in the Council regarding the Holy Spirit; he ignored it even in his second letter to Cledonius, in 382, in the very place where he deplores that the Nicene Creed was insufficient in its third article.[53] How could he thus feign to ignore the *Constantinopolitanum*? Ritter has recently explained this omission, by proposing an interpretation of verses 1703-1708 of the long poem *De vita sua*, his lamentation on the subject of the Council.[54] "Favoring everyone's view," the bishops have troubled the sweet source of the primitive faith, which Nicaea had formerly protected by proclaiming the adorable nature of the Trinity united in Unity: the bishops have mingled with it the bitter streams of their opinions by approving whatever would please the state. And for the length of nearly 100 verses, whose sharp stings were for a long time deliberately ignored, Gregory takes to task these too conciliatory shepherds who introduce Moab and Ammon into the Church. But the creedal formula of Constantinople is strongly stamped with the Basilian economy, thanks, among others, to the mediation of Amphilochius,[55] and doubtless to that of Gregory of Nyssa. In spite of an immediate failure, this policy, thanks to its doctrinal moderation, ultimately rallied the group of Macedonians. It did not impose either of the words *divinity* or *homoousios* (for the Spirit), but it insisted on the theme of sanctification, which captured everyone's attention, and abstained from calling into play the Trinitarian Metaphysics dear to Gregory, and which imposed itself only a generation later. All this was not at all to the liking of the "Theologian" and it was not these themes that he used for the funeral oration of his friend.

VII. Dialogue and Controversy with Eustathius of Sebaste

The treatise on the Holy Spirit is animated with a contained passion which at last is expressed without restraint at the peroration in the portrayal of the storms and the obscure combats in which souls and churches founder.[56] In fact, this apology of faith in the Spirit coincides exactly with the deepest crisis which affected Basil's spiritual friendships; hence, the serene strength of the affirmations is communicated to us in proportion to the sympathy with which we participate in the drama.

After 375, Eustathius is disgraced as traitor and adversary. Of course, Nazianzen's funeral oration imposes a *damnatio memoriae* on this old heretic, whose role in the formation and the evolution of Basil as ascetic, theologian, and bishop is consequently ignored by the hagiographers.[57]

At the very moment of the break, the bishop of Caesarea lashed out at his old friend with harshness. The perverse resources acquired at the schools of rhetoric allowed him to place all the blame on the adversary, turning into reproaches the admirations of the past. But even at this moment it would not occur to Basil to erase these memories nor to hide the confidence he had previously shown Eustathius, not only on the subject of ascesis and spirituality, but in the defence of orthodoxy against the extreme Arianism of Eunomius (Ep. 223, 3).

I have already, in dictionary notices dedicated to Eustathius,[58] mentioned the major texts, in order to establish that Basil, on returning from the University, had understood baptism as a break with every worldly career, an option in favor of the ascetic life which his mother and his sister, under the influence of Eustathius, practiced in the family estate of Annesi. The Eustathian communities, badly organized and in a crisis, were a challenge to the strong personality of this young intellectual who brought out with exactness evangelical norms and gradually gave monachism structures capable of preserving its spirit.

Eustathius, as we mentioned earlier, had been one of the three heads of the anti-Eunomian movement, who with Sylvanus of Tarsus had concluded the Council of Lampsacus by a voyage, one of communion with Rome. Basil admired this old man, considering him "more than a man."[59] He followed his example as a bishop and ascetic; but they belonged to different circles, and their friends pulled them in opposite directions. Eustathius was more than indifferent with regard to a "dogmatic progress" improving the Trinitarian formulae; his interest lay in sanctification, prayer, and the Gospel. The Basilian economy is no doubt stamped with the same spirit, but Basil's firm resolve to achieve an ecumenical recognition of Meletius as bishop of Antioch led him necessarily to tighten up his relations with Alexandria and Rome, that is, to multiply the formal pledges of orthodoxy.[60] By his side, Gregory's zeal and that of the monks of whose restlessness we have heard, drove him in spite of himself in the same direction. As it often happens, any jolt at the extreme left generated reactions at the right, so that it was sheer fancy to wish to stop all evolution; and the agreement with Eustathius was thereby called into question.

Since the beginning of his episcopacy, or maybe during his sacerdotal ministry, Basil built at Caesarea a monastic hospice after the pattern of that of Sebaste; and Eustathius sent him two disciples to organize the house. Intended as a sign of friendship and of communion, this initiative became unfortunately a center of conflicts, for Basil soon felt himself watched in all his actions and conduct.[61]

A suffragan of Eustathius, Theodotus of Nicopolis, had offered hospitality to Meletius, the exiled bishop of Antioch, who for a long time had been badly disposed towards Eustathius. Theodotus was spying on the bishop of Sebaste and interpreting his intentions, convoking to private synods the opposing bishops, and he censured the tolerance which Basil was intent upon using. These are the intrigues we must have in mind when reading the complaints of the metropolitan of Caesarea about the attacks in the dark and the mortal blows dealt by false friends.

In June 372, Basil undertook to play openly the role of mediator; he paid a visit to Sebaste in order to clear up, in all openness, the attitude of Eustathius concerning the Spirit. Two days of passionate discussion resulted in a substantial oral agreement. But Theodotus did not declare himself satisfied, and refused his communion to Basil until the latter should justify his relations with Eustathius by means of a signature, in black and white, at the bottom of a profession of faith whose text should have been elaborated in advance at Nicopolis. In 373, a new visit of Basil to Sebaste extracted this signature out of Eustathius; the document constitutes the 125th letter of the Basilian correspondence. But Eustathius' entourage reacted; a noisy retraction followed the forced signature, with bitter accusations against Basil, suspected of having acted under Apollinarist influence.[62] Since at this point all our information comes from polemical sources, it is difficult for us to understand Eustathius' evolution. Apollinaris, Athanasius' battling companion in defense of the *homoousios,* had indeed played a role in rallying Basil to the Nicene formulations, while his philosophy must have been suspected of Sabellianism by the people of Sebaste. Besides, the controversies which began to rage around his Christology allowed Basil's previous relations with him to be given a compromising tinge. In addition, we see that Eustathius considered that the agreement formulae of faith had a meaning only relative to determinate circumstances: "We must make use of them like physicians, by modifying them to fit the sicknesses."[63] Basil, on the contrary, whatever the distinction he meant to make between *kèrygma* and *dogma,* linked quite as firmly the words and even the syllables of the formulae of faith to divine doctrine, the latter to gnosis (close to *dogma*) and gnosis to resemblance to God, the aim of our vocation.[64] His faith, then, was not at all indifferent to the *kèrygma* of the Bible and of the Church.

For a period of two years, nonetheless, Basil bore in silence opposition and calumnies in the hope of recreating peace. The explosion was all the more violent when, in 375, he addressed an open letter to Eustathius and attempted to justify the break by means of a vast press (or rather correspondence) campaign. This same year he addressed to Amphilochius the treatise on the Holy Spirit.

VIII. Structure of the Treatise

Amphilochius is in a situation quite different from that of Eustathius, of Gregory, or of that old Eusebius of Samosata, the confidant of Basil's first steps in ecclesiastic politics. Amphilochius was, to our knowledge, the first of Basil's personal disciples. Converted by him to the monastic ideal, he was very early thrust on to the see of Iconium whence he would guide the episcopacy not only of Lycaonia, but of the combined churches of southwest Cappadocia. Faithful among the faithful, he it was who requested of Basil the practical instructions which are our three "canonical" letters.[65]

The question which occasioned the treatise was Amphilochius' perplexity before a conflict of liturgical doxologies: Basil had propagated the use of the formula "Glory to the Father with (*meta*) the Son and (*syn*) the Holy Spirit," beside the more usual "through the Son, in the Holy Spirit." Relying on the analogy of the baptismal formula, Basil hoped in this way to diffuse among his flock the concept of the equality of honor due to the three Persons; but he had to explain himself and convince the communities.

The first chapters would be sufficient to resolve the given problem and he does this with a clarity and at a level of abstraction which imply a protracted period of reflection. The rigid Eunomian system required that to each Person should correspond only one preposition which would express its proper nature, but this postulates a linguistic rigor which has nothing to do with the Bible. Basil shows great skill in quoting from both Testaments sufficient texts to overthrow thoroughly these scholastic postulates.

Chapters 6-8, which continue with the same impetus, must be considered as an excursus, for they accumulate observations of the same kind concerning the Christological element of the doxology, while losing sight of the question of the Spirit. At any rate, in Chapters 1-8, Basil addresses Amphilochius in the second person, and the heretic whose views are discussed is mentioned in the third person, unless by exception a rhetorical turn might lead to interpellating him.[66]

Chapter 9 changes in tone. Without any polemic, it exalts the Sanctifier in a mystical language nourished—indirectly, though noticeably—on Plotinus.[67] Some expressions parallel Chapter 18 but Chapter 9 goes further. One wonders what links this chapter to the preceding pages, as well as to the subsequent ones.

Chapters 10-16 and 17-27 form a twofold block whose continuity Dörries has put in relief.[68] They progress in compact dialogue with an adversary whose twenty interventions, often reported as explicit citations, are easy to isolate. This dialogue has nothing fictitious about it, with the supposed adversary obligingly formulating the theses which the author intends to refute, as often happens in writings of controversy. Nor are we dealing here, as in the books *Against Eunomius* by Basil or Gregory of Nyssa, with a preexisting heretical system, with a book taken up section by section and refuted thesis after thesis. Here the adversary follows the movement of the discussion, yields ground, then tries to regain it.

Dörries analyzed this duel. I shall mention only one example, which I myself developed in a specialized article:[69] the final discussion, in Chapter 27, relative to the authority of unwritten tradition. Until then the duel had been pursued by means of Biblical texts; the subject was doubtless the baptismal and creedal formulae such as they were in usage in the Church, but these were being turned to advantage in terms of Matt. 28:19. In the course of his dialectical effort, Basil finally realized that recourse to the Bible can only with difficulty overcome oppositions; and he shows sufficient understanding for his partner not to accuse him of bad faith, but to discover that an element of interpretation, the lived tradition, is necessary in addition to the material evidence of the letter. He thus succeeds, by remembering some Origenist intuitions, in forming the first positive theory of the authority of tradition.

In these Chapters 10-27, the adversary is dealt with in the second person, not by a literary convention, but because in reality he is truly present. However, the tone used varies strangely: certain pages are violent; others, respectful and fraternal. It is clear that these chapters are not thought out in terms of Amphilochius, but the interlocutor is nonetheless considered in a category altogether different from that of the heretic Eunomius, for the proof that one of his theses leads to Eunomian Anomoeanism is equivalent to refuting it by a *reductio ad absurdum*.

It was thus enough for Dörries to bring out the literary genre proper to these chapters by distinguishing it from that of Chapters 1-9, to identify the interlocutor facing Basil here: he can only be the spokesman of the *pneumatomachoi*, namely, Eustathius, backed up perhaps at times by some theologian-friend, more rationalistic and less religious than himself. And what dialogue with Eustathius was, by clearly facing the question of the Holy Spirit, able to give Basil the opportunity to expound his arguments unless it be that meeting at Sebaste, in June of 372, on which occasion Basil succeeded in obtaining in two days a full oral agreement?[70] The debate as a whole is inspired by the dialogue held, while the paragraphs charged with invectives will represent additions dating from 375. The distinction of Chapters 10-16 and 17-27 may correspond to the two consecutive days.

Thus, the nucleus of the treatise of 375 resumes a living, fraternal, passionate, effective conversation. Amphilochius' question regarding the doxologies is indeed the occasion of the treatise, but not its only and sufficient cause. The heart of the discussion is a dramatic debate of an exceptional ecclesial value which develops the points of view most likely to win the adhesion of a fervent but conservative ascetic and which achieves a synthesis in the faith in spite of the oppositions of formulae. Was there a protocol, notes taken on the fly by tachygraphers, as Dörries likes to think?[71] Or did Basil write down his recollections shortly after those heated days? The objections of Eustathius or of his entourage reach us in a very schematized fashion. The Basilian answers may have been improved, clarified, bolstered by new texts. But the physiognomy of the debate may be clearly distinguished.

Basil must have been anxious to take advantage of this dialogue, in which he had given the best of himself; the friendly curiosity of Amphilochius provided him with the occasion for this publication. He introduced his document with Chapters 2-8, more abstract, colder, apt to give anyone who would linger on them a rather unfavorable impression of the work. The magnificent Chapter 9 could have ante-dated the treatise; it could also be a dogmatic and mystical synthesis, the last touch given to the whole statement on an inspired day. Anxious to add further documentation, he concludes the work with Chapters 28-30 in terms of Am-philochius and of the concrete circumstances of 375. This explains why occasionally Chapters 1-8 seem to reassume formulae which are elaborated in Chapters 10-27, for in-stance, with regard to the tradition of the Fathers. As often happens, the chronological order of the redaction of the chapters does not correspond to the order according to which the reader encounters them; hence the difficulties that arise out of analyses that are too academic.

IX. A Monastic Theology

Dörries does not try to hide his own irenic mentality when he observes and praises Basil's respect for the other churches. He does not hide his own pietism any better when he delights in underscoring how much the *dogma* belongs to prayer and to the gifts of the Spirit, not to theological disputes. To the same inclination can be linked his care to show in the Basilian thought a monastic theology anxious to honor the spiritual and sanctifying activity of the Spirit. At the same time, as a professional historian, he has no difficulty in distinguishing this doctrinal tendency from that of an Athanasius, of a Damasus, of a Gregory Nazianzen. He even distinguishes quite well the Basil of 372 from that of 375. The continuity of one and the same personality, and even less the communion of the same orthodoxy, does not impede the historic, concrete, committed character of a profoundly alive and original thought.

Pruche does not appreciate very much this kind of affirmation. In the first place, he "does not quite see how a so-called 'monastic' theology would greatly differ from a theology which would not be such."[72] He is interested in the objective character of the argumentation, not in the personal interests which command its rhythm. More precisely, he objects that the themes introduced are strictly connected to Baptism, which seems to be related to the Christian and to the bishop, more than to the monk.

It would certainly be wrong to oppose in too simplistic a way, especially at this period and in this milieu, monachism and Christian life. Dörries himself has perhaps tended to exaggerate this opposition or this distinction. In an age when infant baptism was but scarcely practiced, monastic initiation was confused with the baptismal option, as was the case with Basil himself. The milieu in which his theology was elaborated was typically episcopal but Basil, Eustathius, and their friends, behaved with an evangelical radicalism, which closely corresponds to what will later be called monachism.[73]

Pruche refuses, in particular, to explain this theology by the monastic influence of the heretic Eustathius. He insists on emphasizing that it is Basil who influences Eustathius, and not the other way around.[74] I fail to see why the two actions would be exclusive of each other. I had proposed to discover in Chapters 10-27 of the treatise, "something of Eustathius' thinking on the sanctifying action of the Spirit;"[75] I believed I had recourse that way to a modest and prudent formula. I did not intend to speak of the objections presented by Basil's adversary and in which can be detected the almost direct expression of the thought of the bishop of Sebaste and of his circle. I was speaking of Basil's own argumentation, in its most dialectic features and I wanted to point out that it did not represent a scholastic and purely logical elaboration built right within a system, but a dialogue, a progression, which leans upon Eustathius' own concessions, such as the themes of sanctification, of adoration, of the magnitude of the works and of the names of the Spirit. Such a tight dialogue, which leads to an assent, is the common work of those who seek God together.

Under such conditions, Basil's intransigence presents nothing contrary to his charity, to the gift of intellect and heart which realizes the difficulties of the other. The economy does not compromise in anything either the understanding of the faith (*dogma*), or even the necessary ecclesial presentation (*kèrygma*). It expresses a properly spiritual scale of values which fits every Evangelic theology, but principally that which receives and honors the work of the Holy Spirit.

NOTES

*This article was originally a conference given at the University of Salamanca in 1975, and published in *Estudios Trinitarios* IX, 1975, pp. 227-243. *Intransigencia e irenismo en san Basilio. Introduccion al "de Spiritu Sancto."* The text has been revised.

[1]St. Jerome, *Dialogus adversus Luciferianos* 19, PL 23, 172c.

[2]Books I and II of *Against Eunomius* occupy col. 497-652 of PG 29; Book III, consecrated to the Holy Spirit, only col. 653-670.

[3]Ep. 258-267.

[4]Ep. 268-269.

[5]The homilies on the Hexaemeron are sometimes dated the last year of Basil's life, for example, J. Bernardi, "La date de L'Hexaéméron de S. Basile," in *Studia Patristica* III (Texte

und Untersuchungen 78). Berlin, 1961, pp. 165-169. The indications are, however, not absolutely decisive.

[6]Basil has reviewed several times the collection of answers which constitutes the Asketicon, but it is difficult to furnish a *terminus ante quem* for the last rearrangement. As for the Moral Rules, the proposition of L. Lebe, "S. Basile et ses Règles morales," in the *Revue Bénédictine* 75, 1965, pp. 193-200, to refer them to the end of Basil's life is totally unconvincing to me.

[7]See especially the Ep. 47, 51, 58-60, but also 53-54 and even 24-25 and 28-30, which are to be placed after Basil's episcopal consecration. See also, in the correspondence of Gregory Nazianzen, Ep. 40-46, which are very significant.

[8]PG 32, 67-218. Critical Edition: C.F.H. Johnston, *The Book of St. Basil the Great, Bp. of Caesarea in Cappadocia, on the Holy Spirit*. A revised text with notes and introduction. Oxford, 1892. Translation by B. Jackson, "St. Basil. The Treatise 'de Spiritu Sancto', the Nine Homilies of the Hexaemeron and the Letters," *A Select Library of Nicene and Post-Nicene Fathers of the Christian Church*, VIII. London, 1894. (Reprinted, Ann Arbor, 1968). On the French edition of B. Pruche, see below n. 16. German translation with brief introduction of 19 p. (accepting the positions of H. Dörries) but without notes, by M. Blum, *Basilius von Cäsarea. Ueber den hl. Geist* (Sophia). Freiburg im Br., 1967.

[9]Ch. 30, §§ 78-79, PG 32, 216B and 217B.

[10]*Abhandlungen der Akademie der Wissenschaften in Göttingen*, Phil.-Hist. Klasse, III, 39. Göttingen, 1956.

[11]*Basilius und das Dogma vom hl. Geist, Lutherische Rundschau* 6, 1956/57, pp. 227-262.

[12] Dörries, H., *Wort und Stunde, I. Gesammelte Studien zur Kirchengeschichte des vierten Jahrhunderts*. Göttingen, 1966, pp. 118-144.

[13]*Patristische Texte und Studien*, 3. Berlin, 1964.

[14]*Forschungen zur Kirchen- und Dogmengeschichte*, 15. Göttingen, 1965.

[15] In *Zeitschrift für katholische Theologie* 87, 1965, pp. 257-308.

[16] *Basile de Césarée sur le Saint-Esprit. Introduction, texte, traduction, et notes* by B. Pruche. (Sources Chrétiennes, 17). Paris, 1945, VII & 226 p.; second edition, (Sources Chrétiennes, 17bis), 552 p., of which 248 p. of introduction.

[17] "Autour du traité sur le Saint-Esprit de saint Basile de Césarée," in *Recherches de Science Religieuse* 52, 1964, pp. 204-232.

[18] *Byzantinische Zeitschrift* 50, 1957, pp. 452-453. I shall use in the rest of the present article the observations proposed in this recension.

[19] IV. Paris, 1961, col. 1708-1712.

[20] XVI. Paris, 1967, col. 26-33.

[21] "Esotérisme et Tradition dans le Traité du Saint-Esprit de saint Basile," in *Oecumenica. Jahrbuch für ökumenische Forschung* 2, 1967, pp. 22-56.

[22] *Wort und Stunde*, (supra n. 12), p. 124, n. 7b.

[23] Cf. St. Athanasius, *Ad Palladium* (PG 26, 1168CD) and *Ad Joannem et Antiochum* (ibid., 1168A); Dörries, *De Spiritu Sancto*, p. 25.

[24] For this whole debate: Gallay, P., ed., *S. Grégoire de Nazianze. Lettres.* I, Ep. 58. (Collection des Universités de France). Paris, 1964, pp. 73-77.

[25] Or. 41, PG 36, 437B; Dörries, *De Spiritu Sancto*, p. 27.

[26] Or. 43, PG 36, 585-589; Dörries, *De Spiritu Sancto*, p. 26.

[27] Conclusion of the article of the *Recherches de Science Religieuse*, (supra n. 17), p. 232: "The silence of St. Basil is then very simply explained by the reasons invoked by Gregory Nazianzen and Athanasius;" on the Holy Spirit, second edition, p. 103, n. 2: "It is not at all necessary by resorting to a complicated reading of the chapters of the book on the Holy Spirit, to look for unavowed motives, whose meaning neither Athanasius nor Gregory would have per-

ceived, and which would make of the Basilian economy something else than what they said it was."

[28]*De Spiritu Sancto*, ch. 10, PG 32, 112B; and ch. 25, 180A.

[29]Ibid., ch. 21, 164A.

[30]Ibid., ch. 29, 205D.

[31]Courtonne, Y., ed., *S. Basile*, Ep. 71, in his *Lettres*, I. Paris, 1957, pp. 166-168. The passage mentioned is in § 1, 1-10.

[32]Ibid., § 1, 10-17; "among the most intimate" obviously refers to Gregory in person.

[33]Ibid., § 2, 29-30.

[34]Dörries, *De Spiritu Sancto*, p. 24.

[35]Gregory, Ep. 59, hides behind this excuse in order to beat a retreat and reaffirm his confidence in Basil.

[36]On these groups, see M. Simonetti, *La crisi ariana nel IV secolo*. (Studia Ephemeridis "Augustinianum," 11). Rome, 1975, pp. 234sqq., 338sqq., and esp. 393-399.

[37]Ibid., p. 405.

[38]Courtonne, Y., ed., Ep. 113, *Lettres de s. Basile*, II. Paris, 1961, p. 16, 10-12.

[39]Ibid., p. 17, 23-24.

[40]Ibid., p. 17, 32-35.

[41]Ibid., p. 17, 39-41. cf. Dörries, *De Spiritu Sancto, p. 19*.

[42]PG 32, 217B.

[43]Courtonne, Ep. 114, p. 18, 14-16.

[44]Ibid., p. 18, 22-26.

[45]Ibid., p. 18, 31-32.

[46]Ibid., p. 19, 38 and 41.

[47] Dörries, *De Spiritu Sancto*, pp. 121-128; *Wort und Stunde*, I, pp. 127-132.

[48]"The Pair Kerygma and Dogma in the Theological Thought of St. Basil of Caesarea" in *The Journal of Theological Studies*, N.S. 16, 1965, pp. 129-142.

[49] "Esotérisme et Tradition," (supra n. 21), pp. 43-48.

[50]See in particular Basil, Ep. 52 (written in 375 according to Dörries, *De Spiritu Sancto*, p. 115, n. 1), where Basil takes

up the defense of the Nicene Creed, while showing a deep understanding even for those who refuse the term *homoousios*: Courtonne, I, p. 134, 23-24.

[51]This difference has often been noted by assuming Gregory's point of view, more inclined as he was to expose his sufferings in great length; see in particular S. Giet, *Sasimes, Une méprise de S. Basile*, Paris, 1941. But one could also study the disappointments brought to Basil by Gregory. We may note in passing that Gregory of Nyssa was not always exactly either what his brother hoped; see Basil, Ep. 58, 59, 100, then 215, which considers him totally inept to fulfill a role of ambassador to Rome. Recently, R. Hübner has shown the tendency of the bishop of Nyssa to absolve one of the principal adversaries of Basil: "Gregor von Nyssa und Markell von Ankyra," in *Ecriture et culture philosophique dans la pensée de Grégoire de Nysse. Actes du Colloque de Chevetogne*, ed. M. Harl. Leiden, 1971, pp. 199-229; cf. R. Hübner, *Gregor von Nyssa, als Verfasser der sog. Ep. 38 des Basilius*, and G. May, *Einige Bemerkungen über das Verhältnis Gregor von Nyssa zu Basileios dem Grossen*, in *Epektasis. Mélanges patristiques offerts au Card. J. Daniélou*. Paris, 1972, pp. 463-490 and 509-515.

[52]Ritter, A.M., *Das Konzil von Konstantinopel*, (supra n. 14), pp. 97-111.

[53]Ep. 102, 2, PG 37, 193C; P. Gallay-M. Jourjon, eds., *Grégoire de Nazianze. Lettres théologiques.* (Sources Chrétiennes, 208). Paris, 1974, p. 70. Gregory's silence has been exploited by many, such as F.J.A. Hort and A. von Harnack, in order to deny the authenticity of the *Constantinopolitanum*, but this position is definitely obsolete.

[54]Ritter, A.M., *Das Konzil von Konstantinopel*, pp. 155-156 and 253-270; Ritter cites Hefele, who already interprets Gregory in the same way.

[55] Cf. Dörries, *De Spiritu Sancto*, pp. 174-176; *Wort und Stunde*, pp. 141-142; Ritter, *Das Konzil von Konstantinopel*, pp. 194-196.

[56]Ch. 30, PG 32, 212AC.

[57]The one who did the most to rediscover the image of the bishop of Sebaste is K. Holl, *Eustathius von Sebaste und die Chronologie der Basilius-Briefe.* Halle, A.S., 1898; we must mention also D. Amand, *L'ascèse monastique de S. Basile de Césarée.* Maredsous, 1948, pp. 52-61.

[58]Cf. supra n. 19 and 20.

[59]Ep. 212, 2 (Courtonne, II, p. 199, 10-12); cf. Ep. 131, 1 (ibid., p. 45, 22-25), 131, 2 (p. 45, 5-6); Ep. 226, 2 (ibid., III. Paris, 1966, p. 26, 45-46).

[60] Cf. Gribomont, J., "Obéissance de charité et liberté envers l'Eglise de Rome," in *Commandements du Seigneur et Libération Evangélique.* (Studia Anselmiana, 70). Rome, 1977, pp. 120-138.

[61]Ep. 119, Courtonne, II, pp. 24-25.

[62]Basil seems so embarrassed by this accusation that it is doubtless not totally without foundation. See G.L. Prestige, *St. Basil the Great and Apollinaris of Laodicea,* London, 1956, and H. De Riedmatten, "La correspondance entre Basile de Césarée et Apollinaire de Laodicée," in *The Journal of Theological Studies,* N.S. 7, 1956, pp. 199-210; 8, 1957, pp. 53-70.

[63]Ep. 226, 3, Courtonne, III, p. 27, 17-19.

[64]*Treatise on the Holy Spirit,* ch. 1 § 2, PG 32, 69B.

[65]Basil, Ep. 188, 199, and 217, entered long ago in the manuscripts of Basil's correspondence; but their own tradition is that of the canonical manuscripts, cf. P.J. Joannou, *Les Canons des Pères Grecs.* (Pontificia Commissione per la redazione del codice di diritto canonico orientale. Fonti. IX. Discipline générale antique. II). Grottaferrata, 1963, pp. 85-159.

[66]For ex., ch. 8, § 20, PG 32, 105A.

[67]H. Dehnhard, op. laud., (supra n. 13), has shown that Basil interprets Plotinus by Origen and Gregory Thaumaturgus, and depends immediately on the summary *De Spiritu,* PG 29, 768-773. The Basilian authenticity of this summary is

not beyond dispute, but this question is secondary for the moment.

[68]*De Spiritu Sancto*, pp. 56-75, and esp. 81-90.

[69] "Esotérisme et Tradition," (supra n. 21).

[70]I point out again that it is not this agreement which turned out to be fragile, but the one which, the following year, Theodotus caused to be imposed on Eustathius in writing.

[71]*De Spiritu Sancto*, p. 85, n. 1. The intervention of tachygraphers is nothing but a hypothesis, which in no way conditions Dörries' conclusions. The obvious fact is that in Chapters 10-27, Basil faces directly the adversaries' spokesman, i.e., Eustathius (on this point, Pruche does not object), and that the only in-depth discussion which is known to have occurred between them is this dialogue at Sebaste in 372, which must therefore in some way be behind the duel of these chapters.

[72]*Recherches de Science Religieuse* 52, 1964, p. 205, n. 8.

[73] See my article "Basile," in *Théologie de la vie monastique.* (Collection "Théologie," 49). Paris, 1961, pp. 99-113.

[74]*Recherches de Science Religieuse* 52, 1964, p. 222.

[75] "Eustathe," in the *Dictionnaire de Spiritualité*, IV, col. 1710.

SAINT BASIL ON THE HOLY SPIRIT—
SOME ASPECTS OF HIS THEOLOGY*

Cyril Karam, Obl. OSB
*(Member of the Monastic Community
of Still River, Mass.)*

Reading St. Basil's "De Spiritu Sancto" in this 1600th anniversary of his death brings back vividly the latter part of the fourth century, so rich in controversy, in creativity, so vibrant with the very life and activity of the Spirit, the Spirit being himself the focal point both of the controversies and of the creative productions of some of the greatest of the Greek Fathers. Our own age, nearing the end of a century, is not too unlike that age. Whether it will have produced writings as great remains to be seen. But the turmoil and the conflict are obvious; and also the work of the Spirit in the Church and in the world at large, which perhaps will produce out of this apparent confusion some order and new life.

St. Basil's treatise is refreshing, and may also prove to be very helpful as we seem to be wrestling in a similar situation to his. I will choose a few themes, therefore, ask a few questions relevant to contemporary problems, and indicate some of Basil's answers and attitudes concerning them.

I.   Background and Basil's Economy

TRINITARIAN THEOLOGY

In the early part of the fourth century, the battle had raged around the Son, the Word. Nicaea had defined his divinity, his consubstantiality with the Father. But, far from resolving the problems and silencing the oppositions, the Council seemed to have added more fuel to the fire. It had used an unscriptural term (*homoousios*), a term that had been the rallying-point of some who had denied real distinction in the godhead (Paul of Samosata). Those who still sympathized with this attitude took shelter behind the Nicene formula to propogate their errors and draw the simple faithful, loyal to Nicaea, into their nets (thus Marcellus of Ancyra). The more orthodox, worried about the term and its possible repercussions, accepted Nicaea, but took exception to the *homoousios* (consubstantial [with the Father]), substituting *homoiousios* (of *like* substance), thereby trying to salvage both the distinctness of "persons" (or *hypostases* as St. Basil would call them at this time), and their equality in nature or essence (*ousia*). This would be the policy of Basil of Ancyra, a policy defended by the Father of Orthodoxy, Athanasius himself—even though by so doing, this same Basil was moving into the camp of the suspected Semi-Arians.

The camps were forming, still in relation to what these men held concerning the Son. Yet, the Holy Spirit was beginning to be the center of the controversy. He had only been mentioned by name in Nicaea—no more. It would be much easier for the heretics to make *him* the target of their attacks.

Athanasius says in his first letter to Serapion that "some have, no doubt, separated themselves from the Arians because of their [the Arians'] blasphemy against the Son of God, but nourish thoughts hostile to the Holy Spirit, claiming that he is not only a creature, but even one of the ministering spirits (cf. Heb. 1:14), and that he differs from the angels only in degree. Now this is only a feigned opposition to the Arians, and a real contradiction of our holy faith. For just as the Arians, by denying the Son, deny also the Father, so also these men, by decrying the Holy Spirit, decry also the Son. The two parties have shared between them the rebellion against the truth and so have achieved, some by opposing the Son and some the Spirit, the same blasphemy against the Holy Trinity" (PG XXVI, 529A-532A).

The Arians were still the adversary; but so are now the *Pneumatomachoi* (adversaries of the Spirit). But, adds Athanasius, *their* opinion "is not foreign to the Arians either.

In fact, once they have denied the Word of God, these naturally rail against his Spirit also" (532B).

But the doctrine of the Trinity must be preserved at all cost. Theophilus of Antioch, in the second century, had probably been the first to use the term *Trias* (*Triad*). But faith in the Three is contemporaneous with Christianity. Baptism had been administered in the Name of the Trinity from the earliest days (cf. Didache 7, 1), and even though the Risen Savior's words in Matt. 28:19-20, "manifestly contain a baptismal formula," yet "any attempt to prove them an interpolation remain unfounded."[1] Profession of faith in the Trinity (e.g. at the occasion of Baptism), embryonic at first, later developing into the "Apostles' Creed," had always been part of the Church's discipline.[2] And so, Trinitarian faith, Trinitarian baptismal formula, Trinitarian profession have always formed the background for theological speculation, and have been the bulwark for preserving orthodoxy.

Yet theology had consistently lagged behind in this area especially. Pneumatology was very slow in developing. Most of the earlier Fathers had found it difficult to avoid a certain subordinationism of Son and Spirit. Origen, who had started with the traditional rule of faith, where Father, Son, and Holy Spirit are united in the same dignity and honor, and had concluded that the Spirit is not "something made or created" (*factura vel creatura*, De Principiis 1, 3, 3) and had also attacked those who lower him to the rank of inferior spirit (De Princ. 2, 7, 3)—St. Basil will take up both arguments—the same Origen said that the Spirit must be considered as an inferior reality in relation to the Word, even though Scripture seems at times to hint at the opposite (Comm. on John 2, 10, 70-12, 90, or 2, 6).

The ambivalence—and apparent ambiguity—of the scriptural texts relating to the Spirit, at least when taken all together, escaped the notice of no one in the early Church. But is Scripture alone sufficient to answer all our queries? We shall see Basil's answer. A year after his death, in 380, his friend Gregory Nazianzen was to say (Sermon 31, 26-28): "The Old Testament announced the Father clearly, but the Son more obscurely. The New Testament has manifested the Son and hinted at the divinity of the Holy Spirit. Now the Spirit himself dwells among us, and supplies us with a clear demonstration of himself. For it was not safe, when the godhead of the Father was not yet acknowledged plainly to proclaim the Son, and when that of the Son was not yet received to burden us further, if I may speak boldly, with the Holy Spirit.... Our Savior had some things which, he said, could not be borne at that time by his disciples (Jn. 16:12)... And again he said that all things should be taught us by the Spirit when he should come to dwell among us" (Jn. 14:26). (This text should not be misconstrued as a forthright denial, but as positing the principle of explication of what is at first implicit.)

The Holy Spirit *had* been at work in the Church. The Church's very life is a "life in the Spirit;" the Church's faith is a vision, albeit dark, of the Triune God. Now was the time ripe for the Church's theology to clearly propound the truth about the Holy Spirit. Yet Basil takes up a policy that was termed by his friends and contemporaries, *oikonomia* ("economy"). For many years he remained silent, prayed, and refused to take an active part in the controversy. Persuaded, finally, by his disciple, Amphilochius of Iconium, he took up his pen and wrote his treatise in defense of the Holy Spirit, without ever calling him "God" or "consubstantial" with the Father and Son. Why?

BASIL'S RETICENCE

We must repeat, first of all, that the period in question, the half-century that separates Nicaea from Constantinople, is one of the most confused in Christian history. Parties were forming and breaking up, fellow partisans were not really in theological agreement, the shades of Arianism, semi-Arianism and orthodoxy (or quasi-orthodoxy) were so numerous that contemporaries were truly baffled. In 380, toward the end of this period, Gregory Nazianzen expressed a feeling of disgust and discouragement at the spectacle of controversy and strife (cf. his 31st *Discourse*).

The most articulate groups ranged from the extreme left: the Anomoeans, who asserted the radical *unlikeness* of the Father and Son (Aetius had been their leader; Eunomius their most brilliant spokesman), to the Homoeans, who professed a *likeness* of Father and Son that was far from producing clarity of thought. In between were Homoiousians of different shades, who confessed some kind of *likeness of substance* in Father and Son, the most orthodox of these being among the followers of Basil of Ancyra. Of the right-wing Homoousians, some, like Gregory Nazianzen, were champions of orthodoxy, but others, like Marcellus of Ancyra and his followers, professed under the term *consubstantial* their Sabellian views, thus reviving the errors of Paul of Samosata condemned a century earlier.

To this must be added the unfortunate and complicated schism in Antioch, which placed Basil, as champion of Meletius (who was in his eyes the only legitimate bishop of Antioch, and who, against the danger of Sabellianism, advocated "three" hypostases in God) on the opposite side from Athanasius and Pope Damasus, who championed his opponent, Paulinus (uncanonically consecrated, but faithful to the Western terminology: "one" hypostasis in God).

In the last chapter of his treatise (c. 30), Basil compares the confusion and the struggles to a naval battle where fleets hurl themselves in hatred and anger against each other, in the midst of a violent storm, with a thick darkness coming over the scene, with torrential rains, winds blowing from every direction, and enormous waves throwing vessel against vessel, creating utter confusion. "Among the combatants, some betray their camp and pass over to the enemy camp during the struggle itself; others find themselves obliged at the same time to repulse the ships thrown against them by the wind, to march against the assailants, and to massacre each other in the rebellion created by ill-will against authority and the desire of many an individual to be the leader" (212A-C).

The description continues, in vivid tones, and Basil returns to describe the actual state of the Church, with the confusion, hatreds, betrayals; some "going over to Judaism by confounding the Persons [the Sabellians], others to Paganism by opposing the natures [the Arians]—the Scriptures 'inspired by God' being unable to appease them, nor the Apostolic traditions to achieve their reconciliation" (213C).

That is why Basil had decided not to join any parties, but to keep silence, as both the Preacher (Eccles. 9:17) and the Prophet (Amos 5:13) give counsel (216A-B). Urged by Amphilochius, he finally yields and breaks the silence which so many had criticized. He takes up the defense of the Holy Spirit, but still hopes that the treatise will be discreetly circulated (217B). He wishes to deal a heavy blow to the blasphemies of a Eunomius or a Macedonius; but he hopes not to antagonize or drive into the enemy camp those many confused minds who joined one or another party with good will and pure intentions, and whom an explicit defense of the divinity of the Holy Spirit, or the use of *consubstantial* in this regard would frighten away. Basil keeps to his "economy." He insists on denying that the Spirit is a *ktisma*, or creature; he also insists on giving him "equal honor" with Father and Son; on showing that the Three, while being quite distinct, are associated in honor, dignity, qualities, and operations by Christ himself and all of Scripture.

In his four letters to Serapion (PG XXVI) Athanasius had, around 360, undertaken the same task. He had shown that the Holy Spirit is neither a creature, *ktisma* (1, 12; 3, 3), nor an angel (1, 17); that he is immutable, *atrepton*, immense, *panta plēroi* (1, 26; 3, 4), and eternal, *aei ēn* (3, 7); that he takes an active part in creation *en tō ktizein estin* (3, 4-5); that sanctification is one, *hena einai ton hagiasmon*, coming to us from the Father, through the Son, in the Holy Spirit

(1, 20). But Athanasius had also said that the Spirit was consubstantial, *homoousios*, with Father and Son (1, 27). This last assertion Basil carefully avoids and, as we already mentioned, he never uses the *homoousios* in his treatise, nor does he ever call the Holy Spirit "God," although he quotes Origen who refers to the "divinity of the Spirit" (204B). But he affirms the Spirit's equality in dignity with the Father and the Son, and insists he should always be numbered (*synarithmeisthai*) with them (c. 17).

Basil's reticence was for the sake of gaining the weak, making himself weak for them. But he also did not wish to go ahead of the Church in her formulation. On the register of theological expression, which is derivative (see later), compromise on words is sometimes necessary. Athanasius saw this as well as Basil. Cyril of Alexandria will also, more than fifty years later. This is especially true when the same words had different meanings in different theological schools.

UNION IN CHARITY

Orthodoxy should always be viewed in conjunction with fellowship (*koinōnia*). Not, of course, in a simple linear relationship, but in a dialectical one. This is another way of saying that charity is just as essential as Faith, is indeed its fulfillment. Yet, concern for one seems to bring about a decline of the other. W. Kasper says the same thing, in relation to identity and relevance. "With its programme of *aggiornamento* the Church runs the risk of surrendering its unambiguousness for the sake of openness. Yet whenever it tries to speak straightforwardly and clearly it risks losing sight of men and their actual problems. If the Church worries about identity, it risks a loss of relevance; if, on the other hand, it struggles for relevance, it may forfeit its identity."[3]

Basil was intensely eager to keep communion with the churches, with Rome, with the various groups that ranged from differing shades of semi-Arianism to perfect orthodoxy. He did not believe in extinguishing the smoking flax. As long as someone agreed not to call the Holy Spirit a creature and gave him equal honor with Father and Son, Basil accepted him in his communion. The more intransigent rejected this attitude and even criticized him severely. He exerted himself to show that both Scripture and Tradition required that we name the Holy Spirit equal in honor, *homotimos*, with the Father and the Son. He certainly believed in the divinity of the Holy Spirit, but for the sake of *koinōnia*, which not only signifies but also produces oneness in faith, he was anxious to require a minimum of profession and to let the Holy Spirit himself infuse his light and his knowledge into the believing heart. The Spirit is the Father's "gift" (as is also the Son); but he is a gift that is not less than God himself, the giver (173B).

But while Basil's concern for unity drove him to require no more of others than the bare minimum in explicit profession, his "ecumenism" implied just as strongly a concern for orthodoxy—the orthodoxy of true honor and worship given to the Spirit, whose divinity is thus acknowledged in an act of worship which could be reconciled only with the right formula.

II. Basil's Theological Argument

Basil has been talked into writing his treatise. He goes into the fray, yet without basically altering his "economic" policy. He will attack the enemy, while coaxing his readers into the fullness of orthodoxy.

In the very first chapter of the treatise, Basil presents the incident which on September 7, 374, on the feast of St. Eupsychus the Martyr, occasioned the controversy. "Recently, as I was praying with the people, glorifying God the Father in this twofold manner: sometimes 'with' (*meta*) the Son, 'together with' (*syn*) the Holy Spirit, and sometimes 'through' (*dia*) the Son, 'in' (*en*) the Holy Spirit, some of those who were present accused us of using strange and even contradictory expressions" (72B-C).

The whole treatise takes the form of an answer to this accusation; but while the attitude of the adversaries is taken up and answered, the richness of Basil's own thought and spirituality comes out quite clearly.

Unbounded rationalism has always tended toward agnosticism, even atheism. Our contemporaries are no exception. But neither was Eunomius in his day. He very confidently asserted that God's simplicity can be adequately expressed in only one simple term: innascibility. Otherwise, all the other names used of God yield us absolutely no light. Thoroughgoing rationalism joined to thoroughgoing agnosticism. The same attitude is reflected in the Anomoean syllogism that Basil quotes in c. 2 of his treatise: "They attempt to show that the Father, Son, and Holy Spirit are not named in a similar fashion, in order to draw an easy proof that they are different in nature. For they have an ancient sophism, invented by Aetius, the leader of this heresy, who wrote in one of his letters that dissimilarity of nature is expressed by dissimilar expressions; and conversely, that things expressed in unlike terms, differ in nature. Aetius backs this with the words of the Apostle: 'One God and Father *from whom* are all things, and One Lord Jesus Christ, *through whom* are all things' (1 Cor. 8:6). Thus, according to him, the natures signified by the terms are in the same relation as the terms themselves. But *through whom* is not like *from whom*. Therefore, the Son is unlike the Father. . . . They accordingly assign to God the Father, as a privilege reserved to him, the expression *from whom*, to God the Son the expression *through whom*, to the Holy Spirit the expression *in whom*. They claim that this use of the particles never varies, the unlikeness of the expressions manifesting, as I said before, the unlikeness of the natures" (73A-B); *through* referring to instrumentality in the work of creation, and *in*, to circumstances of time or place (73C). In other words, according to Aetius, the three particles: *ex*, *dia*, and *en* give us a thorough grasp of Father, Son, and Spirit; and also *all* that can be known about them.

Against this naive use of philosophy, and this obviously tendentious use of Scripture, Basil counters with a threefold attack: confronting rationalism with faith, advocating a thorough and penetrating exegesis, and completing Scripture with Tradition.

FAITH

First of all, philosophy is an intruder which should be kept in its place. Basil shows real knowledge and even erudition in matters of philosophy: in c. 3 he expounds masterfully the doctrine of "causes" and its expression by means of various particles. He even shows in places the influence of Plato, the Stoa, and Plotinus. Yet he consistently refused to allow philosophy and natural reason entrance into the holy of holies. The philosophers are *hoi exōthen* (76A), the "outsiders," and they employ their "vanity and empty deception" to corrupt the purity of the Gospel, "the simple (*haplē*) and 'untechnological' doctrine of the Spirit" (76C). Basil prefers to answer with the Apostles' words: "It is better to obey God than men" (Acts 5:29) (112A). But the Lord has clearly prescribed to the disciples to "baptize all nations in the Name of the Father and of the Son and of the Holy Spirit" (Matt. 28:19), and "has delivered as a necessary and salutary doctrine the coordination of the Spirit with the Father; and if it seems to them that it is not so but that he must be separated, divided (*diaspan*) and relegated to a servile nature, are they not giving more authority to their blasphemy than to the Master's precept?..." (112C-D). It is faith, not philosophy; tradition, not our own constructions which matter. Without these even the saving sacrament becomes worthless: "It is an equal loss to depart [from life] without baptism, and to receive one which is lacking in anything received traditionally" (113A). He is referring here to the Trinitarian formula of faith.

What Basil and other Church Fathers wish to avoid is, in the words of J. de Ghellinck, making the human mind "the measure of the heavenly mysteries; they consider as a sacrilege the desire to reduce to a few syllogisms the way that leads to salvation; they regard as the destruction of the faith the attempt on the part of some to reduce to a dry technical argumentation all that the divinity has been pleased to reveal to us of its intimate life."[4] The heretics, especially the Anomoeans, and now the *Pneumatomachoi,* "replaced by a mechanical dialecticism the whole depth of the Christian religion, the surge of its piety and the infinitude of its mysteries."[5]

On the other hand, the only way to defend the faith in such circumstances is to use the weapons of philosophy for "in itself the dialectical method was only the disciplined exercise of reason. The same dexterity in manipulating it was necessary to ward off the enemy's blows."[6] But it must remain a weapon, and a method, and not claim to give the mind a total grasp over the truth.

Basil uses his power of reasoning and dialectics to uncover and refute the inconsistencies of the adversaries, as well as to analyze the articulations of Tradition, Faith, Symbols, and Rites. He will also demonstrate that reason is indispensable in the area of exegesis, to properly collate texts and "scientifically" bring out their implications; and the implications of Rites and Symbols as well. Finally, after leading to the threshold of Mystery, and there yielding entirely to Faith, Reason must come in again, not to penetrate the Mystery itself, but first to translate it into human and cultural terms, and then to articulate its incarnate expression.

SCRIPTURE

Just as destructive as the misuse of Reason is the attitude which uses Scripture in an uncritical and fragmentary way, and with no depth of understanding. In addition to faith, therefore, as our primary approach, we also need a scientific knowledge of Scripture, as well as an understanding which goes beyond the superficial and mechanical application of terms.

"The goal that is set before us," says Basil "is, insofar as it is possible to human nature, to become like God. [But] no such likeness (*homoiōsis*) is possible without knowledge (*gnōsis*). Now, *gnōsis* is the fruit of instruction, and speech is the beginning of instruction. But speech is made up of syllables and words. So that it is not apart from our goal to investigate even syllables. Though seemingly insignificant questions, they are not unworthy of our attention. On the contrary, since the truth is difficult to hunt, we must follow its tracks on all sides. If piety is acquired like the arts, bit by bit, its neophytes must neglect nothing, for he who would neglect the first elements as insignificant would never reach the height of wisdom" (69B-C).

The heretics confronting Basil insisted that *ex* always referred to the Father, *dia* to the Son, and *en* to the Holy Spirit. That was extremely simplistic. In the first place, far from being the Father's exclusively, *ex* is used in Scripture of the Son as well; and conversely *dia* is not proper to the Son, but is used also for the Father, often meaning "from" (c. 5). These, and the other particles, are not restricted in Scripture to the meaning assigned them by the heretics (c. 4), but show a richness and variety of meanings (c. 8).

The "adversaries of the Spirit," as Basil called them, wish to restrict him to the preposition *en*, because it seems to degrade him (c. 25); but in fact it is no less noble in meaning than *syn*: "on the contrary, when understood properly, it raises the mind to a very great height; that is why we have noticed that it is often used in place of the preposition *syn*" (173C-D). Likewise, creation *by* the Father *through* the Son implies neither imperfection in the former, nor subordination in the latter (136B-C).

On the other hand, in our use of the controverted doxologies, *kai* has the same meaning as *syn*, but the latter is better; for if praising Father *and* Son *and* Holy Spirit emphasizes their distinctness and hence refutes Sabellianism, praising Father *with* Son and *with* Holy Spirit emphasizes their equal dignity and refutes Subordinationism (c. 25). Also, praising the Father *in* the Holy Spirit does not degrade the latter; it merely refers to our weakness, because only *in* him do we reach the Father; but glorifying the Father *with* the Holy Spirit shows his glory as co-equal with the Father's (c. 26).

But even this is not enough. Without the sense of faith, Scripture can be "the letter that kills"—which is what it was for the followers of Eunomius. "Now difficult it is to find a soul in love with knowledge and seeking the truth in order to be cured of its ignorance!... Not to take lightly theological terminology, but to attempt in each word and syllable to discover the hidden meaning, does not belong to those who are slow in the pursuit of piety, but to those who understand the aim of our calling" (68B-69B).

Tradition

Basil's opponents object that the doxology: "Glory to the Father, with (*meta*) the Son, together with (*syn*) the Holy Spirit" is unscriptural. But, answers Basil, the "older" doxology: "through (*dia*) the Son in (*en*) the Holy Spirit" is not found in Scripture either. Should we hold fast to scriptural formulae alone, we would have to abandon both doxologies (see 176A-B). They are both transmitted by "unwritten" (*agraphon*) tradition; and, were we to throw these traditions aside, "we would unknowingly hurt the Gospel in its very essential points; what is more, we would reduce the 'kērygma' to mere words" (188A-B).

By *kērygma* Basil refers to the outwardly professed statements of faith—whether as expressed in Scripture or in Symbols, Council statements, or catechetical instructions. This he carefully distinguishes from *dogma*, its inner *content* (see c. 27) "literally, 'that which is thought'."[7] *Dogma* is the fullness of understanding "which requires a heart enlightened by the Spirit; and this enlightenment is none other than faith, according to its various degrees."[8] Faith, produced by the light of the Spirit, brings about fullness of understanding, or *dogma*. *Dogma*, in turn, gives life to the profession of faith, to the *kērygma*.

For Basil, therefore, *kērygma* and *dogma* do not correspond exactly to Scripture and Tradition, nor to what is consigned to writing, and what has remained oral. He says in fact: "Among the 'dogmas' and 'kerygmas' kept in the Church, we hold some from the written teaching, others we have received 'in mystery', transmitted by the tradition of the Apostles; both have the same force in regard to piety" (188A). Jean Gribomont has studied the contrasts: kerygma-dogma, written-unwritten, as well as the possible meanings of "in mystery" (i.e., in secret; or, as related to the Wisdom hidden in the Mystery of God; or, in relation to the liturgical "mysteries").[9] The examples St. Basil proceeds to give: the sign of the Cross, turning to the East to pray, the words of the "Epiclesis" at the moment of the Consecration of the Eucharist, the blessings of water and oil, the triple immersion at Baptism, the renouncing of Satan—all these examples show that, for him, behind the profession of faith, the *kērygma*, behind the faith and its flowering into *dogma*, lies, deeply imbedded in the Church's memory and awareness, "unwritten" tradition, very closely related to Scripture, alive in the Church's rites and ceremonies—those *mysteria* which both symbolize and protect "in mystery" her awareness of the divine Mystery. The doxology Basil is defending is ultimately rooted, therefore, in unwritten tradition which, with the doxology, conveys, in faith, its correct understanding (the *dogma*). We should note, however, that for Basil "unwritten" does not necessarily mean "oral," because much of it is non-verbal, non-conceptual. This will harmonize with what we shall see later: the non-verbal, transconceptual character of contemplation.

From this we can deduce the sequence: Tradition-Rite-Faith-Profession-Praise, which we find explicitly contained in an argument in c. 27: "If, in accordance with piety, we make, following the tradition of baptism, a public profession of faith in conformity[10] with our baptism (for we must believe as we are baptized), then let it be granted to us, for the same reason, to give praise in conformity with our faith" (193A). Or again, with a touch of irony: "Let them teach us now not to baptize as we were taught, or not to believe as we were baptized, or again, not to glorify as we have believed!" (193C). He says the same thing in his 125th Letter: "It is necessary to be baptized according to what we have received by tradition (*hōs parelabomen*), and to believe as we have been baptized, and thus to praise as we believe, the Father, the Son, and the Holy Spirit."[11]

All this does not exclude but complements Scripture. From the conjunction of Scripture and Tradition come the rites and "mysteries" which are normative of faith. On the other hand, faith alone gives us, as we said before, that understanding which both penetrates the Scriptures, and gives life to the Profession. Faith, enlivened by the Spirit, is the heart of this sequence. It is the most interior point of a circular movement, which, starting with Revelation (implied behind the whole pattern) proceeds through the written and unwritten transmission of *dogmata* and *kērygmata*, to external rites and prayer formulae, to that inner dimension of faith blossoming into *gnōsis* or *dogma*, which moves outwardly again into professions of faith, e.g., the Trinitarian profession at Baptism, this in turn developing into "public proclamation" (Church *kērygma*), and finally terminating in praise of the Trinity—the circular movement returning to its source. This sequence is the central vision of the treatise.

III. Spiritual Presentation

Liturgy and Faith

Let us take Faith in relation to Rite (which precedes it) and Praise (which follows). Rite and Praise include the complex: Sacraments-Eucharist, and Opus Dei. What we are dealing with is, therefore, Liturgy, with all that the word implies. As such, a quarrel over doxologies is hardly worth the attention of a man of Basil's stature. The Treatise on the Holy Spirit is his greatest work as bishop: much more, then, is involved here than mere liturgical formulae. Basil, like all the ancients, had a vivid sense of the importance of liturgy, not merely in giving us the divine life but in guaranteeing and transmitting, in that very gift, both orthodoxy and the instinct for it. This is more than just the "lex orandi, lex credendi" principle, in which the liturgy presupposes and expresses a certain belief, and more than a "legem credendi lex statuit supplicandi" where prayer is somehow normative of faith. It is rather that we are most truly "credentes" *when* we are "orantes."

The Church has always offered us her prayer, the Liturgy, as the true source of faith and sanctification, for both individual and community. Prayer cannot unfold unless preceded by faith; but only *in* prayer and *through* prayer does our faith reach true maturity. For Basil, it is only this life of prayer, the life of the Spirit in us, or our "life in the Spirit," which gives us true knowledge of him.

Thus, it is in his effort to "glorify" the Holy Spirit, that Basil, in spite of his "economic" silence, for once clearly affirms his divinity: "He who is divine by nature (*theion tē phusei*), unlimited in his greatness, powerful in his works, and good in his benefactions, shall we not exalt him and glorify him?" (169A).

Having established his right to use either formula—both are traditional, neither is scriptural, both embody in a context of prayer and praise the content, the "inner meaning" of all that Scripture teaches—Basil presents an attitude which gives primacy to the *lived* faith, to prayer as a means both of knowing God and of communicating with him, to the liturgical celebration as the best means both to proclaim and be one with the truth. Proclamation—*kērygma*—is by no means rejected, but it is made to live through the *dogma* which Tradition keeps alive thanks to the working of the

Spirit in the Church's liturgy. These ideas were also being voiced in the West, as in St. Ambrose's statement that "the mysteries can infuse their light better by themselves than when preceded by instruction."[12]

FAITH AND DOGMATIC FORMULATION

What, then, is the relation of faith to proclamation? What, in other words, is the content, the object of faith? Is it the dogmatic formulations—whether of Scripture or of the documents of the Magisterium? What is orthodoxy? Is it assent of the mind to these formulations?

We think the following analysis is implicit in Basil's words and attitudes. First of all, we must distinguish various levels of formulation. There are primary and secondary or derivative formulae. We have first the normative expressions of Revelation (the inspired words of Scripture); then, sometimes also found in Scripture (as e.g. the invocation of the Trinity in Baptism), the ritual and sacramental formulae, which, together with the symbols and mysteries which accompany and contain them, constitute much of the *agrapha*, the unwritten patrimony of the Church. These two classes must be maintained, defended, proclaimed at all cost. They are normative of faith, of Church teaching, of liturgical practice, of theology. Next we have symbols or professions of faith. These must and do express the faith of the Church, always in conformity with the traditional rites and mysteries (the unchanging core of the Church's liturgical treasure). These also, while being *normatae*, are normative; but they remain within the ambiance of the liturgy.

Then come the Church's more elaborate teachings, her *kērygmata*, the expressions of her "inner understanding" of the faith, the outer manifestation of what Basil calls *dogma*. These are the result of prayer, of controversy, of the effort of numerous minds, struggling for clarity of thought and precision of expression, and finally of the Church's discriminating judgment in the light of the Holy Spirit. This, the

Church's kerygmatic teaching, once achieved, becomes also normative. But, what is gained in clarity sometimes entails a certain loss in depth, in fullness of understanding; and the conquest of one peak brings out more clearly the profiles of the other, yet unconquered peaks.

These proclamations, therefore, while embodying the efforts and fruits of theology, invite these all the more, and are always followed by greater probing, more controversy, further efforts at clarity of thought and precision of expression. It is here, in preparing for the Church's proclamations, and in the research that follows upon them, that theology feels the need for all the apparatus that philosophy and dialectics can offer her; but true theology uses these to defend the different normative proclamations, to clarify their content to the believer, and to bring about and demonstrate the true harmony that exists among them, while the heretics use these to try to "circumscribe" and define the Mystery and make it conform to their natural understanding, thus deviating from the Church's various levels of normative formulations.

The last of these formulations, conforming to all the previous ones, brings us back into the sphere of prayer and liturgy, and therefore into the heart of the Mystery. It is the "praise-proclamation," the doxological formulation—of the type that caused the controversy behind St. Basil's "De Spiritu Sancto."

It is in relation to the second-to-last level that Basil prudently hesitated, and was silent. In an era which saw Marcellus of Ancyra (agreeing in this with the Arian interpretation of the Council) use Nicaea's *homoousios* to propound a kind of Sabellianism, and his successor, Basil, repudiate the same word and adopt the suspected *homoiousios*, precisely to protect the distinction of Persons—a policy which, as we said, received the wholehearted approval of Athanasius— Basil of Caesarea wishes to avoid similar difficulties in relation to the Holy Spirit. Nicaea, which according to

Athanasius (*Oratio III contra Arianos*, 4) wishes simply to assert that "one must say about the Son all that one says about the Father, except the name of Father," had failed to make a clear distinction in terminology between what we would call Person and Nature. It had been understood by many (but not by Basil) as equating the terms *ousia* and *hypostasis*. Athanasius seemed to hesitate, and allowed at one time the assertion of *one*, at another time of *three* hypostases in God. Basil insisted on the latter policy as the only way to avoid both Sabellianism and Arianism (Letter 210, 3-5).[13] [Origen had already used the expression: "three hypostases" (Comm. on John 2, 10, or 6).][14] The Fathers of Constantinople would follow suit.

Basil defended the terminology canonized by the Church, but was very cautious in extending its use himself, for fear of causing confusion. He suggested correctives, but mainly relied on the ritual formulae and proper doxologies to instill faith and orthodoxy in the minds and hearts of his hearers.

But faith and "inner understanding," intrinsically related to the Spirit as they are, remain more important than the formulations, which, without them, become nothing but dead letter. Formulae *must* be used; but, for Basil, "the proposition of the truth may remain sober and discreet, aiming merely at leading the believers to a personal, religious, spiritual assimilation."[15] In this, Basil anticipated the thesis of St. Thomas Aquinas that *the* object of faith lies *behind* and *above* the formulae (which remain indispensable in their mediating role) and is none other than the Mystery (II-II, q. 1, a. 2 ad 2).

PRAYER AND CONTEMPLATION

Formulae must lead the believer, therefore, to a "spiritual assimilation" which is achieved in contemplation, an awareness latent in the light imparted by the Spirit, who is the source of our prayer life.

The Holy Spirit is, according to Basil, "intelligible light,"

phōs noēton (108C). Christian prayer is not a dark uncon-
scious communion with the "utterly unknowable." The
salvation brought about by Christ consists in an assimilation
to God leading to a true "deification;" an assimilation in
which the activity of faith, as a higher knowledge and true
gnosis of God, plays a role of primary importance. Only in
the Word do we recover that likeness with God, lost by sin.
But only the Holy Spirit can lead us into Christ, can sanctify
and enlighten us. If prayer is more excellent than rational
formulation, it is because only *in* prayer do we reach a deeper
and clearer knowledge thanks to the activity of the Spirit.
Only in the Spirit do we gaze on God. "...He, as a sun
taking hold of a most pure eye, will show you in himself the
Image of the Invisible. In the blessed contemplation of the
Image, you will see the unspeakable beauty of the Archetype" (109B). In the light which is the Spirit, we behold the
Son, in whom as in an image, we contemplate the Father
(Letter 226, 3).[16] "As it is written, 'In your light we shall see
the light' (Ps. 35:10), i.e., in the light produced by the Spirit,
we shall see 'the true light which enlightens every man that
comes into the world' (Jn. 1:9)" (153B). It is this action of
enlightening the soul which makes it "spiritual" (in the Spirit)
and therefore "divinizes" it, thus continuing the work begun
in baptism. We are spiritualized, divinized, in that very blaze
and fullness of divine knowledge. In the light of the Holy
Spirit we shall see him who is *the light* for us, who is "light
from light," and in whose countenance the primordial light
and source of all light is seen.

TRANSCENDENCE AND MYSTERY

In this mystical experience we reach the highest point of
the Christian life. We reach an "identification" with the
Triune God, from whom all things proceed. But this God,
who invites us to such intimacy with himself, is in himself
Transcendence and Mystery.

In c. 22, Basil attempts to "prove that the Holy Spirit is in communion of nature with the Father and the Son from the fact that he is as difficult to contemplate as the Father and the Son" (165C). In what does this "difficulty" consist, and how does it prove a "communion of nature"?

First of all, only those who have been thoroughly purified of their passions can attempt this contemplation. This is the first difficulty. Moreover, we have to believe in the risen Christ. Those are incapable of this contemplation "who are given over to the material and carnal life" and who, "for lack of faith in the resurrection, will certainly never see the Lord with the eyes of the heart" (168A). "The carnal man... cannot raise his eyes to the spiritual light (*pneumatikon phōs*) of the truth," while it is given to the disciples "already in this life to attain to the contemplation of the highest mysteries of the Spirit: 'For you are clean already because of the word which I have spoken to you ' (Jn. 15:3)" (168B).

No other "difficulties" are mentioned. It is taken for granted that the believing disciple, once he has been cleansed, can and should aspire to this contemplation—and indeed reach it. But this itself shows the fundamental "difficulty" inherent in this contemplation of the Spirit. Of ourselves, we are incapable of it. Only the power of the Spirit himself can raise us to it. The "world" (the unbelieving and unpurified) cannot "know" him any more than they can know the Father or the Son. All three "are beyond all human thought" (165D). They are utterly transcendent, a mystery totally inaccessible to our reason, our concepts, our language.

In himself, God is unknowable and unutterable. Only faith, a gift of the Spirit, can give us a glimpse of him, but faith is a darkness ("we see now through a glass in a dark manner" [1 Cor. 13:12]), a darkness which sheds light on everything else. That is where our human rational and poetic capacities come into play. They do not produce light beyond the limits of the creatures; but they shine with a new light received from above. But they stop at the threshold of the Mystery. Beyond that point, our concepts and words fail us.

Commenting on Basil's treatise against Euncmius, Louis Bouyer says that, "no concept can be properly applied to the divine essence, in such a way as to deduce his qualities from it. As soon as we come to affirm something true of it in a certain respect, we have to immediately deny it in another, and finally to acknowledge, after saying all that we can, that we neither have said nor could have said anything adequate of it. To the 'kataphasis', which speaks of God by analogy to the creatures, must succeed the 'apophasis', which denies the fact that we can do so strictly speaking."[17]

God is unknowable, ineffable. But, in the words of Lossky, "unknowability does not mean agnosticism or refusal to know God. However, this knowledge will always take place on the road whose proper end is not knowledge but union, deification. It will therefore never be an abstract theology, operating through concepts, but a contemplative theology, raising the minds to those realities which surpass our understanding. That is why the dogmas of the Church often confront human reason under the form of antinomies which are the more insoluble as the mystery they express is more sublime."[18]

Contemplation of the Mystery is baffling to our reason and its concepts. But it is not in itself darkness, contradiction, impenetrability. On the contrary, St. Basil, as we saw, refers to it only in terms of *light*, "intelligible light." Mystical contemplation is non-conceptual, non-verbal; but it *is* knowledge, an awareness. "It is a flower of knowledge," says Journet, "growing on the branch of love, but this knowledge is transconceptual,"[19] yet "enriched with everything that was antecedently clarified by means of concepts."[20] This vision, which was St. Basil's, accepts man as he is and does not reject his dignity or the value of his native powers. On the contrary, these reflect the traits of God's own Son. Yet, they remain incapable of achieving that "divinization" which is our ultimate goal. But, within these very powers, when they yield to the activity of the Spirit, is released a capacity which the Spirit himself enlightens. Our own positive efforts and activities are merely preparatory to the higher activity of the Spirit present in us, who is then able to divinize the "temple" in which he dwells. The Spirit at work within our own spirit, will then lead us from glory to glory, to the fullness of the light of the Trinity.

FAITH AND DOXOLOGY

Beyond words and concepts, but "on the very road which faith opens up by means of concepts,"[21] the Holy Spirit, by his light and love, floods our spirit with that knowledge, that awareness which makes us one with God. But we cannot remain silent. Where the language of propositions, of affirmations and negations, helpful and indispensable once, has been transcended, language must still come to help our efforts. God's word is a communication to us that achieves more than an intellectual awareness. Now, in turn, *our* words carry back to him more than an intellection—the expression of our experience, our enthusiastic praise, filled as it is with that knowledge of God acquired in contemplation. Praise through doxology is the spontaneous outpouring of mystical prayer.

Basil saw clearly that the traditional doxology, by praising the Father *through* the Son *in* the Holy Spirit, focused on the Father, the primordial origin of all being, who reveals himself, objectively *through* his Word and Son, and, in our subjectivity, *in* the Holy Spirit. This revelation of the Father is a revelation also of the Word and Spirit who reveal him, and inasmuch as they reveal him, a revelation of what has been called the "economic Trinity," the Trinity of salvation history. The Father is revealed through his Son, Jesus Christ, in the indwelling Spirit. The doxology therefore which carries us back, in the Spirit, through the Son, to the Father, is quite acceptable. But it is capable of a "subordinationist" interpretation. That was the precise reason why the Arians and the *Pneumatomachoi* insisted on its exclusive use. On the other hand, it could be also taken in a Sabellian sense, if the Word and the Spirit are seen merely as "manifestations" of the one *hypostasis* of the Father. That the Trinity as revealed *in* salvation history, namely the "economic" Trinity, *is* the God of Christians, must be readily admitted. But is there more to the Trinity *in itself* than the threefold "economic" manifestation? If not, then not only Sabellianism, but radical Immanentism might be the outcome. Could it not be that it is in *this* sense, together with an equally radical agnosticism as to our capacity of knowing the Trinity *in itself*, that some contemporary theologians understand K. Rahner's basic thesis: "The Trinity of the economy of salvation *is* the immanent Trinity and vice versa."[22]

We do not intend here to tackle the epistemological question: how can we know God except *as* revealed, hence in his "economic" manifestation. Kept at the level of awareness and clear formulation, the problem is very difficult but it *can* be resolved, in a realist-based theology. But we are dealing here with Mystery, which communicates itself not merely through concepts and other representations, but in a self-giving which is a true identification between the believer and the "object" of faith. Symbol, rite, and ritual formulae are among the means of communicating knowledge of the Mystery, a knowledge which is more a sense of the Transcendent than a mere intellectual awareness. We would like to answer, therefore, with St. Basil: faith and piety require that we praise Father, Son, and Holy Spirit, as transcendent, distinct, and co-equal, with the utmost praise and adoration. For our praise must be in conformity with our baptismal profession and this profession must be in conformity with our faith; this in turn has for its norm the baptismal rite—which came down to us from apostolic tradition. According to this pattern, therefore, we will, in addition to the "subordinative" doxology, use a "coordinative" one. We will praise and glorify "the Father *with* the Son *together with* the Holy Spirit," or, as does "the whole West (or almost), from Illyria to the confines of the inhabited earth" (208C), we shall glorify "the Father *and* the Son *and* the Holy Spirit," thus giving praise *in their very transcendence* to the three distinct, co-equal and co-eternal hypostases.

In the words of B. de Margerie: "It is partly thanks to him [Basil] that the Church continues and will always continue to glorify the Father, the Son, and the Holy Spirit conjointly— 'Gloria Patri et Filio et Spiritui Sancto'."[23]

LIFE IN THE SPIRIT

In what is perhaps the most beautiful chapter of the whole treatise, c. 9, in a style both poetic and theological, Basil gives us a glimpse of his own high contemplation of the Holy Spirit, and a beautiful treatment of the sublimity of the Spirit, of his multiple operations in the souls of believers, and of that "life in the Spirit" which is the goal of our human destiny.

It is to the Spirit that "all those turn who have need of sanctification, to him that rise the desires of all those who live according to virtue, and who are, as it were, refreshed by his breath and assisted in their pursuit of that end which is appropriate to them and befitting their nature. Capable of perfecting others, he himself lacks nothing: he is living, not as relying on a source outside himself, but as leader (*chorēgos*) of life. He does not grow and increase, but is immediate fullness, firmly established in himself, and present everywhere. Source of sanctification, intelligible light, he offers through himself, to every rational power, a kind of clarity for the discovery of the truth. Inaccessible by nature, yet he is reachable because of his goodness. He fills all things with his power but only communicates himself to those who are worthy of him; and this not according to a single measure, but distributing his operations proportionately to our faith. Simple in his substance, yet manifold in his powers, he is wholly present to each being, yet entirely present everywhere. He lets himself be shared without suffering anything, he gives himself in participation without diminishing, like the sunlight which is received by him who enjoys it as if he were alone, and yet enlightens the earth, the sea, and the air. Thus is the Spirit present to everyone capable of receiving him, as if he alone received him; and remaining intact, he pours out his grace, which is sufficient for all. Those who share in the Spirit enjoy him as much as is possible for their nature, but not as much as *he* can give himself to be shared.

"As for the Spirit's intimate union (*oikeiōsis*) with the soul, it does not consist in drawing closer locally (for how could one in a bodily way draw closer to the incorporeal), but in the exclusion of the passions which, having overwhelmed the soul because of its love for the flesh, had separated it from intimacy with God. Therefore, it is only by purifying oneself from the stain of sin, by returning to the beauty of one's nature, by restoring, so to speak, to the royal image its primitive form through purity, it is by doing this alone that one draws close to the Paraclete. And he, like a sun taking hold of an eye which has been purified, will show you in himself the Image of the Invisible; in the blessed contemplation of the Image, you will see the ineffable beauty of the Archetype.

"By him hearts are lifted, the weak are led by the hand, the proficient become perfect. It is he who, by enlightening those who have cleansed themselves of every stain, makes them spiritual through communion with him. As limpid and transparent bodies themselves become sparkling when a ray of light strikes them, and in turn send forth out of themselves a new brightness, in like manner, once the souls which bear the Spirit (*pneumatophoroi*) are enlightened by him, they become spiritual themselves and a source of grace for others.

"From this come foresight of the future, understanding of mysteries, comprehension of hidden things, distribution of charisms, heavenly citizenship, singing with the angelic choirs, joy without end, permanent abode in God, likeness to

God, and finally the supremely desirable object: 'becoming God' " (108B-109C).

Basil's rhapsodizing about the Holy Spirit brings the realization that a proper theology of the Holy Spirit is an essential part of Christian doctrine. A certain lack in this respect has been a weakness in Western theology for many centuries. Also, we see that for St. Basil, contemplation and mystical union are not merely a gazing, in the light of the Spirit, at the Image, seeing in it the Invisible (or Archetype); but first of all a gazing at the light *itself*—a knowledge and contemplation of the Holy Spirit, *in* whom the Son as Image grants us that vision of the Father which *is* divinization.

NOTES

*St. Basil's treatise "De Spiritu Sancto" is found in Migne PG XXXII. I will sometimes refer to the page in this volume, sometimes to the chapter.

¹Franco Bolgiani, "La Théologie de l'Esprit Saint," in *Dieu révélé dans l'Esprit*, (Les quatre fleuves, 9). Paris: Editions Beauchesne, 1979, p. 33.

²Johannes Quasten, *Patrology*, Vol. 1. Utrecht-Antwerp: Spectrum Publishers, 1975, p. 25.

³Walter Kasper, *Jesus the Christ*, New York: Paulist Press, 1977, p. 15.

⁴J. de Ghellinck, S.J., *Patristique et Moyen Age, Etudes d'histoire littéraire et doctrinale*. III, Etude VI, "Un aspect de l'opposition entre Hellénisme et Christianisme. L'attitude

vis-à-vis de la dialectique dans les débats Trinitaires." Paris: Desclée de Brouwer, 1948, p. 303.

[5]Ibid., p. 304.

[6]Ibid., p. 304.

[7]Jean Gribomont, "Esotérisme et Tradition dans le Traité du Saint-Esprit de saint Basile," in *Oecumenica. Jahrbuch für ökumenische Forschung* 2, 1967, p. 43.

[8]Ibid., p. 45.

[9]Ibid., pp. 43-53.

[10] Read: *homoion* (see *Basile de Césarée sur le Saint-Esprit. Introduction, texte, traduction et notes*, by B. Pruche. [Sources Chrétiennes, 17]. Paris: Editions du Cerf, 1945, p. 238, n. 3).

[11]PG XXXII, 549B.

[12]"...inopinantibus melius se ipsa lux mysteriorum infuderit, quam si ea sermo aliquis praecucurrisset." *De Mysteriis*, c. 1, n. 2.

[13]PG XXXII, 772A-777A.

[14]PG XIV, 128A.

[15]Gribomont, op. cit., p. 47.

[16]PG XXXII, 849A.

[17]Louis Bouyer, *Le Fils Eternel*. Paris: Les Editions du Cerf, 1974, pp. 385-386.

[18]Vladimir Lossky, *Théologie mystique de l'Eglise d'Orient*. (Les Religions, 13). Paris: Aubier, Editions Montaigne, 1944, pp. 40-41.

[19]Charles Journet, *Connaissance et inconnaissance de Dieu*. Paris: Desclée de Brouwer, 1969, p. 110.

[20]Ibid., p. 106.

[21]Ibid., p. 101.

[22]Karl Rahner, *Theological Investigations*, Vol. IV, Part Two, "Remarks on the Dogmatic Treatise 'De Trinitate'." New York: The Seabury Press, 1974, p. 87.

[23]Bertrand de Margerie, S.J., *La Trinité Chrétienne dans l'Histoire*. (Théologie Historique, 31). Paris: Editions Beauchesne, 1975, p. 151.

SOME ASPECTS OF THE ANAPHORA OF SAINT BASIL THE GREAT

Brian Keleher
(*Pastor of St. Seraphim's Greek Catholic Church, Toronto, Canada*)

With the exception of the ferial days of Great Lent and three or four other "a-liturgical" days in the course of the Church Year, Christians of the Byzantine Rite (both Catholic and Orthodox) normally use the text of the Ordinary of the Mass called *The Divine Liturgy of Saint John Chrysostom* when they celebrate the Holy Eucharist.[1] However, the use of a different text is required on ten days of the year,[2] particularly the Sundays of Great Lent, Holy Thursday, and Holy Saturday: the Divine Liturgy of Saint Basil the Great. The rubrics of this Liturgy do not differ at all from that attributed to St. John Chrysostom, and except for the Anthem to Our Lady, the people's responses are also identical in both liturgies. They differ only in the text of the various prayers said by the celebrant from the Litany for the Catechumens on, and most particularly in the Anaphora, or the "Eucharistic Prayer," as the Western Church now calls the Preface and Canon. We give here the complete Greek text of St. Basil's Anaphora as presently used, together with a parallel English translation. The translation is not our own, and is given only for convenience; the bibliography lists several other translations and editions of this prayer, and in any case the Greek is essential for any serious study.

Scholars are generally agreed that the present recension of the text, while substantially that of St. Basil himself, does contain some accretions; these are not of any great importance,[3] with one exception at the Epiclesis which we shall discuss below. Those who are familiar with the various Anaphorae in use in the Church, both today and in the past, often consider that of St. Basil to be, on balance, the best of the lot, particularly for its skillful weaving of the biblical themes and quotations, dogmatic teaching on the Blessed Trinity, and earlier forms of the Prayer together with the shape and even the material of the ancient Jewish formularies on which parts of the Christian Anaphora are based. We shall see some examples of these different elements.

Although they do not use it very often, Byzantine Christians hold this Liturgy in very high esteem—as may be seen from its retention on Holy Thursday and at the ancient Paschal Vigil on Holy Saturday—and commonly explain that the so-called *Liturgy of Saint John Chrysostom* is only an abbreviation of the Liturgy of St. Basil for pastoral convenience. Hence we may properly consider the Anaphora of St. Basil the *typical* Anaphora of the Byzantine Rite, and we must criticize those translators and commentators on the Byzantine Liturgy who ignore the text of St. Basil.

The Anaphora of St. Basil is of special interest to Roman Catholics at the present time because the Fourth Eucharistic Prayer of the contemporary *Missale Romanum* is said to be based on the Anaphora of Basil.

And so, to the text itself. We find that the actual "thanksgiving," with which the Prayer opens, is a brilliant synthesis of Scriptural themes recounting the glory of God in Himself and in His Creation, woven into "a magnificent litany of all the titles and all the attributions of the divine persons in the Bible."[4]

The opening expression, *Ho On*, is the standard Greek rendering for the Holy Name of God, *YHWH*, which cannot really be either translated or pronounced—in this the Greeks were wiser than some modern translators of the Bible. When they met this word in either the sacred text of Scripture or in prayer, the Hebrews often substituted the euphemism "Most High;" we might suggest that this would be a better English rendering here. The use of the Holy Name at the beginning of the Prayer stresses the infinite goodness of God in Himself, and hence implies the doctrine that Creation was in no way necessary, but rather a free gift of God's grace.

The phrase *soi prospherein...ten logiken tauten latreian hemon...*provides a difficult problem of translation. Until recently, the key word *logiken* has usually been rendered as either *reasonable* or *rational*, as in the *Quam Oblationem* of the Roman Canon. Recently many translators both of liturgical texts and of the Scriptures have found this traditional rendering unsatisfactory, and the present trend is to speak of "our spiritual offering." However, that will not do, since Greek has a perfectly good word for "spiritual," for one thing, and since the Eucharist is not a purely spiritual offering but involves the material substances of bread and wine which become the material substances of the Body and Blood of Christ. We might suggest that the "reasonable sacrifice" is specifically the sacrifice of *men*, as contrasted to the prayers offered by the Angels (which really are purely spiritual, obviously), or the involuntary obedience offered to God by the rest of the created order, which does not have free will nor the faculty of reason.

From the Preface through the Post-Sanctus, the Prayer is one of Trinitarian praise of the Father, suggesting that at first it was the Angels who offered the most perfect expression of the praise of all creation, in the never-ceasing "Sanctus." The Post-Sanctus states at once that *we sinners* join the Angels in the great Sanctus, reminding us of the belief held by the Fathers that Man was made to replace the fallen angels, and as a creature of body and soul to offer up to God the praise and thanksgiving due Him from all creation. The Prayer continues, recounting the Creation and Fall of Man with the continuing loving care of God, recounting how the Father prepared His People for the coming of Christ, and how eventually God became Man for our salvation and *deification*, "becoming conformable to the body of our lowliness that He might make us conformable to the image of His glory" and reversing the effects of the Fall "that they who died in Adam might be made alive in Thy Christ Himself."

Basil stresses the reality—we may almost say the juridical effect!—of the Incarnation with an interesting turn of phrase *empoliteusamenos to kosmo touto*—having "taken citizenship" in this cosmos. In other words, Our Lord did not simply "appear," or visit here for a while, but He actually made our world His home.

The great importance of the Descent into Hell and the Cappadocian idea of salvation (sometimes irreverently called the Mousetrap Theory) is expressed here, "He went down through the Cross into Hades, to fill all things with Himself and loosed the pains of death, and rose on the third day, *making a way for all flesh to the resurrection from the dead— because it was not possible for the Author of Life to be held bound by corruption.*" In other words, Satan was not sure of the divinity of Christ, and thought that he had won with the Crucifixion—only to discover that he had quite literally bitten more than he could chew, and taken a Prisoner Whom he could not hold. It is, of course, only through our union with God in the Mystical Body of Christ—a union which reaches its highest point in this present age when we celebrate the Eucharist—that we too can gain the resurrection unto eternal life, following that "way for all flesh to the resurrection from the dead" of which St. Basil speaks here.

We may note that St. Basil includes the Second Coming and the Final Judgment in his list of the *mirabilia Dei* for which he gives thanks, thus reminding us that the Eucharistic Sacrifice not only looks back to the Last Supper, Calvary, and the Resurrection, but also forward to the Parousia. The dominical command, "Do this in remembrance of me," absent in the liturgy attributed to St. John Chrysostom, is present in Basil, followed by this aspiration which reminds us of the new acclamation of the Roman Rite: "As often as ye eat this Bread and drink this Chalice, ye proclaim my death and confess my Resurrection." Both texts are based on St. Paul.

The Greek text, and the translations which follow it, are

slightly corrupt at the phrase "Thine own of thine own..." The present text reads *Ta sa ek ton son soi prospheromen...*, but the verb should actually be *prospherontes* (as it is in the Church-Slavonic edition: *prinosjashche*), and hence the whole phrase should be translated:

> Therefore, O Master, we also, having in remembrance His saving Passion, the life-giving Cross, the three days Burial, the Resurrection from the dead, the Ascension into the heavens, the Session at the right hand of Thee, the God and Father, and His glorious and fearful Second Coming,
> Offering Thine own of Thine own unto Thee, in behalf of all and for all,
> We hymn Thee, we bless Thee, we give thanks to Thee, O Lord, and we beseech Thee, our God.

The *Epiclesis*, or invocation of the Holy Spirit, presents some problems for our consideration. As many are aware, over-zealous polemicists of both East and West have created a quite unnecessary and pointless controversy over the "exact moment" of the Consecration, with most Latin theologians insisting on the Words of Institution and most Oriental theologians insisting on the Epiclesis. The whole discussion is really depressing and best avoided, since on both sides the disputants do violence to the most basic ideas of liturgy by taking these few phrases quite out of the context of the Anaphora in which they occur, as though one phrase or the other were somehow "magic words" which all by themselves, apart from the intention of the Church, could effect the Consecration (and at times such thinking has led to practical abberations too grotesque to be described). Happily, cooler heads seem to be prevailing, at least at the moment, and the controversy has died down. We mention it only to disclaim any intention of supporting either of the extreme positions in our own comments on some points to do with the Epiclesis.

First, let us note that the Epiclesis, as the rest of the Anaphora, is addressed to God the Father, asking Him, the

Holy of Holies, to send the Holy Spirit upon us and upon the Gifts. Some popular manuals of the Liturgy have quite incorrectly labeled this section of the Anaphora "Prayer to God the Holy Spirit," which it clearly is not.

So addressing the Father, the celebrant uses an interesting term with reference to the Gifts: "Presenting the *antitypes* of the holy Body and Blood of Thy Christ..." This is a rather curious word, and might perhaps in this context be understood to mean that the Holy Gifts which we receive in Communion are symbols which really are that which they symbolize. A "type" is an image or symbol; usually an "antitype" is that which the type symbolizes. Here the word has posed a problem for translators; most prefer simply to retain the word "antitype" and let the reader draw his own conclusions.

Father Bouyer in his study of this Anaphora points out that the Epiclesis and the Words of Institution are intimately linked by the use in both places of the verb *anadeixai*, which in both cases should best be translated "consecrate." Unfortunately virtually all the published English translations miss the point of the double use of this difficult verb and translate it in each place by quite different words. (In general this Anaphora has yet to receive a really satisfactory English translation).

Many editions, particularly in Church-Slavonic, add after the words "shed for the life (and salvation) of the world" the further prayer "changing them by Thy Holy Spirit." This addition is taken from the Liturgy of John Chrysostom and makes no sense here; it is added, evidently, for polemical reasons.

Likewise many editions interpolate a Troparion addressed to Christ, asking Him to send the Holy Spirit, just before the celebrant blesses the Gifts. Though I am personally fond of this devotional Troparion, it must be admitted that its use at this point not only makes no sense whatever but is an obvious intrusion into a well-constructed prayer. To understand the flow of the Anamnesis-Epiclesis-Diptychs, one should read the text aloud *without* either the Deacon's interjections or the rubrics.

The Anthem to Our Lady is notable for its careful ordering, placing her at the center of created beings "of whom God was incarnate." This hymn is one of the very few places in early Christian worship in which the words "glory to thee" are addressed to anyone other than God Himself.

The long intercessions in both wording and structure reflect the Jewish Eighteen Benedictions very closely, and witness to the carefulness of Basil's scholarship. We may note also that, although they clearly were written in consideration of the needs of the Church in the fourth century, they have lost none of their value today.

Our text, following most of the editions, orders the celebrant to commemorate by name only his own Ordinary, and no other Hierarchs. Some more recent editions require a longer list: the Pope, the Patriarch, and/or the Metropolitan, as well as the local Ordinary. The simpler practice reflects the more ancient understanding of the Bishop as the Head of the local church, and reminds the hearers that every Eucharist is celebrated either by the local bishop or by his delegate. The final intercessions against heresy and schism remind us of Basil's deep concern for orthodoxy of doctrine and the unity of the Church reflected again in the doxology with which the Prayer ends: that we may with *one mouth and one heart* glorify the Most Blessed Trinity.

With its exact structure, its majestic use of themes from Holy Scripture and Sacred Tradition, its dogmatic clarity, and its magnificent intercessions, this Anaphora of St. Basil the Great is not only a precious treasure from the early Church but also a prayer that remains today as appropriate as it was when it was first used. Perhaps we may be forgiven for suggesting that in the present period of liturgical confusion especially those who seek to "compose" new

Eucharistic Prayers would do well first to familiarize themselves with the old ones, and most especially with that of St. Basil...and even, maybe, to decide that the texts which the Church has kept for us throughout all these centuries are of a sufficient richness already.

NOTES

[1]On ferial days of Great Lent the rubrics of the Byzantine Rite forbid the celebration of the full Eucharistic Liturgy and permit only the Liturgy of the Presanctified Gifts—that is, a solemn Vespers and Holy Communion.

In theory, the Byzantine Rite still has another form of the Eucharistic Liturgy called the Divine Liturgy of St. James, but in practice this latter is celebrated only rarely in a few places.

[2]Outside of Great Lent, the Divine Liturgy of Saint Basil is prescribed on his feast day (1 January) and the Vigils of Christmas and Theophany.

[3]For a schematic presentation of the text, showing the different strata of the material, cf. Bouyer, *Eucharist*, pp. 292-6.

[4]Ibid., p. 292

SELECTED BIBLIOGRAPHY

A. Greek Texts of the Anaphora (and Liturgy) of Saint Basil:

1. Catholic edition:

   Iepatikon. Rome, 1950, pp. 167-218. Highly recommended, published by authority of Pope Pius XII, Patriarch Maximos IV of Antioch, and the Sacred Oriental Congregation.

2. Orthodox edition:

   I Theia Leitourgia. Athens: Saliveros, pp. 65-86. Poorly printed, not as fine as the above.

   I Theia Leitourgia. Athens: Apostoliki Diakonia. Authorized by the Church of Greece. Good quality, although sometimes a bit confusing in use.

B. Church-Slavonic Texts:

1. Catholic edition:

   Sluzhebnik. Rome, 1942, pp. 316-407 (the text of Basil alone is available as an off-print). The best Slavonic edition available; published by authority of Pope Pius XII.

2. Edition of the Patriarchate of Moscow and all Russia:

   Sluzhebnik. Vol. II. Moscow, 1977, pp. 357-418. Published by authority of Patriarch Pimen. This is a photo-offset reprint of an edition done before the Russian Revolution, with the commemorations of the Sovereign and Imperial House removed and the commemorations of the Patriarch restored, but no other changes. Primarily of bibliographic interest.

There are several other printings of the Divine Liturgy of Saint Basil in Church-Slavonic, but they do not present anything of special interest.

C. English translations of the Anaphora, or the entire Divine
   Liturgy of Saint Basil the Great (a selected list):

1. Catholic editions: unfortunately the existing Catholic
   translations of the Divine Liturgy of Saint Basil are of
   consistently poor quality, seriously inaccurate, and, in
   our opinion, worthless for scholars and unfitting for
   public worship. Those wishing to confirm our negative
   judgment are invited to compare either the Greek or the
   Church-Slavonic text with any of the following:

   Divine Liturgy of Our Holy Father St. Basil the Great.
   Pittsburgh: Byzantine Seminary Press, 1976. Very
   poor and highly overpriced.

   The Byzantine Liturgy. Bronx, New York: Russian
   Center, Fordham University, pp. 64-74. This pam-
   phlet is at least inexpensive. (Imprimatur of Francis
   Cardinal Spellman).

   Byzantine Daily Worship. Allendale, New Jersey:
   Alleluia Press, 1970. Despite the authorization of
   Patriarch Maximos V of Antioch, the section of this
   book dedicated to the Liturgy of Saint Basil is so hope-
   lessly confused that the Melkite Archbishop in the
   United States has found it necessary to forbid its use.

   Kucharek, Casimir, *Byzantine-Slav Liturgy of St. John
   Chrysostom.* Allendale, New Jersey: Alleluia Press,
   1971. The Anaphora of Saint Basil in a poor English
   translation is given on pages 743-749. This book has
   generally received very negative reviews, and is not
   recommended.

2. Orthodox editions: fortunately for the English-speaking
   world, here we have two good translations of the
   Liturgy of Saint Basil which can be recommended for
   general use (although, of course, no translation can replace the original Greek text):

Service Book... according to the use of the Antiochian Orthodox Christian Archdiocese of New York and all North America, Fourth Edition, 1971, pp. 132-145. This translation was in fact done by Father Stephen Upson. It is faithful, reads well, and can be used nicely in public worship. It includes the Proper "Prayer Behind the Ambo," missing in all the Catholic editions listed above. It does *not* include the commemorations of the Sovereign.

The Divine Liturgy According to St. John Chrysostom with Appendices. New York: Russian Orthodox Greek Catholic Church of America (now the Orthodox Church in America), 1967, pp. 95-111. Based on the Church-Slavonic text of Moscow. On the whole good, despite a few problems. Does not have the commemorations of the Sovereign or the "Prayer Behind the Ambo."

Robertson, J.N.W.B., ed., *The Divine Liturgies*. London, 1894, pp. 344-385. The Greek text with a parallel English translation. Unfortunately long out of print, this edition is invaluable, and it would be a very worthwhile reprint. The translation is not perhaps suitable for liturgical use, but its careful accuracy is of great help to students.

D. Commentaries:

Orlov, M., *Liturgia sviatavo Vasilia Velykavo*, First Critical Edition. St. Petersburg, 1905, (in Russian). Despite its age, this remains far and away the most important study on the Liturgy of Saint Basil. Like so much else, it has long been out of print, and it is greatly to be hoped that someone will decide to reprint it soon (perhaps during this Basilian Year).

Bouyer, Louis, *Eucharist*, Theology and Spirituality of the Eucharistic Prayer. Notre Dame, 1968. Includes the best published English discussion of the Eucharistic Prayer.

Bouyer, Louis, *Liturgical Piety*. Notre Dame, 1954. Contains an important discussion on "The Anaphora," a note on "Epiclesis," and "Verba Consecrationis," based on the Anaphora of Saint Basil.

E. Discography:

There is only one complete recording of the Divine Liturgy of Saint Basil the Great; fortunately it is a very good one. *Die heilige Basilius-Liturgie im slawish-byzantinischen Ritus*, sung in Church-Slavonic by the Schweizer Romanos Chor (male chorus directed by Father Ludwig Pichler of the Pontifical Russian College, Rome). Duraphon HD 224. Beautiful traditional Slav chant, very well executed.

THE DIVINE LITURGIES

OF OUR FATHERS AMONG THE SAINTS

JOHN CHRYSOSTOM

AND

BASIL THE GREAT

WITH THAT

OF THE PRESANCTIFIED

PRECEDED BY THE HESPERINOS AND THE ORTHROS

EDITED WITH THE GREEK TEXT BY

J. N. W. B. ROBERTSON.

From the rising of the sun even unto the going down my Name is glorified among the nations, and in every place incense is offered to my Name, and a clean Sacrifice; for my Name is great among the nations, saith the Lord Almighty.   MALACHIAS, i. 11.

This do ye in remembrance of me.
LUKE, xxii. 19.

LONDON:

DAVID NUTT, 270—271 STRAND, W. C.

1894.

ΑΙ ΘΕΙΑΙ ΛΕΙΤΟΥΡΓΙΑΙ

ΤΩΝ ΕΝ ΑΓΙΟΙΣ ΠΑΤΕΡΩΝ ΗΜΩΝ

ΙΩΑΝΝΟΥ ΤΟΥ ΧΡΥΣΟΣΤΟΜΟΥ

ΚΑΙ

ΒΑΣΙΛΕΙΟΥ ΤΟΥ ΜΕΓΑΛΟΥ

ΣΥΝ ΤΗι

ΤΩΝ ΠΡΟΗΓΙΑΣΜΕΝΩΝ

ΗΓΟΥΜΕΝΟΥ ΤΟΥ ΕΣΠΕΡΙΝΟΥ ΚΑΙ ΟΡΘΡΟΥ

ΕΚΔΟΘΕΙΣΑΙ ΜΕΤΑ ΑΓΓΛΙΚΗΣ ΜΕΤΑΦΡΑΣΕΩΣ ΥΠΟ

Ι. Ν. W. B. ΡΟΒΕΡΤΣΩΝΟΣ.

Ἀπὸ ἀνατολῶν ἡλίου καὶ ἕως δυσμῶν τὸ Ὄνομά μου δεδόξασται ἐν τοῖς ἔθνεσι, καὶ ἐν παντὶ τόπῳ θυμίαμα προσάγεται τῷ Ὀνόματί μου, καὶ Θυσία καθαρά· διότι μέγα τὸ Ὄνομά μου ἐν τοῖς ἔθνεσι, λέγει Κύριος Παντοκράτωρ.
Μαλαχίου, Α΄. II.

Τοῦτο ποιεῖτε εἰς τὴν ἐμὴν ἀνάμνησιν
Λουκᾶ, ΚΒ΄. 19.

ΕΝ ΛΟΝΔΙΝΩι,

DAVID NUTT, 270—271 STRAND, W. C.

1894.

according to the multitude of thy mercy; that we may be worthy to offer to thee this rational and unbloody Sacrifice for our own sins, and for the errors of the people: which accepting at thy holy, and heavenly, and intellectual .Altar, for an odour of a sweet smell, in return send down on us the grace of thy Holy Spirit. Look upon us, O God, and behold this our worship, and accept it, as thou didst accept the gifts of Abel, the sacrifices of Noe, the holocausts of Abraham, the priestly-ministrations of Moses and Aaron, the peace-offerings of Samuel. As thou didst accept from thy holy Apostles this true worship, so also from the hands of us, sinners, accept these Gifts in thy beneficence, O Lord; that, being vouchsafed to minister blamelessly at thy holy Altar, we may find the reward of faithful and wise stewards, in the fearful day of thy righteous recompense.

After the conclusion of the holy Symbol (See page 295), the Deacon saith aloud:

Let us stand well, let us stand with fear: let us attend to offer in peace the holy Anaphora.

The Choir: A mercy of peace, a sacrifice of praise.

The Priest, having turned to the people, saith aloud:

The grace of our Lord Jesus Christ, and the

κατὰ τὸ πλῆθος τοῦ ἐλέους σου· ἵνα γενώμεθα ἄξιοι τοῦ προσφέρειν σοι τὴν λογικὴν ταύτην καὶ ἀναίμακτον Θυσίαν ὑπὲρ τῶν ἡμετέρων ἁμαρτημάτων, καὶ τῶν τοῦ λαοῦ ἀγνοημάτων· ἣν προσδεξάμενος εἰς τὸ ἅγιον, καὶ ὑπερουράνιον, καὶ νοερόν σου Θυσιαστήριον, εἰς ὀσμὴν εὐωδίας, ἀντικατάπεμψον ἡμῖν τὴν χάριν τοῦ Ἁγίου σου Πνεύματος. Ἐπίβλεψον ἐφ' ἡμᾶς, ὁ Θεός, καὶ ἔπιδε ἐπὶ τὴν λατρείαν ἡμῶν ταύτην, καὶ πρόσδεξαι αὐτὴν, ὡς προσεδέξω Ἄβελ τὰ δῶρα, Νῶε τὰς θυσίας, Ἀβραὰμ τὰς ὁλοκαρπώσεις, Μωσέως καὶ Ἀαρὼν τὰς ἱερωσύνας, Σαμουὴλ τὰς εἰρηνικάς. Ὡς προσεδέξω ἐκ τῶν ἁγίων σου Ἀποστόλων τὴν ἀληθινὴν ταύτην λατρείαν, οὕτω καὶ ἐκ τῶν χειρῶν ἡμῶν τῶν ἁμαρτωλῶν πρόσδεξαι τὰ Δῶρα ταῦτα ἐν τῇ χρηστότητί σου, Κύριε· ἵνα, καταξιωθέντες λειτουργεῖν ἀμέμπτως τῷ ἁγίῳ σου Θυσιαστηρίῳ, εὕρωμεν τὸν μισθὸν τῶν πιστῶν καὶ φρονίμων οἰκονόμων, ἐν τῇ ἡμέρᾳ τῇ φοβερᾷ τῆς ἀνταποδόσεώς σου τῆς δικαίας.

Μετὰ τὴν συμπλήρωσιν τοῦ ἁγίου Συμβόλου (Ὄρα σελ. 294), λέγει ὁ Διάκονος ἐκφωνῶς·

Στῶμεν καλῶς, στῶμεν μετὰ φόβου· πρόσχωμεν τὴν ἁγίαν Ἀναφορὰν ἐν εἰρήνῃ προσφέρειν.

Ὁ Χορός· Ἔλεον εἰρήνης, θυσίαν αἰνέσεως.

Ὁ Ἱερεὺς ἐκφώνως, ἐστραμμένος πρὸς τὸν λαόν·

Ἡ χάρις τοῦ Κυρίου ἡμῶν Ἰησοῦ Χριστοῦ, καὶ ἡ

love of the God and Father, and the communion of the Holy Spirit, be with you all (**And he blesseth the people**).

The Choir: And with thy spirit.

The Priest: On high let us have our hearts (pointing with his hand).

The Choir: We have them with the Lord.

The Priest: Let us give thanks to the Lord.

The Choir: Meet and right is it (See page **297**).

The Priest prayeth secretly:

Thou the 'Existing', Master, Lord, God, Father, almighty, adorable, meet it is indeed, and right, and becoming the majesty of thy holiness, to praise thee, to hymn thee, to bless thee, to adore thee, to give thanks to thee, to glorify thee, the only really existing God, and to offer to thee with a contrite heart, and a spirit of lowliness, this our rational worship; for thou art he that hath bestowed on us the knowledge of thy truth. And who is sufficient to utter thy mighty acts, to make all thy praises to be heard, or to tell of all thy wonders at every season? Master of all things, Lord of heaven and earth, and of every creature, visible and invisible, who sittest upon the throne of glory, and beholdest the depths, unoriginate, invisible, incomprehensible, uncircumscribed, immutable, the Father of our Lord Jesus Christ the great God and Saviour of our hope: who is the image of thy goodness, seal of equal type, shewing in himself

ἀγάπη τοῦ Θεοῦ καὶ Πατρός, καὶ ἡ κοινωνία τοῦ Ἁγίου Πνεύματος, εἴη μετὰ πάντων ὑμῶν (Καὶ εὐλογεῖ τὸν λαόν).

Ὁ Χορός· Καὶ μετὰ τοῦ πνεύματός σου.

Ὁ Ἱερεύς· Ἄνω σχῶμεν τὰς καρδίας (δεικνύων ἅμα τῇ χειρί).

Ὁ Χορός·Ἔχομεν πρός τὸν Κύριον.

Ὁ Ἱερεύς· Εὐχαριστήσωμεν τῷ Κυρίῳ.

Ὁ Χορός·"Ἄξιον καὶ δίκαιον ("Ὅρα σελ. 296).

Ὁ Ἱερεύς ἐπεύχεται μυστικῶς·

Ὁ Ὤν, Δέσποτα, Κύριε, Θεέ, Πάτερ παντοκράτορ, προσκυνητέ, ἄξιον ὡς ἀληθῶς, καὶ δίκαιον, καὶ πρέπον τῇ μεγαλοπρεπείᾳ τῆς ἁγιωσύνης σου, σὲ αἰνεῖν, σὲ ὑμνεῖν, σὲ εὐλογεῖν, σὲ προσκυνεῖν, σοὶ εὐχαριστεῖν, σὲ δοξάζειν τὸν μόνον ὄντως ὄντα Θεόν, καὶ σοὶ προσφέρειν, ἐν καρδίᾳ συντετριμμένῃ καὶ πνεύματι ταπεινώσεως, τὴν λογικὴν ταύτην λατρείαν ἡμῶν· ὅτι σὺ εἶ ὁ χαρισάμενος ἡμῖν τὴν ἐπίγνωσιν τῆς σῆς ἀληθείας. Καὶ τίς ἱκανὸς λαλῆσαι τὰς δυναστείας σου, ἀκουστὰς ποιῆσαι πάσας τὰς αἰνέσεις σου, ἢ διηγήσασθαι πάντα τὰ θαυμάσιά σου ἐν παντὶ καιρῷ; Δέσποτα τῶν ἁπάντων, Κύριε οὐρανοῦ καὶ γῆς, καὶ πάσης κτίσεως ὁρωμένης τε καὶ οὐχ ὁρωμένης, ὁ καθήμενος ἐπὶ θρόνου δόξης, καὶ ἐπιβλέπων ἀβύσσους, ἄναρχε, ἀόρατε, ἀκατάληπτε, ἀπερίγραπτε, ἀναλλοίωτε, ὁ Πατὴρ τοῦ Κυρίου ἡμῶν Ἰησοῦ Χριστοῦ, τοῦ μεγάλου Θεοῦ, καὶ Σωτῆρος τῆς ἐλπίδος ἡμῶν· ὅς ἐστιν εἰκὼν τῆς σῆς ἀγαθότητος, σφραγὶς

thee the Father, living Word, true God, the wisdom before the ages, life, sanctification, power, the true light; from whom the Holy Spirit hath appeared, the Spirit of truth, the grace of adoption, the earnest of the future inheritance, the first-fruits of eternal good things, the life-giving power, the source of sanctification; of whom enabled, every rational and intellectual creature worshippeth thee, and to thee sendeth up the everlasting doxology, for all things are thy servants. For thee do praise Angels, Archangels, Thrones, Dominations, Principalities, Authorities, Powers, and the many-eyed Cherubim: about thee stand in a circle the Seraphim, one with six wings, and another with six wings; and with twain they cover their faces, and with twain their feet; and with twain flying, they cry one to another, with unceasing mouths, with never silent doxologies:

The Priest aloud:

Singing, vociferating, crying, and saying the triumphal Hymn:

The Choir: Holy, Holy, Holy, Lord of Sabaoth: the heaven and the earth are full of thy glory.

Hosanna in the highest:

Blessed is he that cometh in the Name of the Lord:

Hosanna in the highest.

Then the Deacon doth the same as in the Liturgy of Chrysostom.

And the Priest prayeth secretly:

ἰσότυπος, ἐν ἑαυτῷ δεικνὺς σὲ τὸν Πατέρα, Λόγος ζῶν, Θεὸς ἀληθινός, ἡ πρὸ αἰώνων σοφία, ζωή, ἁγιασμός, δύναμις, τὸ φῶς τὸ ἀληθινόν· παρ' οὗ τὸ Πνεῦμα τὸ Ἅγιον ἐξεφάνη, τὸ τῆς ἀληθείας Πνεῦμα, τὸ τῆς υἱοθεσίας χάρισμα, ὁ ἀρραβὼν τῆς μελλούσης κληρονομίας, ἡ ἀπαρχὴ τῶν αἰωνίων ἀγαθῶν, ἡ ζωοποιὸς δύναμις, ἡ πηγὴ τοῦ ἁγιασμοῦ· παρ' οὗ πᾶσα κτίσις λογική τε καὶ νοερὰ δυναμουμένη, σοὶ λατρεύει, καὶ σοὶ τὴν ἀΐδιον ἀναπέμπει δοξολογίαν, ὅτι τὰ σύμπαντα δοῦλα σά. Σὲ γὰρ αἰνοῦσιν Ἄγγελοι, Ἀρχάγγελοι, Θρόνοι, Κυριότητες, Ἀρχαί, Ἐξουσίαι, Δυνάμεις, καὶ τὰ πολυόμματα Χερουβίμ· σοὶ παρίστανται κύκλῳ τὰ Σεραφίμ, ἓξ πτέρυγες τῷ ἑνί, καὶ ἓξ πτέρυγες τῷ ἑνί· καὶ ταῖς μὲν δυσὶ κατακαλύπτουσι τὰ πρόσωπα ἑαυτῶν, ταῖς δὲ δυσὶ τοὺς πόδας· καὶ ταῖς δυσὶ πετόμενα, κέκραγεν ἕτερον πρὸς τὸ ἕτερον, ἀκαταπαύστοις στόμασιν, ἀσιγήτοις δοξολογίαις·

Ἐκφώνως ὁ Ἱερεύς·

Τὸν ἐπινίκιον ὕμνον ᾄδοντα, βοῶντα, κεκραγότα, καὶ λέγοντα·

Ὁ Χορός· Ἅγιος, Ἅγιος, Ἅγιος, Κύριος Σαβαώθ· πλήρης ὁ οὐρανὸς καὶ ἡ γῆ τῆς δόξης σου.

Ὡσαννὰ ἐν τοῖς ὑψίστοις·

Εὐλογημένος ὁ ἐρχόμενος ἐν Ὀνόματι Κυρίου·

Ὡσαννὰ ὁ ἐν τοῖς ὑψίστοις.

Ἐνταῦθα ὁ Διάκονος τὰ αὐτὰ ποιεῖ, ὡς ἐν τῇ τοῦ Χρυσοστόμου Λειτουργίᾳ.

Ὁ δὲ Ἱερεὺς ἐπεύχεται μυστικῶς·

With these blessed Powers, O Master, lover of man, we also, sinners, cry aloud and say: Holy art thou, indeed, and all-holy, and there is no measure of the majesty of thy holiness; and pure in all thy works, for in righteousness and true judgement hast thou brought all things upon us: for having fashioned man, taking clay from the earth, and honouring him, O God, with thine own image, thou didst place him in the Paradise of pleasure, promising him immortality of life, and enjoyment of eternal good things, in the keeping of thy commandments; but when he disobeyed thee the true God, that created him, and was led astray by the guile of the serpent, and subjected to death by his own transgressions, thou didst banish him in thy righteous judgement, O God, from the Paradise into this world, and madest him return to the earth whence he was taken, providing for him the salvation of regeneration, which is in thy Christ himself. For thou didst not turn away utterly from thy creature which thou madest, O Good One, nor forget the work of thy hands, but didst visit it in divers manners through the bowels of thy mercy: thou didst send forth Prophets; thou wroughtest mighty things through thy Saints that were pleasing to thee in each generation; thou spakest to us by the mouth of thy servants the Prophets, foretelling us the salvation to come; thou gavest a law for help; thou didst appoint Angels as Guardians. But when the fulness of the times came, thou spakest to us in thy Son himself,

Μετὰ τούτων τῶν μακαρίων Δυνάμεων, Δέσποτα φιλάνθρωπε, καὶ ἡμεῖς οἱ ἁμαρτωλοὶ βοῶμεν καὶ λέγομεν· Ἅγιος εἶ, ὡς ἀληθῶς, καὶ πανάγιος, καὶ οὐκ ἔστι μέτρον τῇ μεγαλοπρεπείᾳ τῆς ἁγιωσύνης σου, καὶ ὅσιος ἐν πᾶσι τοῖς ἔργοις σου, ὅτι ἐν δικαιοσύνῃ καὶ κρίσει ἀληθινῇ πάντα ἐπήγαγες ἡμῖν· πλάσας γὰρ τὸν ἄνθρωπον, χοῦν λαβὼν ἀπὸ τῆς γῆς, καὶ εἰκόνι τῇ σῇ, ὁ Θεός, τιμήσας, τέθεικας αὐτὸν ἐν τῷ Παραδείσῳ τῆς τρυφῆς, ἀθανασίαν ζωῆς καὶ ἀπόλαυσιν αἰωνίων ἀγαθῶν, ἐν τῇ τηρήσει τῶν ἐντολῶν σου, ἐπαγγειλάμενος αὐτῷ· ἀλλὰ παρακούσαντα σοῦ τοῦ ἀληθινοῦ Θεοῦ, τοῦ κτίσαντος αὐτόν, καὶ τῇ ἀπάτῃ τοῦ ὄφεως ὑπαχθέντα, νεκρωθέντα τε τοῖς οἰκείοις αὐτοῦ παραπτώμασιν, ἐξώρισας αὐτὸν ἐν τῇ δικαιοκρισίᾳ σου, ὁ Θεός, ἐκ τοῦ Παραδείσου εἰς τὸν κόσμον τοῦτον, καὶ ἀπέστρεψας εἰς τὴν γῆν, ἐξ ἧς ἐλήφθη, οἰκονομῶν αὐτῷ τὴν ἐκ παλιγγενεσίας σωτηρίαν, τὴν ἐν αὐτῷ τῷ Χριστῷ σου. Οὐ γὰρ ἀπεστράφης τὸ πλάσμα σου εἰς τέλος, ὃ ἐποίησας, Ἀγαθέ, οὐδὲ ἐπελάθου ἔργου χειρῶν σου, ἀλλ' ἐπεσκέψω πολυτρόπως διὰ σπλάγχνα ἐλέους σου· Προφήτας ἐξαπέστειλας· ἐποίησας δυνάμεις διὰ τῶν Ἁγίων σου, τῶν καθ' ἑκάστην γενεὰν εὐαρεστησάντων σοι· ἐλάλησας ἡμῖν διὰ στόματος τῶν δούλων σου τῶν Προφητῶν, προκαταγγέλλων ἡμῖν τὴν μέλλουσαν ἔσεσθαι σωτηρίαν· νόμον ἔδωκας εἰς βοήθειαν· Ἀγγέλους ἐπέστησας φύλακας. Ὅτε δὲ ἦλθε τὸ πλήρωμα τῶν καιρῶν, ἐλάλησας ἡμῖν ἐν αὐτῷ τῷ Υἱῷ σου, δι' οὗ καὶ τοὺς αἰῶνας ἐποίησας· ὃς, ὢν ἀπαύγασμα

through whom thou madest the ages also: who, being the effulgence of thy glory, and the impress of thy hypostasis, and upholding all things by the word of his power, deemed it not usurpation to be equal to thee, the God and Father; but, being God before the ages, appeared upon the earth, and mingled with men; and incarnate of a holy Virgin, emptied himself, taking the form of a servant, becoming conformable to the body of our lowliness, that he might make us conformable to the image of his glory. For since through man sin entered into the world, and through sin death, it pleased thine Only-begotten Son, that is in the bosom of thee, the God and Father, become of a woman, the holy Theotokos, and ever-virgin Mary, become under the law, to condemn sin in his flesh; that they who died in Adam, might be made alive in thy Christ himself; and dwelling in this world, giving precepts of salvation, and withdrawing us from the error of idols, he brought us to the knowledge of thee, the true God and Father, having acquired us to himself for a peculiar people, a royal priesthood, a holy nation; and having cleansed us in water, and hallowed us by the Holy Spirit, he gave himself a ransom to death, wherein we were held, sold under sin; and descending through the Cross into Hades, that he might fill all things with himself, he loosed the pains of death; and rising again the third day, and making for all flesh a way to the resurrection from the dead (because it was not possible that

τῆς δόξης σου, καὶ χαρακτὴρ τῆς ὑποστάσεώς σου, φέρων τε τὰ πάντα τῷ ῥήματι τῆς δυνάμεως αὐτοῦ, οὐχ ἁρπαγμὸν ἡγήσατο τὸ εἶναι ἴσα σοὶ τῷ Θεῷ καὶ Πατρί· ἀλλὰ, Θεὸς ὢν προαιώνιος, ἐπὶ τῆς γῆς ὤφθη, καὶ τοῖς ἀνθρώποις συνανεστράφη· καὶ ἐκ Παρθένου ἁγίας σαρκωθείς, ἐκένωσεν ἑαυτόν, μορφὴν δούλου λαβών, σύμμορφος γενόμενος τῷ σώματι τῆς ταπεινώσεως ἡμῶν, ἵνα ἡμᾶς συμμόρφους ποιήσῃ τῆς εἰκόνος τῆς δόξης αὐτοῦ. Ἐπειδὴ γὰρ δι᾽ ἀνθρώπου ἡ ἁμαρτία εἰσῆλθεν εἰς τὸν κόσμον, καὶ διὰ τῆς ἁμαρτίας ὁ θάνατος, εὐδόκησεν ὁ Μονογενής σου Υἱός, ὁ ὢν ἐν τοῖς κόλποις σοῦ τοῦ Θεοῦ καὶ Πατρός, γενόμενος ἐκ γυναικός, τῆς ἁγίας Θεοτόκου, καὶ ἀειπαρθένου Μαρίας, γενόμενος ὑπὸ νόμον, κατακρῖναι τὴν ἁμαρτίαν ἐν τῇ σαρκὶ αὐτοῦ· ἵνα οἱ ἐν τῷ Ἀδὰμ ἀποθνῄσκοντες, ζωοποιηθῶσιν ἐν αὐτῷ τῷ Χριστῷ σου· καὶ ἐμπολιτευσάμενος τῷ κόσμῳ τούτῳ, δοὺς προστάγματα σωτηρίας, ἀποστήσας ἡμᾶς τῆς πλάνης τῶν εἰδώλων, προσήγαγε τῇ ἐπιγνώσει σοῦ τοῦ ἀληθινοῦ Θεοῦ καὶ Πατρός, κτησάμενος ἡμᾶς ἑαυτῷ λαὸν περιούσιον, βασίλειον ἱεράτευμα, ἔθνος ἅγιον· καὶ καθαρίσας ἐν ὕδατι, καὶ ἁγιάσας τῷ Πνεύματι τῷ Ἁγίῳ, ἔδωκεν ἑαυτὸν ἀντάλλαγμα τῷ θανάτῳ, ἐν ᾧ κατειχόμεθα πεπραμένοι ὑπὸ τὴν ἁμαρτίαν· καὶ κατελθὼν διὰ τοῦ Σταυροῦ εἰς τὴν Ἅδην, ἵνα πληρώσῃ ἑαυτοῦ τὰ πάντα, ἔλυσε τὰς ὀδύνας τοῦ θανάτου· καὶ ἀναστὰς τῇ τρίτῃ ἡμέρᾳ, καὶ ὁδοποιήσας πάσῃ σαρκὶ τὴν ἐκ νεκρῶν ἀνάστασιν (καθότι οὐκ ἦν δυνατὸν κρατεῖσθαι ὑπὸ τῆς φθορᾶς τὸν

the author of life, should be holden of corruption), he became the first-fruits of those that have fallen asleep, the first-born from the dead, that he might be in all things first among all; and ascending into the heavens, he sat down at the right hand of thy majesty in the highest; who shall also come to render to each one according to his works. But he hath left us as memorials of his saving Passion, these, which we have set forth, according to his commandments; for being about to go forth to his voluntary, and famous, and life-giving death, in the night wherein he gave himself up for the life of the world, taking bread into his holy and undefiled hands, and shewing it to thee, the God and Father, and giving thanks, blessing, hallowing, breaking,

Then aloud:

He gave to his holy Disciples and Apostles, saying: Take, eat ye: this is my Body, which for you is broken, unto remission of sins.
The Choir: Amen.

And the Priest secretly:

In like manner taking the Chalice also of the fruit of the vine, mingling it, giving thanks, blessing, hallowing

Then aloud:

He gave to his holy Disciples and Apostles, saying: Drink ye all of it: this is my Blood, of the new testament, which for you and for many is poured out, unto remission of sins.
The Choir: Amen.

ἀρχηγὸν τῆς ζωῆς), ἐγένετο ἀπαρχὴ τῶν κεκοιμημένων, πρωτότοκος ἐκ τῶν νεκρῶν, ἵνα ἦ αὐτὸς τὰ πάντα ἐν πᾶσι πρωτεύων· καὶ ἀνελθὼν εἰς τοὺς οὐρανούς, ἐκάθισεν ἐν δεξιᾷ τῆς μεγαλωσύνης σου ἐν ὑψηλοῖς· ὃς καὶ ἥξει ἀποδοῦναι ἑκάστῳ κατὰ τὰ ἔργα αὐτοῦ. Κατέλιπε δὲ ἡμῖν ὑπομνήματα τοῦ σωτηρίου αὐτοῦ Πάθους, ταῦτα, ἃ προτεθείκαμεν, κατὰ τὰς αὐτοῦ ἐντολάς· μέλλων γὰρ ἐξιέναι ἐπὶ τὸν ἑκούσιον, καὶ ἀοίδιμον, καὶ ζωοποιὸν αὐτοῦ θάνατον, τῇ νυκτὶ ἦ παρεδίδου ἑαυτὸν ὑπὲρ τῆς τοῦ κόσμου ζωῆς, λαβὼν ἄρτον ἐπὶ τῶν ἁγίων αὐτοῦ καὶ ἀχράντων χειρῶν, καὶ ἀναδείξας σοὶ τῷ Θεῷ καὶ Πατρί, καὶ εὐχαριστήσας, εὐλογήσας, ἁγιάσας, κλάσας,

Εἶτα ἐκφώνως·

Ἔδωκε τοῖς ἁγίοις αὐτοῦ Μαθηταῖς καὶ Ἀποστόλοις, εἰπών· Λάβετε, φάγετε· τοῦτό μου ἐστι τὸ Σῶμα, τὸ ὑπὲρ ὑμῶν κλώμενον, εἰς ἄφεσιν ἁμαρτιῶν.
Ὁ Χορός· Ἀμήν.

Ὁ δὲ Ἱερεὺς μυστικῶς·

Ὁμοίως καὶ τὸ Ποτήριον ἐκ τοῦ γεννήματος τῆς ἀμπέλου λαβών, κεράσας, εὐχαριστήσας, εὐλογήσας, ἁγιάσας,

Εἶτα ἐκφώνως·

Ἔδωκε τοῖς ἁγίοις αὐτοῦ Μαθηταῖς καὶ Ἀποστόλοις, εἰπών· Πίετε ἐξ αὐτοῦ πάντες· τοῦτό ἐστι τὸ Αἷμά μου, τὸ τῆς καινῆς διαθήκης, τὸ ὑπὲρ ὑμῶν καὶ πολλῶν ἐκχυνόμενον, εἰς ἄφεσιν ἁμαρτιῶν·
Ὁ Χορός· Ἀμήν.

This do ye in remembrance of me: for as often as ye eat this Bread, and drink this Chalice, ye proclaim my death, and confess my Resurrection.

Wherefore, O Master, we also, having in remembrance his saving Passion, the life-giving Cross, the three days Burial, the Resurrection from the dead, the Ascension into the heavens, the Session at the right hand of thee, the God and Father, and his glorious and fearful second Coming,

Aloud:

Thine own of thine own do offer to thee, in behalf of all, and for all.

The Choir: Thee we hymn, thee we bless, to thee we give thanks, O Lord, and beseech thee, our God.

The Priest, bowing his head prayeth secretly:

Therefore, O all-holy Master, we also, sinners, and thine unworthy servants, who have been vouchsafed to minister at thy holy Altar, not through our righteousness (for we have done nothing good upon the earth), but through thy mercies and thy compassions, which thou hast richly poured out upon us, taking courage, draw near to thy holy Altar; and presenting the antitypes of the holy Body and Blood of thy Christ, beseech thee, and implore thee, O Saint of Saints, by the good will of thy goodness, for thy Holy Spirit to come upon us, and upon

---

Ὁ Ἱερεὺς ἐπεύχεται μυστικῶς·

Τοῦτο ποιεῖτε εἰς τὴν ἐμὴν ἀνάμνησιν· ὁσάκις γὰρ ἂν ἐσθίητε τὸν Ἄρτον τοῦτον, καὶ τὸ Ποτήριον τοῦτο πίνητε, τὸν ἐμὸν θάνατον καταγγέλλετε, καὶ τὴν ἐμὴν ἀνάστασιν ὁμολογεῖτε·

Μεμνημένοι οὖν, Δέσποτα, καὶ ἡμεῖς τῶν σωτηρίων αὐτοῦ Παθημάτων, τοῦ ζωοποιοῦ Σταυροῦ, τῆς τριημέρου Ταφῆς, τῆς ἐκ νεκρῶν Ἀναστάσεως, τῆς εἰς οὐρανοὺς Ἀνόδου, τῆς ἐκ δεξιῶν σοῦ τοῦ Θεοῦ καὶ Πατρὸς Καθέδρας, καὶ τῆς ἐνδόξου καὶ φοβερᾶς δευτέρας αὐτοῦ παρουσίας,

Ἐκφώνως·

Τὰ σὰ ἐκ τῶν σῶν σοὶ προσφέρομεν κατὰ πάντα, καὶ διὰ πάντα.

Ὁ Χορός· Σὲ ὑμνοῦμεν, σὲ εὐλογοῦμεν, σοὶ εὐχαριστοῦμεν, Κύριε, καὶ δεόμεθά σου, ὁ Θεὸς ἡμῶν.

Ὁ Ἱερεύς, κλίνας τὴν κεφαλήν, ἐπεύχεται μυστικῶς·

Διὰ τοῦτο, Δέσποτα πανάγιε, καὶ ἡμεῖς οἱ ἁμαρτωλοὶ καὶ ἀνάξιοι δοῦλοί σου, οἱ καταξιωθέντες λειτουργεῖν τῷ ἁγίῳ σου Θυσιαστηρίῳ, οὐ διὰ τὰς δικαιοσύνας ἡμῶν (οὐ γὰρ ἐποιήσαμέν τι ἀγαθὸν ἐπὶ τῆς γῆς), ἀλλὰ διὰ τὰ ἐλέη σου καὶ τοὺς οἰκτιρμούς σου, οὓς ἐξέχεας πλουσίως ἐφ᾿ ἡμᾶς, θαρροῦντες προσεγγίζομεν τῷ ἁγίῳ σου Θυσιαστηρίῳ· καὶ προθέντες τὰ ἀντίτυπα τοῦ ἁγίου Σώματος καὶ Αἵματος τοῦ Χριστοῦ σου, σοῦ δεόμεθα, καὶ σὲ παρακαλοῦμεν, Ἅγιε Ἁγίων, εὐδοκίᾳ τῆς σῆς ἀγαθότητος, ἐλθεῖν τὸ Πνεῦμά σου τὸ Ἅγιον ἐφ᾿ ἡμᾶς, καὶ

these laid out Gifts, and bless them, and hallow, and make—

The Deacon putteth down the Fan, which he was holding (or the Veil), and cometh nearer to the Priest; and bowing his head, pointeth with his Orarion to the holy Bread, saying secretly:

Bless, Master, the holy Bread.

And the Priest, standing erect, thrice signeth the holy Gifts with the sign of the Cross;—first holy Bread, saying:

This Bread the precious Body itself of our Lord, and God, and Saviour Jesus Christ,

The Deacon: Amen.

And again, pointing with his Orarion to the holy Chalice:

Bless, Master, the holy Chalice.

And the Priest, blessing, saith:

And this Chalice, the precious Blood itself of our Lord, and God, and Saviour Jesus Christ,

The Deacon: Amen.

And again, pointing with his Orarion to both the holy Things:

Bless, Master, both.

And the Priest, blessing both, saith:

Which was poured out for the life and salvation of the world,

The Deacon: Amen. Amen. Amen.

And having bowed his head to the Priest, and said, Be mindful, holy Master, of me a sinner.

ἐπὶ τὰ προκείμενα Δῶρα ταῦτα, καὶ εὐλογῆσαι αὐτά, καὶ ἁγιάσαι, καὶ ἀναδεῖξαι —

Ὁ Διάκονος ἀποτίθησι τὸ Ῥιπίδιον, ὅπερ ἐκράτει (ἢ Κάλυμμα), καὶ ἔρχεται ἐγγύτερον τοῦ Ἱερέως· καὶ ὑποκλίνας τὴν κεφαλήν, δεικνύει τῷ Ὠραρίῳ τὸν ἅγιον Ἄρτον, καὶ λέγει μυστικῶς·

Εὐλόγησον, Δέσποτα, τὸν ἅγιον Ἄρτον.

Καὶ ὁ Ἱερεύς, ἀνιστάμενος, σφραγίζει τρὶς τὰ ἅγια Δῶρα· πρῶτον τὸν ἅγιον Ἄρτον, λέγων·

Τὸν μὲν Ἄρτον τοῦτον, αὐτὸ τὸ τίμιον Σῶμα τοῦ Κυρίου, καὶ Θεοῦ, καὶ Σωτῆρος ἡμῶν Ἰησοῦ Χριστοῦ,

Ὁ Διάκονος· Ἀμήν.

Καὶ αὖθις ὁ αὐτός, δεικνύων σὺν τῷ Ὠραρίῳ τὸ ἅγιον Ποτήριον·

Εὐλόγησον, Δέσποτα, τὸ ἅγιον Ποτήριον.

Ὁ δὲ Ἱερεὺς εὐλογῶν, λέγει·

Τὸ δὲ Ποτήριον τοῦτο, αὐτὸ τὸ τίμιον Αἷμα τοῦ Κυρίου, καὶ Θεοῦ, καὶ Σωτῆρος ἡμῶν Ἰησοῦ Χριστοῦ,

Ὁ Διάκονος· Ἀμήν.

Καὶ τρίτον ὁ αὐτός, δεικνύων μετὰ τοῦ Ὠραρίου ἀμφότερα τὰ Ἅγια·

Εὐλόγησον Δέσποτα, τὰ ἀμφότερα.

Καὶ ὁ Ἱερεὺς εὐλογῶν ἀμφότερα, λέγει·

Τὸ ἐκχυθὲν ὑπὲρ τῆς τοῦ κόσμου ζωῆς καὶ σωτηρίας,

Ὁ Διάκονος· Ἀμήν. Ἀμήν. Ἀμήν.

Καὶ τὴν κεφαλὴν ὑποκλίνας τῷ Ἱερεῖ, καὶ εἰπὼν τό, Μνήσθητί μου, ἅγιε Δέσποτα, τοῦ ἁμαρτωλοῦ, μεθίστα-

he shifteth to the place where he stood before, taking withal the Fan again, as before.

And the Priest prayeth:

And to unite us all, that partake of the one Bread and of the Chalice, to one another unto communion of the one Holy Spirit, and cause that none of us may partake of the holy Body and Blood of thy Christ unto judgement, or unto condemnation; but that we may find mercy and grace with all the Saints that have ever pleased thee, Forefathers, Fathers, Patriarchs, Prophets, Apostles, Preachers, Evangelists, Martyrs, Confessors, Teachers, and every righteous spirit in faith made perfect:

Then censing the holy Table in the front, he saith aloud:

Especially our All-holy, undefiled, exceedingly blessed, glorious Lady, Theotokos, and ever-virgin, Mary:

The Choir singeth:

In thee rejoiceth, O full of grace, the whole creation, the system of Angels, and the race of men, thou hallowed Temple, and rational Paradise, glory of virgins, of whom God was incarnate, and became a little child, our God who is before the ages; for thy womb he made a throne, and thy belly he rendered wider than the heavens. In thee rejoiceth, O full of grace, the whole creation: glory to thee.

ται ἐν ᾧ πρότερον ἵστατο τόπῳ, λαβὼν καὶ τὸ Ῥιπίδιον αὖθις, ὡς πρότερον.

Ὁ δὲ Ἱερεὺς ἐπεύχεται μυστικῶς·

Ἡμᾶς δὲ πάντας, τοὺς ἐκ τοῦ ἑνὸς Ἄρτου καὶ τοῦ Ποτηρίου μετέχοντας, ἑνώσαι ἀλλήλοις εἰς ἑνὸς Πνεύματος Ἁγίου κοινωνίαν, καὶ μηδένα ἡμῶν εἰς κρίμα, ἢ εἰς κατάκριμα ποιῆσαι μετασχεῖν τοῦ ἁγίου Σώματος καὶ Αἵματος τοῦ Χριστοῦ σου· ἀλλ' ἵνα εὕρωμεν ἔλεον καὶ χάριν μετὰ πάντων τῶν Ἁγίων, τῶν ἀπ' αἰῶνός σοι εὐαρεστησάντων, Προπατόρων, Πατέρων, Πατριαρχῶν, Προφητῶν, Ἀποστόλων, Κηρύκων, Εὐαγγελιστῶν, Μαρτύρων, Ὁμολογητῶν, Διδασκάλων, καὶ παντὸς πνεύματος δικαίου ἐν πίστει τετελειωμένου·

Εἶτα θυμιῶν τὴν ἁγίαν Τράπεζαν κατέμπροσθεν, λέγει ἐκφώνως·

Ἐξαιρέτως τῆς Παναγίας, ἀχράντου, ὑπερευλογημένης, ἐνδόξου, Δεσποίνης ἡμῶν Θεοτόκου, καὶ ἀειπαρθένου Μαρίας·

Ὁ Χορὸς ψάλλει·

Ἐπὶ σοὶ χαίρει, Κεχαριτωμένη, πᾶσα ἡ κτίσις, Ἀγγέλων τὸ σύστημα, καὶ ἀνθρώπων τὸ γένος, ἡγιασμένε Ναέ, καὶ Παράδεισε λογικέ, παρθενικὸν καύχημα, ἐξ ἧς Θεὸς ἐσαρκώθη, καὶ παιδίον γέγονεν, ὁ πρὸ αἰώνων ὑπάρχων Θεὸς ἡμῶν· τὴν γὰρ σὴν μήτραν θρόνον ἐποίησε, καὶ τὴν σὴν γαστέρα πλατυτέραν οὐρανῶν ἀπειργάσατο. Ἐπὶ σοὶ χαίρει, Κεχαριτωμένη, πᾶσα ἡ κτίσις· δόξα σοι,

Εἰ δέ ἐστιν ἡ Μεγάλη Πέμπτη·

Τοῦ Δείπνου σου τοῦ μυστικοῦ ("Ορα σελ. 348).

Εἰ δέ ἐστι τὸ Μέγα Σάββατον·

Σιγησάτω πᾶσα σάρξ βροτεία ("Ορα σελ. 348).

Ὁ Διάκονος, λαβὼν παρὰ τοῦ Ἱερέως τὸ Θυμιατήριον, θυμιᾷ τὴν ἁγίαν Τράπεζαν κύκλῳ· ὕστερον δὲ μνημονεύει τὰ Δίπτυχα τῶν Κεκοιμημένων. Μνημονεύει δὲ καθ' ἑαυτὸν καὶ ὧν βούλεται, Ζώντων καὶ τεθνεώτων.

Ὁ δὲ Ἱερεὺς ἐπεύχεται μυστικῶς·

Τοῦ ἁγίου Ἰωάννου, Προφήτου, Προδρόμου, καὶ Βαπτιστοῦ· τῶν ἁγίων ἐνδόξων καὶ πανευφήμων Ἀποστόλων· τοῦ Ἁγίου (τοῦ δεῖνος), οὗ καὶ τὴν μνήμην ἐπιτελοῦμεν, καὶ πάντων σου τῶν Ἁγίων· ὧν ταῖς ἱκεσίαις ἐπίσκεψαι ἡμᾶς, ὁ Θεός· καὶ μνήσθητι πάντων τῶν προκεκοιμημένων ἐπ' ἐλπίδι ἀναστάσεως ζωῆς αἰωνίου (μνημονεύει ὧν βούλεται ὀνόματα τεθνεώτων), καὶ ἀνάπαυσον αὐτούς, ὅπου ἐπισκοπεῖ τὸ φῶς τοῦ προσώπου σου.

Ἔτι σοῦ δεόμεθα· Μνήσθητι, Κύριε, τῆς ἁγίας σου Καθολικῆς καὶ Ἀποστολικῆς Ἐκκλησίας, τῆς ἀπὸ περάτων ἕως περάτων τῆς οἰκουμένης, καὶ εἰρήνευσον αὐτήν, ἣν περιεποιήσω τῷ τιμίῳ Αἵματι τοῦ Χριστοῦ σου· καὶ τὸν ἅγιον Οἶκον τοῦτον στερέωσον μέχρι τῆς συντελείας τοῦ αἰῶνος.

Μνήσθητι, Κύριε, τῶν τὰ Δῶρά σοι ταῦτα προσκομισάντων, καὶ ὑπὲρ ὧν, καὶ δι' ὧν, καὶ ἐφ' οἷς αὐτὰ προσεκόμισαν.

But if it be the Great Fifth-day:
Of thy mystic Supper (See page 349).
But if the Great Sabbath:

Let all mortal flesh be (See page 349).
The Deacon, receiving the Censer from the Priest, censeth the holy Table all round; and finally commemorateth the Dyptichs of those that have fallen asleep. And to himself he maketh mention of such also as he pleaseth, living and dead.

And the Priest prayeth secretly:

The holy John, Prophet, Precursor, and Baptist; the holy, glorious and all-famous Apostles; Saint N, whose memory also we celebrate, and all thy Saints; at whose supplications, visit us, O God: and be mindful of all those that have heretofore fallen asleep in the hope of a resurrection to life eternal (here by name he maketh mention also of such of the dead as he pleaseth), and give them repose, where the light of Thy countenance beholdeth.

Again, we beseech thee:—Be mindful, O Lord, of thy holy Catholic and Apostolic Church, which is from end to end of the universe, and give peace to her, whom thou hast purchased with the precious Blood of thy Christ, and stablish this holy House until the end of the world.

Be mindful, O Lord, of those that have offered to thee these holy Gifts, and of those for whom, and through whom, and on account of whom they have offered them.

24

Be mindful, O Lord, of those that bear fruit and do good works in thy holy Churches, and are mindful of the poor: recompense them with thy rich and heavenly graces; bestow on them heavenly things for things earthly, eternal things for things temporal, incorruptible things for things corruptible.

Be mindful, O Lord, of those that are in deserts, and mountains, and dens, and caves of the earth.

Be mindful, O Lord, of those that live in virginity, and reverence, and asceticism, and grave manner of life.

Be mindful, O Lord, of our most pious and faithful Kings, whom thou hast given the right to reign upon the earth: crown them with the shield of truth, with the shield of good will; overshadow their head in the day of battle; strengthen their arm; exalt their right hand; confirm their kingdom; subdue beneath them all the barbarous nations, which desire war; bestow on them profound and inviolate peace; speak good things to their heart for thy Church and all thy people; that in their calm, we may lead a tranquil and quiet life, in all piety and gravity.

Be mindful, O Lord, of every Principality and Authority; also of our brethren in the Palace, and of all the Army: preserve the good in thy goodness; make the evil to be good in thy beneficence.

Μνήσθητι, Κύριε, τῶν καρποφορούντων καὶ καλλιεργούντων ἐν ταῖς ἁγίαις σου Ἐκκλησίαις, καὶ μεμνημένων τῶν πενήτων· ἄμειψαι αὐτοὺς τοῖς πλουσίοις σου καὶ ἐπουρανίοις χαρίσμασι· χάρισαι αὐτοῖς ἀντὶ τῶν ἐπιγείων τὰ ἐπουράνια, ἀντὶ τῶν προσκαίρων τὰ αἰώνια, ἀντὶ τῶν φθαρτῶν τὰ ἄφθαρτα.

Μνήσθητι, Κύριε, τῶν ἐν ἐρημίαις, καὶ ὄρεσι, καὶ σπηλαίοις, καὶ ταῖς ὀπαῖς τῆς γῆς.

Μνήσθητι, Κύριε, τῶν ἐν παρθενίᾳ, καὶ εὐλαβείᾳ, καὶ ἀσκήσει, καὶ σεμνῇ πολιτείᾳ διαγόντων.

Μνήσθητι, Κύριε, τῶν εὐσεβεστάτων καὶ πιστοτάτων ἡμῶν Βασιλέων, οὓς ἐδικαίωσας βασιλεύειν ἐπὶ τῆς γῆς· ὅπλῳ ἀληθείας, ὅπλῳ εὐδοκίας στεφάνωσον αὐτούς· ἐπισκίασον ἐπὶ τὴν κεφαλὴν αὐτῶν ἐν ἡμέρᾳ πολέμου· ἐνίσχυσον αὐτῶν τὸν βραχίονα· ὕψωσον αὐτῶν τὴν δεξιάν· κράτυνον αὐτῶν τὴν βασιλείαν· ὑπόταξον αὐτοῖς πάντα τὰ βάρβαρα ἔθνη, τὰ τοὺς πολέμους θέλοντα· χάρισαι αὐτοῖς βαθεῖαν καὶ ἀναφαίρετον εἰρήνην· λάλησον εἰς τὴν καρδίαν αὐτῶν ἀγαθὰ ὑπὲρ τῆς Ἐκκλησίας σου, καὶ παντὸς τοῦ λαοῦ σου· ἵνα ἐν τῇ γαλήνῃ αὐτῶν ἤρεμον καὶ ἡσύχιον βίον διάγωμεν, ἐν πάσῃ εὐσεβείᾳ καὶ σεμνότητι.

Μνήσθητι, Κύριε, πάσης Ἀρχῆς καὶ Ἐξουσίας, καὶ τῶν ἐν τῷ Παλατίῳ ἀδελφῶν ἡμῶν, καὶ παντὸς τοῦ Στρατοπέδου· τοὺς ἀγαθούς, ἐν τῇ ἀγαθότητί σου διατήρησον· τοὺς πονηρούς, ἀγαθοὺς ποίησον ἐν τῇ χρηστότητί σου.

Be mindful, O Lord, of the people standing around, and of those that are absent through reasonable causes, and have mercy on them and on us, according to the multitude of thy mercy: fill their store-chambers with every good thing; preserve their unions in peace and concord; rear up the babes; guide the youth; support the aged; encourage the faint-hearted; collect the scattered; bring back the wandering, and unite them to thy holy Catholic and Apostolic Church; free those that are vexed with unclean spirits; voyage with those that voyage; travel with those that travel; defend the widows; shield the orphans; deliver the captives; heal the sick. Of those that are in tribunals, and mines, and exile, and bitter slavery, and all affliction, and necessity, and distress, be mindful, O God, and of all that beseech thy great tenderness of heart; also of those that love us, and of those that hate us, and of those that have enjoined us, unworthy as we are, to pray for them. And of all thy people be mindful, O Lord our God, and up-on all pour out thy rich mercy, granting to all their petitions unto salvation. And of whom we have not been mindful through ignorance, or forgetfulness, or multitude of names, be thou thyself mindful, O God, who knowest the age and the appellation of each one, who knowest each one from his mother's womb. For thou, O Lord, art the helper of the helpless, the hope of the hopeless, the saviour of the tempest-tost, the harbour of the voyager, the healer of the

Μνήσθητι, Κύριε, τοῦ περιεστῶτος λαοῦ, καὶ τῶν δι εὐλόγους αἰτίας ἀπολειφθέντων, καὶ ἐλέησον αὐτοὺς καὶ ἡμᾶς, κατὰ τὸ πλῆθος τοῦ ἐλέους σου· τὰ ταμεῖα αὐτῶν ἔμπλησον παντὸς ἀγαθοῦ· τὰς συζυγίας αὐτῶν ἐν εἰρήνῃ καὶ ὁμονοίᾳ διατήρησον· τὰ νήπια ἔκθρεψον· τὴν νεό-τητα παιδαγώγησον· τὸ γῆρας περικράτησον· τοὺς ὀλι-γοψύχους παραμύθησαι· τοὺς ἐσκορπισμένους ἐπισυνά-γαγε· τοὺς πεπλανημένους ἐπανάγαγε, καὶ σύναψον τῇ ἁγίᾳ σου Καθολικῇ καὶ 'Αποστολικῇ 'Εκκλησίᾳ· τοὺς ὀχλουμένους ὑπὸ πνευμάτων ἀκαθάρτων ἐλευθέρωσον· τοῖς πλέουσι σύμπλευσον· τοῖς ὁδοιποροῦσι συνόδευσον· χηρῶν πρόστηθι· ὀρφανῶν ὑπεράσπισον· αἰχμαλώτους ῥῦσαι· νοσοῦντας ἴασαι. Τῶν ἐν βήμασι, καὶ μετάλλοις, καὶ ἐξορίαις, καὶ πικραῖς δουλείαις, καὶ πάσῃ θλίψει, καὶ ἀνάγκῃ, καὶ περιστάσει ὄντων, μνημόνευσον, ὁ Θεός, καὶ πάντων τῶν δεομένων τῆς μεγάλης σου εὐσπλαγχνίας· καὶ τῶν ἀγαπώντων ἡμᾶς, καὶ τῶν μισούντων, καὶ τῶν ἐντειλαμένων ἡμῖν τοῖς ἀναξίοις εὔχεσθαι ὑπὲρ αὐτῶν. Καὶ παντὸς τοῦ λαοῦ σου μνήσθητι, Κύριε ὁ Θεὸς ἡμῶν, καὶ ἐπὶ πάντας ἔκχεον τὸ πλούσιόν σου ἔλεος, πᾶσι παρέχων τὰ πρὸς σωτηρίαν αἰτήματα. Καὶ ὧν ἡμεῖς οὐκ ἐμνημονεύσαμεν δι ἄγνοιαν, ἢ λήθην, ἢ πλῆθος ὀνομά-των, αὐτὸς μνημόνευσον, ὁ Θεός, ὁ εἰδὼς ἑκάστου τὴν ἡλικίαν καὶ τὴν προσηγορίαν, ὁ εἰδὼς ἕκαστον ἐκ κοι-λίας μητρὸς αὐτοῦ. Σὺ γὰρ εἶ, Κύριε, ἡ βοήθεια τῶν ἀβοηθήτων, ἡ ἐλπὶς τῶν ἀπηλπισμένων, ὁ τῶν χειμα-ζομένων σωτήρ, ὁ τῶν πλεόντων λιμήν, ὁ τῶν νοσούν-

sick: be thou thyself all things to all men, who knowest each one, and his petition, each house, and its need. Deliver, O Lord, this City (or, Abode), and every city, and country, from famine, plague, earthquake, flood, fire, sword, incursion of foreigners, and civil war.

Then he saith aloud:

Among the first be mindful, O Lord, of our Archbishop N., whom grant to thy holy Churches in peace, safe, honoured, healthful, attaining to length of days, and rightly dividing the word of thy truth.

And the Deacon, standing by the Door, saith: Of N., the all-sacred Metropolitan (or, Bishop as the case may be).

And for him that offereth these holy Gifts, &c., as far as, and for all, men and women.

The Choir: And for all, men and women.

And the Priest prayeth secretly:

Be mindful, O Lord, of every Bishopric of the Orthodox, who rightly divide the word of thy truth.

Be mindful, O Lord, according to the multitude of thy compassions, of my unworthiness also: forgive me every transgression, voluntary and involuntary, and do not, on account of my sins, withhold the grace of thy Holy Spirit from these laid out Gifts.

Be mindful, O Lord, of the Presbytery, of the Diaconate in Christ, and of every Sacer-

των ἰατρός· αὐτὸς τοῖς πᾶσι τὰ πάντα γενοῦ, ὁ εἰδὼς ἕκαστον, καὶ τὸ αἴτημα αὐτοῦ, οἶκον, καὶ τὴν χρείαν αὐτοῦ. Ῥῦσαι, Κύριε, τὴν Πόλιν (ἢ, τὴν Μονὴν) ταύτην, καὶ πᾶσαν πόλιν, καὶ χώραν, ἀπὸ λιμοῦ, λοιμοῦ, σεισμοῦ, καταποντισμοῦ, πυρός, μαχαίρας, ἐπιδρομῆς ἀλλοφύλων, καὶ ἐμφυλίου πολέμου.

Εἶτα ἐκφωνεῖ·

Ἐν πρώτοις μνήσθητι, Κύριε, τοῦ Ἀρχιεπισκόπου ἡμῶν (τοῦ δεῖνος)· ὃν χάρισαι ταῖς ἁγίαις σου Ἐκκλησίαις ἐν εἰρήνη, σῶον, ἔντιμον, ὑγιᾶ, μακροημερεύοντα, καὶ ὀρθοτομοῦντα τὸν λόγον τῆς σῆς ἀληθείας.

Καὶ ὁ Διάκονος λέγει, πρὸς τῇ Θύρᾳ στάς·
(Τοῦ δεῖνος) Πανιερωτάτου Μητροπολίτου (ἢ, Ἐπισκόπου ὅστις ἂν ᾖ).

Καὶ ὑπὲρ τοῦ προσκομίζοντος τὰ ἅγια Δῶρα ταῦτα· καὶ τὰ λοιπὰ μέχρι τοῦ, καὶ πάντων καὶ πασῶν.
Ὁ Χορός· Καὶ πάντων καὶ πασῶν.

Ὁ δὲ Ἱερεὺς ἐπεύχεται μυστικῶς·

Μνήσθητι, Κύριε, πάσης Ἐπισκοπῆς Ὀρθοδόξων, τῶν ὀρθοτομούντων τὸν λόγον τῆς σῆς ἀληθείας.

Μνήσθητι, Κύριε, κατὰ τὸ πλῆθος τῶν οἰκτιρμῶν σου, καὶ τῆς ἐμῆς ἀναξιότητος· συγχώρησόν μοι πᾶν πλημμέλημα ἑκούσιόν τε καὶ ἀκούσιον· καὶ μή, διὰ τὰς ἐμὰς ἁμαρτίας, κωλύσῃς τὴν χάριν τοῦ Ἁγίου σου Πνεύματος ἀπὸ τῶν προκειμένων Δώρων.

Μνήσθητι, Κύριε, τοῦ Πρεσβυτερίου, τῆς ἐν Χριστῷ Διακονίας, καὶ παντὸς Ἱερατικοῦ Τάγματος· καὶ μηδένα

dotal Order, and put none of us to confusion, who surround thy holy Altar. Visit us in thy beneficence, O Lord: manifest thyself to us in thy rich compassions; bestow on us duly-tempered and advantageous air; give peaceful showers to the earth for fruit-bearing; bless the crown of the year of thy bounty; stay the schisms of the Churches; quench the ragings of the nations; quickly destroy the uprisings of heresies, by the power of thy Holy Spirit; accept us all in thy Kingdom, making us children of the light and children of the day; bestow on us thy peace and thy love, O Lord our God; for thou hast given us all things.

Aloud:

And grant us with one mouth, and one heart, to glorify, and hymn thine all-honourable and majestic Name, of the Father, and of the Son, and of the Holy Spirit, now, and ever, and unto the ages of the ages.

The Choir: Amen.

And the rest as in the Hierurgy of Chrysostom (See page 309), except the following Prayers.

Prayer of the Ektene (See page 311).

O our God, the God of salvation, do thou teach us to give thanks to thee worthily for thy benefits, which thou hast done, and still doest toward us. Do thou, our God, who acceptest

---

ἡμῶν κατεαχύνης, τῶν κυκλούντων τὸ ἅγιόν σου Θυσιαστήριον. Ἐπίσκεψαι ἡμᾶς ἐν τῇ χρηστότητί σου, Κύριε· ἐπιφάνηθι ἡμῖν ἐν τοῖς πλουσίοις σου οἰκτιρμοῖς· εὐκράτους καὶ ἐπωφελεῖς τοὺς ἀέρας ἡμῖν χάρισαι· ὄμβρους εἰρηνικοὺς τῇ γῇ πρὸς καρποφορίαν δώρησαι· εὐλόγησον τὸν στέφανον τοῦ ἐνιαυτοῦ τῆς χρηστότητός σου· παῦσον τὰ σχίσματα τῶν Ἐκκλησιῶν· σβέσον τὰ φρυάγματα τῶν Ἐθνῶν· τὰς τῶν αἰρέσεων ἐπαναστάσεις ταχέως πάντας κατάλυσον, τῇ δυνάμει τοῦ Ἁγίου σου Πνεύματος· πάντας ἡμᾶς πρόσδεξαι εἰς τὴν Βασιλείαν σου, υἱοὺς φωτὸς καὶ υἱοὺς ἡμέρας ἀναδείξας· τὴν σὴν εἰρήνην καὶ τὴν σὴν ἀγάπην χάρισαι ἡμῖν, Κύριε ὁ Θεὸς ἡμῶν· πάντα γὰρ ἀπέδωκας ἡμῖν.

Ἐκφώνως·

Καὶ δὸς ἡμῖν, ἐν ἑνὶ στόματι, καὶ μιᾷ καρδίᾳ δοξάζειν, καὶ ἀνυμνεῖν τὸ πάντιμον καὶ μεγαλοπρεπὲς Ὄνομά σου, τοῦ Πατρός, καὶ τοῦ Υἱοῦ, καὶ τοῦ Ἁγίου Πνεύματος, νῦν, καὶ ἀεί, καὶ εἰς τοὺς αἰῶνας τῶν αἰώνων.

Ὁ Χορός· Ἀμήν.

Καὶ τὰ λοιπὰ ὡς ἐν τῇ τοῦ Χρυσοστόμου Ἱερουργίᾳ (Ὅρα σελ. 308), ἐκτὸς τῶν ἑξῆς Εὐχῶν.

Εὐχὴ τῆς Ἐκτενοῦς (Ὅρα σελ. 310).

Ὁ Θεὸς ἡμῶν, ὁ Θεὸς τοῦ σώζειν, σὺ ἡμᾶς δίδαξον εὐχαριστεῖν σοι ἀξίως ὑπὲρ τῶν εὐεργεσιῶν σου, ὧν ἐποίησας, καὶ ποιεῖς μεθ᾽ ἡμῶν. Σὺ ὁ Θεὸς ἡμῶν, ὁ

FINAL PROFESSION OF A MONK
Feast of the Immaculate Conception, December 8, 1974

Thomas Keating, OCSO
(Abbot of St. Joseph's Abbey,
Spencer, Mass.)

Brother, I know how well you are prepared for this moment of consecration. Since our ritual calls for a little exhortation, I would like to bring to your mind a few thoughts that might crystallize your deepest feelings at this time.

Man is designed in the form of a cross. In the account of the creation of the first man, we are reminded that "he was made out of the dust of the earth"—his horizontal dimension; and that "God breathed into his face the breath of life," the invasion of man by charity—his vertical dimension. Thus, man is created in a kind of tension. He seems to have been designed in God's evolutionary plan to rise out of the unconsciousness of the beasts and to move toward God-consciousness. There remains something in man that wants to go back to where he was: the downward pull which seeks psychological oblivion in the instinctual spontaneity of animal life. And yet at the same time, there is in man this hunger for God, for more life, for higher consciousness.

It is precisely this tension, which is the actual situation of man, that Jesus has taken completely to himself and with which he has identified himself. And when he says to us, "Come, follow me," he certainly means that we should accept, as he did, the actual situation that we find ourselves in. That creative tension has been greatly intensified by original sin, and made all the more dramatic, poignant, and crucial by Christ's redemption.

Monastic life addresses itself to this fundamental and primary situation in which human nature finds itself and gives it a decisive thrust in the direction of God-consciousness. The basic principle out of which the monastic thrust emerges is the commitment to poverty, a vow which is not too well understood today, because of the very difficult connotations of that word in our times. A good translation of what the vow means for monks might be this: it is the promise to develop a non-possessive attitude. It begins with what we usually mean by the vow of poverty, which is the renunciation of outward possessions. By entering into the common life, we agree to possess nothing of our own. The other vows are all contained in this attitude, like a growing tree that puts forth branches, and eventually leaves and fruit.

A further development in the non-possessive attitude is represented by the vow of chastity, which is a non-possessive attitude toward your own body. This is expressed by the wholehearted acceptance of the monastic life style with its commitment to chastity, vigils, abstinence and fasting, silence and solitude, and the other observances. These observances will not produce the fruits of monastic life unless they are practiced with this growing interior attitude of non-possessiveness or poverty of spirit.

The ripe fruit of this attitude, when it has fully developed, is the willingness to give up a possessive attitude even over our own will. The most intimate part of us, that part which Our Lord himself has pointed to with his finger and said, "Unless you deny your inmost self, you cannot be my disciples," is our will, our judgment. While St. Benedict presents obedience as a kind of synopsis of his whole ascetical thrust, it might also be expressed in terms of this deepening, growing attitude of poverty of spirit—the non-possessive attitude toward one's inmost self. This, dear Brother, is the most important attitude to bring to the commitment you are about to make.

What is poverty of spirit, ultimately, if not a commitment to powerlessness? The permanent state of powerlessness is what most characterizes the poor; it is what makes poverty so grinding and difficult. That is why monastic life has to be permanent. It is not enough to submit your body to the monastic life style and to practice obedience to the Rule and an abbot for a certain number of years. The perpetual commitment to stability, which is the promise to live in one place and with the same group of brothers for life, opens you up to a whole new dimension of poverty, to a kind of refinement of all the attitudes developed during your long period of formation. It is a commitment to advance with giant strides along the path of freedom, which is what a non-possessive attitude makes possible. Freedom from everything. Freedom to let God act. Freedom to express God in every human situation, relationship, and action.

The term of the asceticism of the Rule you are professing this morning is to make you truly present with the whole of your being to every moment and to every action of your life. Extraordinary gifts are always given by God to bring us to the ordinary—to what is right under our nose—to the obvious, which is, especially, that God is present everywhere and in everything, giving himself to us. If at first the Rule must be your master and the abbot your teacher, it is eventually the Spirit who must be your teacher and the Spirit expressing himself as your master through events. No one can obey this master without a great deal of preparation, without a sensitivity that has been matured through the other forms of obedience, and through the other forms of poverty. To be free to run and leap in God's presence, to be wholly yourself on every occasion, to express God's way of living human life—these are the ripe fruits of discipline.

A most beautiful way to describe what Benedict means by obedience is *the discipline of the Spirit*. Of course, this disposition can belong to any Christian, but I shall describe it in terms of a monk. The discipline of the Spirit is a contract with God by which you *believe* that everything that happens is his way of bringing you to purity of heart.

The discipline of the Spirit is what *happens*. It does not matter *what* happens. What is necessary is to see the Spirit's action bringing events and people in and out of your life in order to free you from what Paul calls the *outer man*—the man that is headed downward, who wants to go back to the psychological oblivion, to the *unconsciousness* of the beasts. And on the other hand, there is the *inner man* who is renewed every day by the Spirit, who reaches out in hunger for more life, for eternal life, for *God-consciousness*.

What is God-consciousness if not what Paul calls the *mind* of Christ? The mind of Christ is his realization that he *is* the Son of God. It is his attitude of utter confidence and rest in the bosom of the Father; and this is the consciousness that is yours—yours in the degree of your freedom, in the degree of your non-possessive attitude toward all reality. If you submit to the discipline of the Spirit, it does not matter what you do; everything is God's action in you and through you. So you sleep, so you get up, so you eat your breakfast, brush your teeth, go to work, pray. It is all God's because you have given everything to him.

Our Lady was created immaculate, but you can become pure of heart. May the Spirit give you this grace in all its fullness! That is our prayer as we welcome you into the community of the dispossessed.

FINAL PROFESSION OF A MONK
April 1, 1978

The final profession of a monk is not just a juridical act, though it certainly has juridical consequences. The rite of profession is not just a very special kind of blessing. For one thing, it is a permanent blessing, and many rites of blessing are not. The rite of profession is not just a commitment on your part, Brother, because you have already made a number of commitments to monastic life: entering the sacred precincts of the monastery, receiving the novice's habit, making and renewing temporary profession. However, this is a new and more serious commitment. If the rite of profession is not just a juridical act, a very special blessing, or a new and more serious commitment, what is it?

It is a covenant: something you do, something God does—a permanent agreement between you and God. It is this characteristic of permanency which makes it a true consecration, though it is not, strictly speaking, a sacramental consecration. The rite of profession expresses this idea of permanency by following the pattern of liturgies for the consecration of persons which are true sacraments, such as a Solemn Baptism, the Diaconate, the Priesthood, the Episcopate. This pattern appears in the Litany of the Saints, which we will sing; in the essential form, which is your pronouncement of profession; in the solemn prayers that follow; and in the bestowal of the symbols of office or of charism—in your case, the monk's cowl. Your side of the covenant is expressed in the brief dialogue we just held, in which you asked for "the mercy of God and of the Order."

Through this rite, God through His Church ratifies the covenant. What makes it permanent is God's consent and blessing. Thus, the rite of profession is more what God does than what we do. For after we have done everything, it is still nothing compared with what God does in this sacred rite. What is impossible for you, is possible for God. You are exchanging what you are and what you have been, for what you want to be. It is God who makes you a monk.

This covenant with God is not between two abstractions, but is a personal encounter. Just as baptism is incorporation into the whole Christ, Head and members, so final profession is incorporation into Christ in this monastic community— into the body of Christ present in this place, in these concrete people. The community, in fact, receives you as the sign of Christ's acceptance. In accepting and serving one another, we make the "sacrament" of monastic profession a reality. Though I use the term "sacrament" in a broad sense, there is an ancient monastic tradition which understood it in the strict sense—Christ taking possession of our commitment and making it His own.

In the monastic community, fraternal charity—the give and take, the ups and downs, the trial and struggles of every-day life—is the visible sign that makes Christ present. Through the wear and tear of the daily humdrum routine, we are to become one with Jesus, one with the Father in and through Jesus, and one with one another in the Holy Spirit. The love with which God loves the sacred humanity of His only-begotten Son is extended to us. Jesus is in us, we are in Him, and the Gospel, that is to say, the total message of Christ—His teaching and example, His humanity and divin-ity, His very life and presence—is extended to this place and time, and proclaimed to all creation by the witness of the community.

FINAL PROFESSION OF A MONK
October 28, 1978

Brother, on this joyful occasion and at this moment when you are about to make your final vows as a Cistercian monk, I would like to talk to you about *vocation*. Vocation means "call." A religious vocation is nothing new. Those of us who have received it are just invited to continue the tradition already instituted by Our Lord in the persons of his first disciples. Moreover, each individual vocation is a continuum, an ongoing process which never ends, and which is filled with new beginnings. We might distinguish three important stages of it. The case histories of the first disciples of Jesus suggest this. There is the first call, then a probationary period. There is a second and definitive call, based on a stable response to the first invitation. The second call always requires efforts to imitate the example of Jesus. Finally, there is the ultimate call. Let us look at these three calls in the lives of the first disciples. This will help us locate where you are at this precise moment in relation to the development of your own vocation.

Everybody remembers the charming description of the call of the disciples, Andrew and John. They were fascinated by the presence of Jesus as he walked along the shore, and when John the Baptist pointed him out, saying, "That man is the Lamb of God, who takes away the sins of the world," they followed him and spent all that day with him.

There were others whom Jesus personally called, like Matthew from the tax collector's box. But in no case was the first call their definitive call. They were just trying out their vocation, just as many fervent postulants and novices start out following Christ in the monastic way of life with the greatest sincerity. Sometimes there are things they have not taken into consideration. Time sifts motives like nothing else does, and many perceive that their call leads in another direction; or at least that this particular vocation is not for them.

You have been following Jesus for a long time now, and at some point in that following you heard the second call—one that is essential in order to be ready for total commitment— and that is the call to *imitate* Jesus, not just to follow him. All Christians must follow Jesus. But the call to imitate him strikes extremely close to home. It is much more intimate, searching, and demanding. It is a call to the unique love of Christ, a call to respond to what he has done for you with an equal response.

The first disciples did not make out too well when they first started imitating Jesus. Actually, he never asked them whether they wanted to or not. He just chose them. Nothing is said in the Gospel about their choosing him. He reminded them about who chose who at the Last Supper. "You have not chosen me," he said. "I have chosen you." In any case, when he started talking about the difficulties and trials that were involved in this intimate service of him, they got scared and spooked. And when the difficulties actually started happening—when he entered into his passion and they per- ceived that they were being invited to imitate *this*—they all left him and fled. Their example is like a mirror in which we observe ourselves and our own weaknesses, struggles, and failures.

Benedict in the Rule describes these various calls of Jesus in the twelve degrees of humility. He writes: "The third degree of humility is that a monk for the love of God subject himself to his superior in all obedience, imitating the Lord, of whom the Apostle says: 'He was made obedient even unto death.' "

How nice it is to be called! How pleasant to be singled out as a chosen one! How wonderful to imitate Christ!—*except* "unto death." That is why final profession, which is a com- mitment to do just that, needs preparation, practice, and time.

When Our Lord rose from the dead, the light of his Risen Life was reflected back on the long spiritual journey he had taken with his disciples, and they saw that he alone was the source of all their strength. They also perceived that his passion is not an isolated event. It is *one* with his Risen Life. In the light of Christ's Risen Life, pain is joy—and joy is pain. There is no difference, because Christ has made them one in himself. Pain is lost in the joy of the Resurrection, and that joy is already possessed in participating in Christ's passion. This is the ultimate call that the original disciples of Jesus received. And it is now yours.

It is so important to realize what the end of monastic life is. It is not a one-time call. It is a continuous call, becoming more urgent, more vibrant, more exciting, more *alive!* It is a call not only to follow him and walk behind him—servants do that; not only to imitate him and walk beside him— friends do that. Even though to be his friend is to be his constant companion, there is a further call—the ultimate call—to which your commitment this morning is inviting you to respond. It requires a deeper plunge into the mercy of God, a deeper realization of your friendship with Christ. It is the call to live *in* Christ and *with* Christ.

Benedict warns us that it is not enough to make up our minds to imitate the obedience of Christ "even unto death." We have to *do* it! In the fourth degree of humility he tells the monk that "meeting in this obedience with difficulties and contradictions, and even injustice, he should with a quiet mind hold fast to patience, and enduring, neither tire nor run away; for the Scripture says, 'He that shall persevere to the end shall be saved.' "

Imitating Christ means accepting opposition, humiliation, and even injustice. Monastic life is not exempt from all the things everybody else in the world has to endure. But it is a commitment to imitate Christ in them, and this commitment is what changes the bitter experience of them, little by little, into the realization that even in the midst of suffering we are rising again. Each trial is a resurrection, and the grace of that resurrection enables us to see Christ's passion, not as something that happened in the distant past, not as something that Christ endured for us once and for all, but something that he is doing for us *right now!*—and something that is inseparable from his Resurrection. You are dying! You are rising again! Neither matters, because you are called to be *in* Christ and *with* Christ. His glory makes your own suffering insignificant. You are now being called, dear Brother, not only to follow Christ, not only to imitate Jesus, but to experience his very *life!*—to experience his dying and his triumphant Resurrection at every moment! Everything in creation is his gift, and each gift is his way of expressing over and over again, in innumerable ways, one and the same thing—his love for you. What he has begun, he will fulfill. Only your timidity or lack of trust can prevent it. Launch out with total abandon upon the ocean of confidence. Cast away all fears, and open your heart to the love of God in Christ Jesus.

FINAL PROFESSION OF A MONK
Easter Saturday, April 21, 1979

The story of Mary Magdalen's encounter with Jesus after His resurrection is about the return of someone to the Garden of Paradise.* This Gospel pericope magnificently manifests the great themes of the Paschal Vigil, which are being repeated in various ways throughout this wonderful week of feasts, and indeed throughout the whole of Paschal time. The *Exultet* sang of three great benefits of the Paschal Night, the night that reenacted in a dramatic way the redemption which our Savior won for us through His passion, death, and resurrection. "The power of this night," the liturgy sang exultantly, "dispels the darkness of sin, wipes away all guilt, and restores lost innocence." The hymn recounts still other benefits, but these are enough to start with. The return to "lost innocence" is not a matter of returning to childhood, but to the original innocence that our first parents enjoyed in the Garden of Paradise, where their acquaintance with God was so intimate and so entrancing that they scarcely ever thought about themselves; at least they did not even know what clothes they had on, or rather off, until after the Fall. Lost innocence is lost intimacy with God, and *that* is what is being restored by the feast of the Resurrection in our lives as Christians, and especially in your life as a monk. If you are not headed for the Garden of Paradise, you are going in the wrong direction. If you have any doubt about the direction that every prayer, observance, and moment have in this way of life, you have not the intuition of Mary Magdalen. The Garden of Paradise is not a geographical location. It is a state of consciousness; an exalted awareness of God's presence; indeed, it is an ever more penetrating experience of God through faith, confidence, and love.

This incident is a kind of reverse image of the fall of our first parents. Mary Magdalen stands weeping at the tomb. With her unbearable longing to find Christ, she looks in and sees the angels. They question her, but she scarcely notices them or their dazzling robes. What does she care about angels, when her heart is passionately seeking for the body of Christ? She turns around, still weeping, and sees the gardener, or at least someone who seemed to be the gardener. The man said to her, "Why are you weeping? Whom are you looking for?" That question focused all the intense desires of her heart. She did not have to say what her tears expressed, but she tried to explain that she was searching for the body of the Lord.

Jesus said, "Mary!" To be called by name is to experience inwardly that He loves you. Your name stands for who you really are. To be called by name signifies that He knows you through and through—knows every one of your faults, weaknesses and sins—and still loves you; not just puts up with you, but *loves* you, wants you to become His own and to fill you with His Divine Spirit. Mary realized in that moment how much Jesus loved her and that all her sins were forgotten. She turned to Him saying just one word, but one which expressed more than many words the whole ardent longing of her heart to be united to Him.

When our first parents heard the voice of God in the Garden, they headed for the woods. They were afraid of His voice, afraid to be confronted by Him. But one who loves moves in the opposite direction. Mary plunged into His arms and hung on to Him in such a way that He had to say, "Stop clinging to me!" Then He sent her away to bear witness to the truth of His resurrection. Our first parents were thrown out of the Garden, but Mary was *sent*, because now the Garden was inside of her, and she could never leave it.

There are three ascending levels of contemplation in this Garden, three levels of faith, which are suggested by the text itself; and these should be your three principal activities as a monk in the particular Garden of Paradise which you are choosing.

The first is the ability to see God in all things. Mary herself was not equal to doing this, until she had first heard Christ calling her by name, assuring her of His love for her. You cannot see God in all things unless you first have been assured, in your inmost being, that He loves you.

The second level of faith is the ability to see all things as God's gift. Mary expressed this awareness when she responded to His call with her own word, "Rabboni!" That is, "I know you, too, and I love you." You cannot see all things as God's gift unless you first realize that you love Him.

The third level of faith is the ability to see God giving Himself in all things. That is what is suggested by the message Jesus sent to His disciples: "I am ascending to my Father"— that is easy to accept—"and to *your* Father!" That is unheard of! That is the great good news we are all waiting to hear! God is not just the Father of Our Lord Jesus Christ, but through the passion, death, and resurrection of Jesus, has extended the identical love with which He loves His only-begotten Son to all who are incorporated into Him, through His Blood and the reception of His Spirit. It is the knowledge that God is also *our* Father that reestablishes the lost intimacy of Paradise. Innocence is restored, the innocence of being always in communion with God instead of chatting with ourselves; of being able to forget about our own interests, because God's interests are going on inside of us all the time. God's life is springing up in us as living water; as faith that has no more doubt; as hope that reaches out for boundless love and union, because its Source is boundless; for the will of God is to communicate the maximum of Himself to us.

In all we do as monks, the eternal values flowing from the intimate knowledge of Christ are springing up within us all the time; and they are so interwoven with the insignificance of our daily lives that it is impossible to distinguish them anymore. But you can know what is happening when you hear the words of Christ: "Go and tell my disciples. I ascend to my Father and your Father." In other words, go back into ordinary life, into the details of your daily work, into the routine of eating and sleeping. Do all the ordinary things you always do, but now in the full consciousness that God is giving Himself to you in every cup of water, in the flowers we see in front of us, in the Eucharist we are about to break, in your brothers, in your sorrows, in your difficulties. And yet, not just difficulties, not just sorrows, but *God* communicating Himself to you, and you sharing in the mystery of His presence without even reflecting upon it, with spontaneity and joy in fullness of life. This is the sense, it seems to me, in which our monastic Fathers understood our way of life as a return to Paradise; a return to the consciousness of God's love within us, and coming to us in everything, all the time.

NOTES

*John 20:11-18.

JESUS STILL IN AGONY?

Meditation on a Negro Spiritual

Louis Dupré

*(T.L. Riggs Professor in Philosophy of
Religion, Yale University, New Haven, Conn.)*

"Were you there when they crucified my Lord?"

I cannot escape the question. To be present at the Lord's
Passion belongs to the heart of my faith. But how could I be
present? By commemorating an historical fact? How could
any event of the past concern me deeply in the present, even
the agony and death of the Redeemer? To "commemorate"
Jesus' Passion is to take it out of the present: he who merely
remembers knows the pain and suffering of the past to have
ended in the subsequent triumph of the resurrection. Celebrating the Passion, then, means no more than a yearly recall
of the past for the purpose of renewing my awareness of the
victorious, permanent reality of the present.

Not satisfied with such a reenacted commemoration Christian piety has always sought a more intimate presence. Hence
men and women of all Christian ages have attempted to feel
in their own lives what Jesus felt *then*: his agony and rejection
when no triumph was in sight. To be with him in the *present*
of his suffering, rather than anticipating an outcome which
he never knew, is to be where he really was. It is also to be at
the heart of redemption. For to be redeemed is not a present
result of past suffering: it is that suffering itself working *now*.
And so, in our feelings and desires we come to be present to
his hour. But feelings soon turn to ashes and two hours later
we often have difficulty remembering how we felt. Then the
question returns: "Were you there when they crucified my
Lord?" Does the present of his Passion contain no more substance than the fleeting present of my feelings? Is there no
way to be where he *really* is and to be united to his agony in a
lasting manner?

Yes, there is. But only by entering into the dark reality of my own suffering, loneliness, and failure. Only in the brokenness and pain of life am I with him where he continues to live his agony. Unfortunately when thinking of Jesus' Passion we only recall his willingness, his innocence and, above all, his uniquely redemptive mission. Even to the suffering of the saints we attribute exceptional meaning and dignity: following a clearly perceived vocation they entered willingly into what we assume them to have known as a dark night of purification. But my own suffering! Is it anything more than the pain of thinskinned selfishness, the disappointment of vulgar ambitions, the frustration of unpurified desires, and the loneliness of emotional stinginess? How dare I call "suffering" what possesses so little dignity? Whenever I lift my eyes to the crucified Savior it is mainly to move beyond my petty misery, certainly not to move into it. And so life goes by drifting from saintly but sterile aspirations to complacent forgetfulness.

Nevertheless that very suffering of mine, however despicable and even sinful in its origins, *is* Jesus' agony in me. I find a comparison with Jesus' Passion almost blasphemous. But I forget that all suffering is lowly and humiliating, that it all began with a curse. His as well as mine. Whether pain has its roots in private weakness and failure, or whether it is inflicted by an entire universe of weakness and failure, the effect remains the same. Suffering means always failure to him who suffers. Jesus' words on the cross—My God, my God, why have you forsaken me?—do not express the attitude of one who is performing a clearly understood, effective sacrifice. They say what suffering has said from the beginning of the world and what it says in me now: In this I am hopelessly alone.

A great deal has been written about the purifying, strengthening qualities of suffering. These qualities may be known to him who has suffered, but not to him who suffers. Within my actual suffering I detect no meaning. I experience it as absurdly gratuitous and it would cease to exist or, at least, lose its sting, if I could only discover a universal meaning in it. To suffer is to be alone. No one can follow the sufferer into this most private world. Physicians and psychologists may attempt to alleviate human pain and to do so they classify and universalize. They speak of depression, feeling of loss, loss of meaning, and the like. But none of these terms describes the intensely private experience of pain. It is like nothing else and, in it, I am like no one else. Indeed, it is the only part of myself that is exclusively me, that bears my name. No one enters this most intimate dwelling. "Were you there when they crucified my Lord?" Yes, Lord, I was there in the only way I could be present to your suffering: in the solitude of my own pain.

But my present suffering derives from such lowly sources: wrong decisions in the past and neurotic inclinations in the present.... Whatever the undignified causes of my suffering—and they are all undignified in a cursed world, for Jesus as well as for me—my suffering is all I am, my very existence—dignified or not! It is isolation with no past to comfort and no future to hope for, the empty desert of a bleak, unending present. Nor is there peace in this desert, infested as it is with the howling, barking, roaring animals of frustrated desires, broken expectations, tormenting visions of an impossible future. Its blank nothingness means not peace but absence, the lack of fulfillment which I need to be whole. "Were you there when they laid him in the tomb?" Yes, Lord, I was there in the tomb of my loneliness.

We tend to think of the desert as mystical fulfillment. But the desert of the soul is one from which God also has withdrawn. Its emptiness signals rejection. Does God ever answer the cry: Why have you forsaken me? Most times we suppress the question as impious. I know I cannot expect a divine interference for every pain that strikes me. After all, this world follows a course of its own and a cause—self-inflicted or other-inflicted—must have its effect. True, but deep down

I cannot help feeling lost in a machinery the designer of which chose to ignore my anticipated distress. Thus Jesus also felt lost when petty fanaticism and gratuitous resentment, rather than a grand, predetermined scheme of salvation brought him to the cross. "Were you there when they nailed him to the tree?" Yes, Lord, I was there suffering my own rejection, especially by God.

Many of us today, particularly the young and the old, feel hopelessly lost. We want to love, to give ourselves, to commit ourselves and we fail. Or, beyond rejection, some feel so rejectable that they dare not stretch out their hand. And occasionally a man or a woman cannot bear the pain any longer, seeing no other choice but to return the gift of life which parents and generations of ancestors had so carefully prepared for him or for her. Thinking of the last hour of such a person—his utter loneliness—"sometimes it causes me to tremble, tremble, tremble." Not only for their horror but also for the "ordinary hopelessness" of everyday life.

"Were you *there* when they nailed him to the tree?" Was I *there* in my suffering? For that is where he is being crucified—in me, not in Jerusalem. There stands the tree from which grace flows. For grace is not a pipeline from which each taps according to his needs. Grace is my individual election, my being called by my name. It is as personal as my suffering. Indeed, it is my suffering. For in this world there can be no grace but through redemptive suffering, through Jesus' death—in me. This then was God's election: the utter rejection of Gethsemani and of Calvary. In my life: my deserved suffering, my unholy loneliness, my impatient mediocrity. And yes, also my inability to accept this humiliating pain. That also makes part of God's agonizing grace. "Were you there when they laid him in the tomb?" Yes, Lord, I was there in my powerlessness, unable even to say "yes" to that powerlessness.

It is a temptation to think that only the saint's suffering redeems, that he alone knows about the dark night. In all suffering life is on trial and rebellion forms an essential part of that ordeal. Evil, my private evil as it stands revealed in my own suffering, that becomes the channel of God's grace, my unique bond with Jesus in his agony. But to find it I must move into that sorrow—without covering it up or embellishing it with non-existent virtue. Walk into the bleak desert of my life, and be *there.* Perhaps I shall be able to accomplish no more than silently accept my inability to accept. But no more is expected: to confront my bitterness, rebellion, greed, jealousy, rage, impatience is to encounter Jesus' agony in my own.

Yet to move not only into my own suffering. For as the poet says: "To rest in our own suffering is evasion of suffering. We must learn to suffer more." To find Jesus' agony also in those private worlds of others around me, which I am so reluctant to explore and so unable to comprehend. Here also I must accept without understanding Jesus' agony in the uncouth, the uncivilized, the unlovable. This then is the triumph of the cross: that degradation unredeemable has become the sign of God's grace, that rejection has become the call of election and that hopelessness itself henceforth witnesses to the presence of redemption. It has been written: "A curse comes to being as a child is formed..." Over the beginning of all life stands the sign of failure. How it will fail, we do not know—as a murderer or a saint—but it will fail enough to make its mother weep. The joyous mystery of Good Friday is that the failure itself has become redemptive. Jesus fails in me. That is the mystical union, the only one, between God and me: Jesus in agony in me.

COMING SOON!

Word and Spirit, 2 — 1980
Dedicated to St. Benedict and St. Catherine of Siena

Reserve your copy by ordering now!

From: St. Bede's Publications
      Box 132
      Still River, Massachusetts 01467